"Magnificent storytelling, Masterfully writ
powerful Jewish Crime Syndicate and the
organized crime. A must have for any Mob enthusiast.

Frank Monastra,
Cleveland organized crime writer
Author *Brancato "Mafia Street Boss"* and *Gangland Cleveland Style*

"Alan Geik gives us an intimate portrait of a nice Jewish family in the orbit of the 20th Century 'kosher nostra.' We know the big names – Schultz, Lansky, Rothstein— but it's the little stories that give this book the firsthand feel of its *haymish* Jewish mob uncles, men who weren't to be trifled with."

Eric Dezenhall
Mafia historian
The AmericanMafia: The Rise and Fall of Organized Crime in Las Vegas
Author *The Devil Himself*—a novel inspired by Meyer Lansky's personal notes detailing the mob's battle against the Nazis on American streets.

"Alan Geik offers a fascinating look at many of the country's major underworld figures from New York to Las Vegas and beyond. He and his family are central characters in this riveting first-person account. This is a beautifully written book that you won't be able to put down — an instant Mob classic."

Larry Henry
Senior Reporter at Gambling.com, author of "The Mob in Pop Culture" for The Mob Museum in Las Vegas

---

"Excellent read! Whether you are a first timer or an experienced student of organized crime, *Uncle Charlie Killed Dutch Schultz* has you covered. Highlighting lesser known but equally fascinating characters in the nation's 20th century underworld. Alan Geik expertly guides the reader through decades of collaborations between the Jewish and Italian mobs. Highly recommended."

Casey McBride
Mob historian
Curator *Uncle Frank's Place*, the social media site dedicated to all things Mafia boss Frank Costello

---

"From Jews going 'beyond the Pale' fleeing Russian pogroms to 'the more money, the louder it talks' days of Arnold Rothstein and Prohibition ending with the 1986 Commission Case, Alan Geik takes the reader on a colorful tour of American organized crime from the Jewish mob's view."

Gary Jenkins
Gangland Wire Podcast

"It is not often you get an insider's view of a notorious gangland figure like Charles Workman, aka 'the Bug'—the man known to have shot and killed the infamous Dutch Schultz. This book has great insight into the Jewish underworld, told through the eyes of a family descendant."

Nev Morgan
Organized Crime Journalist at the National Crime Syndicate

"*Uncle Charlie Killed Dutch Schultz* is a gripping story of family and crime. Geik does a magnificent job expanding on familiar stories by adding personal insight obtained directly from the infamous characters portrayed throughout the book. Additionally, Geik delves into the life and crimes of his relatively unknown uncle, George Gordon, whose connections to top hoodlums in New York, Cleveland, Las Vegas, and Miami will establish him as a powerful underworld figure to all mob enthusiasts."

Avi Bash,
Author of *Organized Crime in Miami*
and Co-Author of *Los Angeles Underworld*.

"A fascinating account of a mobster who is rarely discussed but was involved in pivotal moments in gangland history. I recommend "Uncle Charlie Killed Dutch Schultz" to any reader who wants to broaden their knowledge of the mob in the 20th century."

James Gladwish
Producer/host of *Organized Crime Shortz* YouTube channel

UNCLE CHARLIE KILLED DUTCH SCHULTZ

THE JEWISH MOB: A FAMILY AFFAIR

ALAN GEIK

This is a work of non-fiction. No names have been changed or characters invented. The author has relied upon original documents—such as Senate hearing transcripts, newspaper articles, and arrest records—and otherwise on dialogue spoken or heard by him to the best of his recollection. Some quotes have been edited for brevity or clarity; some are compilations from several conversations.

Sonador Publishing
160 Alewife Brook Pkwy #1162
Cambridge, MA 02138
sonadorpublishing.com
info@sonadorpublishing.com

First published in the United States in 2022
Printed in Massachusetts

Print ISBN 978-0-578-87735-8
Ebook 978-0-578-87736-5

Library of Congress Control Number: 2022915572

To find out more about the author and his works visit

www.alangeik.com
TWITTER @AlanGeik
INSTAGRAM@alangeik
And
Facebook @Alan Geik
and Alan Geik author

Cover Design: Brianna Harden
Interior Layout: Melanie Calahan

To our parents, Reba and Lou
and our Brother, Bernard

Also by Alan Geik

Glenfiddich Inn
A novel set in WWI era Boston and New York

ACKNOWLEDGMENTS . . . AND HOW THIS ACCOUNT BEGAN

Four years ago my favorite cousin, Ira, called me. He urged me to find one of the many online websites devoted to organized crime. “Could you do it now?” He asked. He was excited. I did so.

The home page featured a black-and-white photo of a police lineup from the 1930s. The characters looked as one might expect in a B gangster movie—dark suits, ties, black overcoats, fedoras. “Ok, so what?” I said to myself.

“That’s my father on the right.” Ira said, indicating which criminal in the lineup was my late Uncle Sol. I never would have recognized him as such a young man.

“My father is on the gangster home page—not Uncle George, not Charlie. Not any of them. My father.” He laughed. We both did.

Throughout my youth our much beloved Uncle Sol had been a smalltime criminal—mail fraud, bad checks, larceny, embezzlement. Neither movies were made nor books written about him. New York City newspapers never featured him in their regular articles about the intrigues of organized crime.

Uncle Sol was unlike Uncle George Gordon—who for decades operated illegal gambling casinos in Ohio as part of the Cleveland

Syndicate, and later owned hidden interests in Las Vegas and Havana casinos. Uncle George was linked with other well-known underworld figures and celebrity gangster groupies like George Raft and Frank Sinatra, who treated him as royalty.

Uncle Sol also lacked the mob stature of Charlie Workman, a hitman for Murder Inc., the hired assassins for organized crime in the 1930s. I didn't meet Uncle Charlie until the mid-1960s after he served twenty-three years for Dutch Schultz's murder.

Nor did Uncle Sol have the visibility of the other members of our extended family—the Jewish Mob.

Sammy Kass was the close associate of Waxey Gordon, the Prohibition era mob boss. Sammy was arrested in 1951 with Waxey in a drug bust on Manhattan's East Side. After a long prison sentence Sammy became part of mob boss Tony Salerno's inner circle. That association proved to be of great importance to the ongoing success of our father's Garment Center trucking business.

Johnny Eder, the least violent mobster of them all, was a high-class fence. He had great insight into the workings of the Jewish gangsters and is one of the more thoughtful contributors to this chronicle.

They, and the others who inhabit this history, were constant figures in our lives growing up—when they weren't in jail that is. Despite this criminal lifestyle appearing normal to us as children it was always expected that we would never adopt it for our own.

We were not exactly the makings of second-generation gangster wannabes.

Iris is an attorney, and Bernard was an NYPD detective and later our guardian in our father's mob-sanctioned Garment Center trucking business.

I received an M.Sc. at the London School of Economics and Political Science and taught for a few semesters at the Kingston College of Technology outside of London. Returning to New York City, I became a film editor at the Wide World of Sports and later at Paramount Pictures in Hollywood. I also had a twenty-five-year run in Los Angeles as a public radio on-air host of Afro-Cuban music. Our younger cousin Ira became a suburban dad (now grandfather) and successful corporate executive.

I note here that it later occurred to us three siblings that we shared one skill fundamental to our chosen vocations: Don't interrupt a subject when they are on a roll. So we didn't interrupt these characters, and over the years compiled the many personal insights transcribed here.

Our parents were lifelong observers of these characters and often filled in the blanks in the fascinating (certainly to us) drama and often tragicomedy of their lives. We grew up hearing the "inside" stories of events that sometimes conformed to what we read about in breathless newspaper accounts or saw on the screen, sometimes the oral histories did not conform so well. Their stories were often told and retold with humorous punch lines that made us laugh, no matter how grim the setting.

When I related to my sister Iris our Cousin Ira's amused sharing of his father's higher standing in social media than our other uncles, she urged me to write this history. As a girl, and later young woman, Iris had the advantage of also hearing the poignant tales of the wives and girlfriends of these men. She later shared them with me—unfortunately, when I was a young man they didn't interest me as much as they do now.

I intentionally left most of the women's tales out of this account as they deserve their own attention. Iris is intent on doing that, much to my delight. She will title her book *View From the Women's Table*.

Iris and Cousin Ira deserve the credit for my publishing this book. A third person I must acknowledge is Mark Swartz, whom I met in 1969 when I was living in Manhattan. He was, at the time, a salesman in the Garment Center, and he understood the mob control of that industry. Coincidentally, he worked next door to our father's newly formed trucking company on West 37th Street. Mark recalled passing by many times and seeing someone standing by the door with a gun in his pocket. (It wasn't my father, who had neither a gun nor a driver's license.)

Mark loved hearing the stories about the criminal element, and after almost fifty years still laughs about them as much as I do. He, too, urged me, "Write it down."

Many thanks to Andy Ross, my insightful editor who made many suggestions that greatly enhanced the story.

William Barrow of Cleveland State University tracked down photos and newspaper articles relating to the Cleveland Syndicate, which plays such an important part in this story.

Prof. Ellen Belcher at the Lloyd Sealy Library, John Jay College of Criminal Justice guided me through the many sources and photographs at that institution. I thank her for that.

I have to thank the following friends and family for their appraisals of this story as it developed: Iris Geik, Johanna Geik, Lida Gellman, Chris Johnson, Roy Strassman, Henry Horbaczewski, Bonnie Kent, Marilyn Romero, Wendy and Anthony Marcisofsky of Copper Cat Books in Las Vegas, Christopher Koefoed, Gary Cox, Joe and Eileen La Russo, Archie Purvis, Barry Altschul, Howard Dratch, Jerry Cohen and David Bellel.

My wife, Yvette Palomo Perales, deserves special thanks, as she so often waited patiently as I tried to extract myself from these characters who still remain of endless fascination in our popular culture.

Burton Turkus Papers, Special Collections, Lloyd Sealy Library, John Jay College of Criminal Justice/CUNY

My Uncle Sol (far right) in a 1934 NYPD lineup. Cousin Ira brought this photo of his father to my attention. It was the impetus for this tale of our family characters who were part of organized crime, and so part of American folklore.

* * *

While writing this, I came to understand that what we know of as "organized crime" began on a few streets in Lower Manhattan in the early 1920s. The Italians and Jews who came of age on those streets—some of them narrators on these pages—would within a few years control the largest cash flow of any industry in America, and it would remain under their control for the next sixty years.

* * *

A few matters:

The reader should note that the main characters in this account were easily accessible and went about their lives with no expectation that they would be of such interest forty, fifty and sixty years later. I certainly never expected to be writing about them at this time in my life.

The internet and cable television gave rise to entertaining and informative organized crime documentaries often featuring reporters and historians who have devoted decades of their careers to this genre. I applaud their efforts. My writings here are largely personal remembrances of a far less complicated time.

Also, although my siblings and I lacked a common bloodline to Charlie Workman that absence was more than compensated for by his gratitude toward my father, who was one of the trusted bearers of mob financial support to Charlie's family during his twenty-three year incarceration. They knew each other since childhood. Both Charlie and his wife were close to our parents before and after his incarceration.

Uncles Charlie and George were pre-teenage criminal partners and both graduated to be hired gunmen and enforcers by the time they were eighteen. They warned my father, a few years younger, off of any criminal activities—a warning he largely respected for the rest of his life.

After he was released from prison in 1963 Uncle Charlie embraced us as family. My brother, a soon-to-be NYPD detective, had a special connection with Charlie who had the assurance of a strong law enforcement advocate through unofficial channels if a bothersome issue would ever come up with his parole status.

Charlie always referred to us as his "niece and nephews." I could never imagine calling him anything other than "Uncle Charlie."

Another observation—

Throughout my youth, people in this criminal world would often say that they grew up in poverty, and crime was a way out. My father, a lifelong fan of popular music, pointed out that George Gershwin, the great American composer, and Meyer Lansky, an architect of organized crime and who has a recurring role in this account, both were raised in poverty at the turn of the twentieth century. Gershwin grew up in Williamsburg and Lansky on the Lower East Side, the two neighborhoods connected by the Williamsburg Bridge.

Yet by the mid-1920s Gershwin had composed his timeless jazz symphony *Rhapsody in Blue*, while the equally youthful Lansky was well on his way into lifelong criminality.

This is my way of noting that it is not my intention to normalize the criminal activities of these characters. They often victimized the most vulnerable in our society as well as hard working union members and owners of small businesses. I am just presenting a history with as little judgment as possible.

Also, many of the events mentioned here are well known to the devoted readers of the organized crime genre. The "Mad Dog" Coll murder, the ascendance of Lucky Luciano and Meyer Lansky, Arnold Rothstein's history, Jews fighting Nazis on America's streets before World War II, the formation and abrupt end to Murder, Inc., and the killing of Dutch Schultz are already well documented. However, I found it necessary to revisit these events, though as lightly as possible, for the readers who are not as familiar with this history and also to give context to the characters central to this story.

Similarly, a number of the photos (especially the mug shots) of these characters are easily recognizable to those immersed in this genre, but hopefully they are new, and of interest, to other readers.

In the case of Uncle Charlie—he was incarcerated during many of the family events that he would have no doubt attended—so we are lacking photos, other than those already in this book.

I can however report that many of the other characters' photographs are straight out of family albums— at weddings, bar mitzvahs and nightclub celebrations—and often presented here alongside their F.B.I, and local law enforcement mug shots.

I had the good fortune to know them, and I think that even as a child I understood that they were not the same as my friends' family members—not by a long shot (as they would say).

CONTENTS

PROLOGUE

Uncle Charlie killed Dutch Schultz in the Palace Chophouse, a Newark, New Jersey bar, at about 10:15 p.m., October 23, 1935. Dutch Schultz, a feared mob boss, had been plotting to kill Thomas Dewey, the New York State special prosecutor, recently hired by the governor to investigate organized crime, especially Schultz. The other mob guys reasoned that killing a state prosecutor would bring heat onto their very profitable rackets, so they called on Louis "Lepke" Buchalter, the head of Murder Inc., organized crime's hit squad, to find a suitable assassin to kill Schultz instead, and so put an end to his not very good idea.[1]

Lepke picked one of his most reliable gunmen—Uncle Charlie, who, six years later, was convicted of the killing and spent the next twenty-three years in New Jersey prisons. Mendy Weiss, another high-ranking gunman, was Uncle Charlie's partner for the hit on Schultz, which also included the assassinations of three of Schultz's guys. Weiss was spared a long prison sentence for the Schultz gang rubouts, as he was electrocuted in Sing Sing prison in 1943 for an unrelated murder.

Charlie "The Bug" Workman's legal downfall was the result of another hit man, Abe "Kid Twist" Reles, who turned state's evidence on many of his longtime colleagues—Uncle Charlie being one of them. During the months of those mobster trials, Kid Twist was hidden away under police protection at the Half Moon Hotel in Coney Island. One evening in November 1941, he exited through his bedroom window and splattered onto the hotel's sun deck six stories below.

Reles' police guards claimed he had been trying to escape. Others thought it more likely those same police guards helped him through the window, since he landed twenty feet from the building—and, besides, escaping through a sixth-floor window with a few cheap bed sheets tied together rarely proves successful. It's probably no coincidence that, the next day, Reles was scheduled to testify against another Murder Inc. boss, Albert Anastasia, called by some "The Lord High Executioner."

Anyway, he was, many years later, a kindly man to me—Uncle Charlie, that is. I don't know whether Reles or Anastasia were kindly men, and it is irrelevant to this tale.

* * *

Many of our characters, or their families, came from Eastern Europe beginning in the 1880s in waves of tens of thousands to America—a land that held out a promise different from anywhere else. Many were escaping the terrifying pogroms enacted in Poland, Russia, Romania, and other lands that had become nightmares for Jews.[2]

They brought with them invaluable knowledge: literacy that began before the Old Testament was written, and skills passed on from their ancestors, who were the first traders throughout the Middle East and the Mediterranean 1,500 years before Christ.

They also brought their own language: Yiddish—a mixture of German, Hebrew and smatterings from every Jewish ghetto in Eastern Europe. It was the language that bonded Jewish communities throughout Europe for hundreds of years—revolutionaries in the

Balkans, shoemakers and rabbis in Polish and Romanian ghettos, and the farmers and horse thieves of Russia.

In July 1901 one of the millions of Jewish refugees arrived on Manhattan Island. Unlike most of the others, he had not come directly across the Atlantic on a barely seaworthy ship crammed with wretched souls. He had made that tortuous voyage earlier. Now he arrived on a train from Montreal. How he ever found himself in Canada is lost to history.

Along with his few possessions, twenty-five-year-old Isaac Gelchevsky carried a childhood memory that would sear through him for the rest of his life. As an eight-year-old boy, Isaac had gone with his father, Schmuel, to a weekly market in a nearby Russian village. Cag, a Roma, Schmuel's sometimes-horse-trading partner, came along.[3] Cag attached two horses to the back of the cart, hoping to sell them.

Cag had sold one of the two horses, and Schmuel three bags of beets Isaac pulled from the sparse garden next to the hovel his family occupied. On their return trip home, five men standing at a bend in the narrow path turned toward them when they heard the cart approach. A Cossack officer moved to the middle of the path. He waved for them to stop.[4] They did.

The Cossack's casual manner reassured Isaac—after all, any involvement with the Cossacks could be humiliating for the Jews, or even life threatening. It was always best to avoid them.

Isaac later remembered the Cossack introducing himself pleasantly as Captain Petro Razin of the Terek Cossacks. The captain walked around the cart.

"What did you sell?" He asked.

"A horse and beets," Schmuel said, then quickly pulled out a bottle of vodka and gave it to Captain Razin. Most Jews knew that vodka in the hands of these people would sometimes be enough for safe passage, but other times vodka could fuel insane violence by ignorant peasants like these.

Captain Razin informed them that two horses had been stolen a few days before from a farm an hour's ride away. He was sure Cag had stolen the horses. Cag denied it.

The captain turned from casual interrogator to raging attacker. He pulled Cag out of the cart.

One of his men thrust a tree branch sharpened to a point with small barbs into Cag's rib cage. The barbs rendered it impossible to remove the branch without causing even more grievous injury. Captain Razin kicked Cag into a thick stand of bushes, to die a sure, slow death.

The captain in what seemed like a flash, pulled Schmuel onto the path and ordered a man to bring forth his horse and mount Schmuel on the animal. Another man quickly lofted a rope over a sturdy tree branch and, before Isaac could even gasp, his father was hanging limply from the tree. It all occurred in swift seconds.

The captain pointed down the road and told Isaac to run back to his village with a warning: "Tell the Jews never to steal from the Christians."

Isaac learned years later that his father and Cag were indeed part-time horse thieves, and he just happened to be with them when their luck ran out.

Schmuel Gelchevsky was my great-grandfather.

Somewhere, either on board a ship, or at the Canadian crossing, an impatient, possibly drunken immigration officer invented the surname "G-E-I-K" from "Gelchevsky." Immediately upon his arrival in New York City Isaac disappeared into the Lower East Side—a tangle of narrow streets overflowing with Jews, Italians, Irish and Chinese, each to their own wretched slum.

Isaac Gelchevsky, now Geik, was my grandfather.

* * *

So it seems like the Lower East Side is the right place for this story to begin. It is also where I, as a young boy, first spent time with the by then semi-retired criminals and heard their reminiscences of brazen, often violent acts that at the time they were recounted were not in the very distant past, as they are now.

---

[1] Louis Buchalter was known since his earliest criminal days as "Lepke," the diminutive of "Lepkele," his mother's Yiddish name for "Little Louis." It proved to be convenient for New York newspaper headline writers throughout the 1930s and 1940s who simply identified him as "Lepke"—an abbreviation as well known in the city as "FDR" and later "Ike." We'll refer to him mostly as Lepke, and sometimes as Lepke Buchalter.

[2] Pogrom—an organized massacre of an ethnic group, in particular Jews, in Russia or Eastern Europe.

[3] Roma: Also known as the Romani people, as *gitanos* in Spain, as *gitan* in France, and by other names that translate as "travelers." Wherever the Roma lived, they were also referred to as "gypsies," a derogatory term used to describe this ethnic group that had migrated throughout the world over the course of many centuries.

[4] Cossacks: A people of southern Russia and Ukraine noted for their horsemanship and military skill. They were fiercely loyal to the Czars (the rulers of Russia) and feared by Jews everywhere for their indiscriminate violence.

POLICE DEPARTMENT
CITY OF NEW YORK

No. B62038

Name Abe Reles
Alias "Kid Twist"
Residence 42 Vn Siclen Ave
Crime Homocide (gun)
Age 32 Height 5' 3½"
Weight 140 Build G.
Hair Bro Eyes Bro
Color W Comp Dk
Born Brooklyn
Occupation Luncheonette
Date of Arrest 2-2-40
Officer Healy 75th Sqd
Remarks

F.R. CLASS

Burton Turkus Papers, Special Collections, Lloyd Sealy Library, John Jay College of Criminal Justice/CUNY.

Abe Reles, one of the dozens of times he was arrested. When Brooklyn District Attorney O'Dwyer had him picked up for vagrancy on February 2, 1941, Reles didn't know that he would never be on the streets again.

New York Public Library Digital Collections

Every Eastern-European Jewish family had a story of near escape from these Jew-hating Cossacks. During World War II a number of Cossack military units joined forces with Hitler's invading army against their own Soviet government. The British captured thousands of them, and at the end of the war they were returned to the Soviet Union. Most were immediately executed, and the rest sent to the Siberian gulags (prison camps), never to be seen again.

"Fuck 'em..." I'm sure Old Grandpa Isaac Geik would have said that.

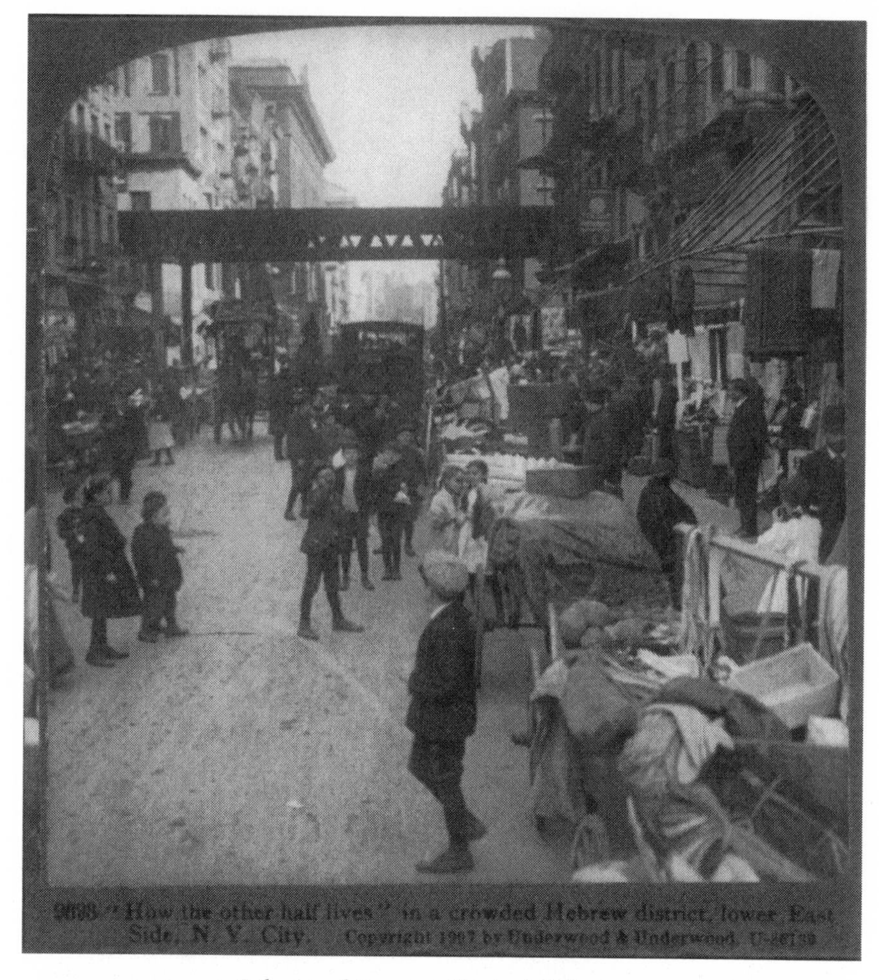

“How the other half lives” in a crowded Hebrew district, lower East
Side, N. Y. City.
Copyright 1907 by Underwood & Underwood.

Library of Congress Digital Collections

1907 photo originally captioned "'How the Other Half Lives' in a crowded Hebrew district on the Lower East Side, N.Y. City"

By 1910 the Lower East Side of Manhattan had a population density greater than that of Calcutta, India. Not just criminals came from these streets but also well-known figures in entertainment, business and even a U.S. Supreme Court justice, Felix Frankfurter.

THE LOWER EAST SIDE—MANHATTAN, NY, 1922

The scarred kitchen table was the center of activity in the crowded tenement apartment. It was Bessie Geik's kitchen. The bathtub in another corner of the kitchen now doubled as a workbench, with a plywood plank balanced on top supporting pots and pans Bessie used to fill catering orders she received from neighborhood shop owners.

For Lower East Side tenement dwellers, the smells of food on every compacted apartment landing would be the one common memory that would never vanish despite their later more affluent circumstances. Stuffed cabbage, as well as *cholent*—a Jewish Sabbath dish of meat and vegetables—would endure as lifetime comfort foods.

The rabbi from a nearby synagogue sometimes called Bessie with an order for a wedding party. Every dime Bessie squeezed out above her costs was a godsend.

Isaac, Bessie's husband, an itinerant worker, sometimes found mechanic's work on the transit system now connecting all the boroughs of New York City, or as the handyman of their building, a tenement on Ludlow Street, in the center of the Lower East Side, the most crowded few blocks in all of America.

Isaac's naturally harsh voice rendered his all-too-often raging drunkenness ever more threatening to Bessie and their six children—

and even to himself, as he was regularly beaten senseless by the Irish cops he provoked into unwinnable violent encounters.

Prohibition had been enacted in 1920—an idiotic federal law promoted by Midwestern farm belt Protestants terrorized by imagined hordes of drunken immigrants rampaging through the cities speaking incomprehensible languages, wearing rags, and, worst of all, they were mostly Catholics and Jews.[1]

Cartoons in many of the nation's 10,000 daily newspapers demonized these immigrants. They were depicted as inebriated on cheap booze, violating women, thieving, and committing every act of depravity.

The lives of everyone around Bessie's kitchen table would soon change because of this new prohibition on the sale and distribution of alcoholic beverages. It would last thirteen years. Some would be destined for fame and fortune in a still to-be organized criminal underworld, others for long prison sentences or untimely death.

Little did the self-righteous Protestants know that Prohibition would unleash the greatest crime wave in American history and the corruption of the police, judges and government officials everywhere —even in their own small towns.

Of Bessie's three boys, her middle son, George, was already lost to the streets. Now twelve years old, George was wise to everything the city had to offer—for the past four years he and his friends had been shoplifting and stealing from fruit and vegetable carts lining the narrow streets.

Louis, seven years old, was in awe of his older brother, George—an awe that would last a lifetime.

The difference in age between George's gang and that of young Louis put them worlds apart. Louis could only dream of the exploits he overheard in mumbled tones and cryptic references.

Late one afternoon Bessie commanded George and Ruby, George's closest friend who would remain so for the rest of their lives, to carry two-gallon cans of krupnik over to Morris', a clothing store on Essex Street, a few minutes walk.[2]

Morris was surprising his wife with a birthday party and she always loved Bessie's krupnik: a soup of leeks, potatoes, carrots, and a few strands of shredded chicken.

George and Ruby entered the store near closing time. They would remember many details, not always the same ones, as the events later that night moved them down the path so many other neighborhood boys had already taken.

Morris Mandel came out of a side room separated by a gray curtain. He started to ask what they wanted, but he saw the cans and understood. He gestured toward a counter. They put the cans on it. Morris turned away. He lifted a battered metal box from under another counter. He opened it—both boys could see it was loaded with cash. Morris counted out a few bills and reached into his pocket for change. He laid the money on the counter next to the soup cans. He waved for them to take the money. They quickly reached for it.

"Come back tomorrow and you can pick up the cans. Bessie will want them," he said, turning back toward the curtain. "Dank dine mutter ba mir (thank your mother for me)."

George nodded. He and Ruby left. As soon as the door closed behind them, they looked at each other. They guessed how much was in the box. Neither could be sure, they had never seen so many bills before. Ruby had something else in mind—the cheap lock on the frame of a dirty window behind the counters had caught his attention. It secured the bottom and top window frames together. It was rusted, maybe not even locked—he couldn't tell in that one furtive glance.

Ruby detoured into the alleyway. George followed.

They walked up to the window halfway down the alley that ended in a brick wall. They both saw the covered garbage pail only a few feet past the window. Ruby tipped it—it was empty. It would be easy to move.

"Let's get this money to your mother. We'll come back later. All we need is a flashlight and a knife to slip in the crack between the bottom and top window frame. I bet that lock will fall right off."

George listened.

They walked quickly toward Ludlow Street. Ruby stopped on a corner, nodding his head in the direction of the hardware store on the corner of Rivington Street. Barrels of nails and wire lined the front of the dirty store window. *Orvitz's Hardware* was painted with minimal flourish on a hanging sign.

"Go across the street and keep walking home. I'll catch up to you," Ruby said. George nodded.

Soon Ruby ran out of the store, a man in a smeared apron waddling after him. The man stopped at the corner. "Haltz gonif! (Stop thief!)," he shouted. He watched Ruby run off, then turned back toward his store.

George continued walking. Ruby slid up alongside George. He pointed to a soiled bag in his hand, opening it enough for George to peer inside.

"It's a Soldier Boy flashlight. It's made out of nickel. It's from the war. I saw it in a magazine. I always wanted one. Now we just need one of your mother's knives."

They returned to the third-floor apartment and gave Bessie the money. She gestured toward the pots on the stove. They were too excited to eat, but they were aware of the wretched lives around them, people struggling for pennies. They knew never to pass up food offered.

Charlie Workman sat with young Louis at the table, talking to Bessie. Charlie was thirteen years old, a year or two older than George and Ruby. He lived in Brownsville, a neighborhood in Brooklyn, but along with many of the other young Jewish boys he often found his way back to the Lower East Side via a short ride on the subway system that was now extending out to the most distant parts of the city. Bessie's kitchen was often Charlie's destination, and prowling the streets with George, Ruby and the others in their growing gang was his thrill—and a thrill for them all.

Ruby slid into the seat next to Charlie. "Can you go over to Morris' clothing store on Essex tomorrow? Pick up mom's cans? We shouldn't go. We'll tell you later." Charlie laughed at the younger boys. He knew a theft was in the works. George also understood it wouldn't be wise for the two of them to turn up again at the clothing store right after it was robbed.

Louis, the boy sitting with Charlie, was my father. He was later known as Bim, or Big Lou. Charlie Workman would be a lifelong friend and family of my Uncle George and my parents. Dad was one of the people who brought his family mob financial support during Charlie's twenty three years in prison. Once he was released from prison my NYPD detective brother Bernard always stood ready to intervene on Uncle Charlie's behalf with any parole officer issues. Uncle Charlie would always refer to Bernard and me as his nephews—I could never imagine calling him anything other than Uncle Charlie but let me not get ahead of the story.

* * *

George and Ruby pushed the garbage can under the window in the alley. The dark side street was not likely to be travelled by casual walkers. Ruby jumped on the can and pulled Bessie's knife from his pocket. He pushed it into the window frame close to the lock, then slashed the knife across the frame. George could hear the lock snap.

"As easy as cutting a piece of challah (braided bread)" Ruby said, as he lifted the bottom window. George handed him the flashlight. Ruby crawled onto a workbench inside the window and disappeared into the darkness. George watched the wavering light illuminating three racks of clothing on hangars along the wall.

A few minutes later Ruby handed out a bag with two metal objects and disappeared again. He returned, climbing through the window onto the garbage pail and dropping to the alleyway. They walked cautiously back to Ludlow Street. George held the bag close—they knew the Irish cops were always on the lookout for Jewish street kids just like them.

"Look in the bag," Ruby said. George opened it.

"I saw those two candle holders when we were in the store before," Ruby said. "They're valuable. They're silver. I saw them in a magazine one time. I think they're worth a lot. I don't know what to do with them."

"Maybe Johnny Eder has a way to get rid of them. He runs errands for that pawn shop uptown," George said.

Johnny Eder, another one of the gang who spent many evenings in Bessie's kitchen, was the most sophisticated. He read books and knew about museums—that was enough to make him different.

"There are also these three rings," Ruby said, reaching in his pocket. He looked at them carefully. "This one looks expensive."

"What about the cash?" George asked.

They moved into a doorway. Ruby counted out forty dollars. It was a fortune. Rings, silver candleholders, cash. They would never waste time stealing from pushcarts again—it could never again be this exciting. A golden door had popped open to the Promised Land. Ruby and George wanted their place in it.

---

1 Prohibition: The Volstead Act—the Eighteenth Amendment to the Constitution. It prohibited the manufacture and sale of alcohol in the U.S. It was in effect between 1920 and 1933. It quickly led to the opening of thousands of illegal saloons—called speakeasies—throughout the country.

2 Ruby was born Reuben Koloditsky in 1910. He changed his name to Ruby Kolod when he later became a full-time criminal—Uncle George became George Gordon. Many criminals changed their names so as not to embarrass their families. Their new names also made them more "American."

Author's family album

Isaac and Bessie Geik, my father's parents. When I was younger, I wondered why most of the other boys' immigrant grandfathers were furniture makers, bakers, taxi drivers or Garment Center workers while mine had to be carried out of Prohibition-era speakeasies by Uncle George and his crew.

Isaac also liked to fight drunken street battles with Irish cops—always a losing proposition. Isaac was a patriarch to a generation of young men who would be at the core of organized crime throughout much of the 20th century.

GETTING CONNECTED, 1925

The nighttime burglary of Morris Mandel's clothing store three years earlier merged into just one of dozens of robberies, shakedowns, stealing coins from younger boys shooting craps, and loading illegal booze onto trucks. For some there was another side job that had a fifty-year history on the Lower East Side—providing muscle for unions or employers, whoever paid the most, in the turbulent labor wars in New York City. The boys who three years ago sat in Bessie Geik's kitchen in that stifling tenement at 89 Ludlow Street were now out on the streets of the Lower East Side—full time.

Uncle George, Ruby, Uncle Charlie, Johnny Eder—along with two new additions to their crew, Sammy Kass and Sol "Blubber" Bloom—and others were ready for anything. The grimness of their parents' lives was not in the cards for them. They now they had role models: older men they could see every day scheming on the street corners.

"Sure, we knew who the criminals were," Uncle Charlie said, reminiscing forty-five years later. "The way they dressed, the way they talked. It was like they owned the streets. They were the ones we wanted to be like. Looking back, they were only ten years older than us, but we knew they were the ones to be connected with."

"Connected," that was the word. Connections would create a roadmap for these teenagers who already knew the city was ripe for every crime. Groups of thieves roamed neighborhoods stealing everything, hijacking trucks, and extorting businesses. Payrolls going from banks to the small factories around the city were better paydays for the criminals than for the employees. It was all cash back then and often carried by a bookkeeper or the uncombative son of a shop owner. Easy targets.

A cottage industry of criminality was exploding on the streets of Manhattan and it was happening thanks to the do-gooder Midwestern Protestants from places nobody on the Lower East Side had ever heard of. Prohibition kick-started the biggest government make-work crime program the Lower East Side, or anywhere else in America, would ever see.

The joining together of young Italians and Jews of the Lower East Side taking advantage of this Criminal Land of Plenty emerged from a long history. Their ancestors had traded with each other even before there was a Roman Empire—especially the Sicilians who since antiquity had seen traders and conquerors come to their island jutting out into the Mediterranean, and who always managed to keep themselves as a tightly wound clan right through their arrival on these Manhattan streets at the turn of the twentieth century.[1]

Back in the Old Country, Northern Italians considered the Sicilians "less white," equating them with "Africans." The Sicilians met the same prejudice in America from the white nationalists as did the Jews.

In the early 1890s a mass lynching of eleven Italians in New Orleans by a frenzied white rabble shocked the nation. Attacks on Italian communities throughout America intensified. The recently arrived Italians and Jews on the Lower East Side recognized each other as outcasts in the New World.

No such close fellowship existed between the Jews and Italians with the Irish Americans. The Jews and Italians arrived at the turn of the century from Europe or were born in America in the first years of the twentieth century. When they arrived, New York City was controlled by Irish Catholics who themselves had landed en masse fifty years earlier, refugees from the devastating British-induced Potato Famine. The Irish soon moved to the core of the city's corruption—an unyielding corruption even for a crusader as fearless as Theodore Roosevelt, the New York City police commissioner in the mid-1890s, then governor of New York, and later the President of the United States.

Tammany Hall, originally a benefit society for impoverished Irish immigrants, soon controlled the city payroll, from mayoral candidates down to the lowest job in the farthest reaches of the Bronx and Staten Island. Italians and Jews need not apply.

The distrust of the Irish ran even deeper for the Jews; the Irish Catholics echoed the same anti-Semitism the Jews had encountered for centuries in Europe. The Irish were the bearers of the centuries old taunt "Christ killers," a view not strongly embraced by the Italians, also Catholics.

The Jewish and Italian criminals believed that Irish gangsters would betray their own at every turn. They were easy for the Irish police to flip, or so it seemed to the Jews and Italians—newspapers reported Irishmen testifying against former partners, even family members. This was sinful to the Jews and Italians. They accepted as truth that the Irish were undisciplined, more ready for drunken bar fights than to plan the details of crimes.

Uncle Charlie later joked, "There's never been an Irish criminal who wouldn't fuck up a wet dream." I laughed. I imagined that to be an expression he picked up in Trenton State Penitentiary. He added as 'proof:' "One time I was going to do a job with this Irish guy, Bones. He never showed up. I found out that he got drunk the night before, shot his girlfriend and then shot a cop in the street. For what? Who knows? A fuckin' idiot."

Of course, Jewish and Italian gangsters also become witnesses for the prosecution against their onetime allies, especially if they feared they were in line to get "whacked" by their bosses. This recounting even begins with Yiddish-English speaking informant Abe "Kid Twist" Reles' exit from a sixth-floor window in 1941 while under close police protection. His testimony was devastating to Murder Inc. and led to Sing Sing executions and many lengthy prison sentences for his one-time fellow hitmen.

The Irish also had their own views of their ethnic gangster rivals. Jimmy Breslin, a Queens, New York, card-carrying Irishman, journalist and lifelong watcher of New York's underworld wrote, "A true Sicilian in America today must smoke in the subway... [He] goes three blocks out of his way for the privilege of going the wrong way on a one-way street."[2]

---

1 Italy's protective attitude towards their Jewish communities only ten years later—during the nightmare of Fascism in Europe—was recounted in Howard M. Sachar's *Farewell España* (New York: Alfred A. Knopf, Inc., 1995), It is an engrossing history of the Jews in Spain and the diaspora after their expulsion in 1492.

"The typical Italian family could neither understand nor emotionally accept the gratuitous persecution of the Jewish family next door." (*Farewell España*, p. 242)

At no time during the Hitler years leading up to the war, or during the war years, did anti-Semitism have as popular a base in Italy as it did throughout the rest of Europe. No number of personal appeals by the Nazi high command to Mussolini or other Italian officials to turn over Jews achieved the desired results.

An October 1943 communiqué by the SS commandant in Rome regarding a roundup of Jews stated, "The behavior of the Italian people was unalloyed passive resistance, which in some individual cases amounted to active assistance... . A great mass of people even tried to cut off the police from the Jews." (*Farewell España*, p. 247)

As a result of the countless acts of personal courage and determination by the Italians to protect their neighbors, members of one of the oldest Jewish communities in Europe, at least 80% of Italian Jews survived the Holocaust. (*Farewell España*, p. 247)

2 *The Gang That Couldn't Shoot Straight*, Jimmy Breslin (New York: Viking Press, 1969).

UNCLE CHARLIE TALKS ABOUT MOSES, 1970

These characters, despite their criminality, shared a sense of destiny as Jewish people. The trauma of their parents' humiliation and precarious existence in Eastern Europe was never lost on them. They had since childhood heard dramatic tales of escapes from the random violence as well as the tragic endings of innocent victims who didn't escape the violence. Most of the young criminals never attended synagogues or practiced Hebrew rituals, but they were aware of their history far back into antiquity.

On a rainy afternoon in 1970 I was with Uncle Charlie, my father and two old friends of theirs from Ludlow Street days. We were in Dubrow's on Seventh Avenue, a self-service restaurant featuring a lengthy steam table abundant with Jewish and American comfort food. I often gravitated to Dubrow's when I visited the Garment Center—old family friends leaning over cups of cold coffee were always welcome sights.

Charlie tossed a piece of rye bread back into the small wire basket. "The bread in prison was fresher than this." As he laughed at his own joke, a large mural on a wall caught his attention: an artist's rendition of a building, perhaps a Roman temple, with people in the foreground in modern suits and dresses, not togas. Somehow he linked the mural to Moses.

"Did Moses lead anyone out of Egypt?" Charlie asked nobody in particular. "Was Moses really found in a wicker basket in the reeds alongside the Nile? Did any of it really happen?" He thought a moment. "It's gotta be bullshit."

* * *

The legend of three-month-old Moses hidden on the banks of the Nile by a mother who couldn't bear that her firstborn son die as mandated by the Pharaoh didn't sit well with Uncle Charlie. He pointed out that the Pharaoh's Nile River teemed with crocodiles.

"Who ever heard of a mother hiding her child in the fucking reeds next to a river filled with crocodiles? It's gotta be bullshit." I imagined Charlie having animated discussions in New Jersey prison yards many times over his twenty-three years in jail with other convicts who might have just been passing through the yard with only five- or ten-year sentences.

"Do you know there was supposed to be 600,000 warriors in the Exodus?" Charlie added. "With women and children that would have been way more than a million people! If that were true, then by the time the first people arrived in the Promised Land the last people would still be leaving Egypt. It just doesn't sound right."

The other men listened without committing to a response.

It wasn't the first time I was aware of how men, old friends like these, had reconnected after a lifetime of such different experiences. A diner at another table would never pick out which one of these four men had spent twenty-three years in prison for murder—and had been, thirty years earlier, one of the most feared gunmen in the city. There was no indication at the table that Uncle Charlie elicited greater respect than anyone else.

* * *

Fifteen years later I was reminded of Uncle Charlie's history lesson. I stood just two feet in front of a mural covering every inch of the walls and ceiling of a tomb in the Valley of the Nobles near Luxor, Egypt.

I marveled that someone, maybe four thousand years earlier, had stood in my exact spot painting in such intricate detail daily life along the Nile. The colors were still as bright as a poster in the lobby of any movie theatre in the world, the desert having immunized them from moisture for several millennia.

Life along the Nile River was depicted in detail: a young boy walking a dog on a leash, and women with colorful makeup on their faces. And yes, there were the crocodiles—good reason to find it curious that a mother would think of saving her child by placing him in harm's way.

Mel Brooks had his own addition to the Exodus saga in his comedy *History of the World Part One*: Moses descends Mt. Sinai with fifteen commandments etched onto three tablets God had given to him. He drops one tablet, it smashes on a rock, and Moses shrugs, "Ok, so there are only Ten Commandments."

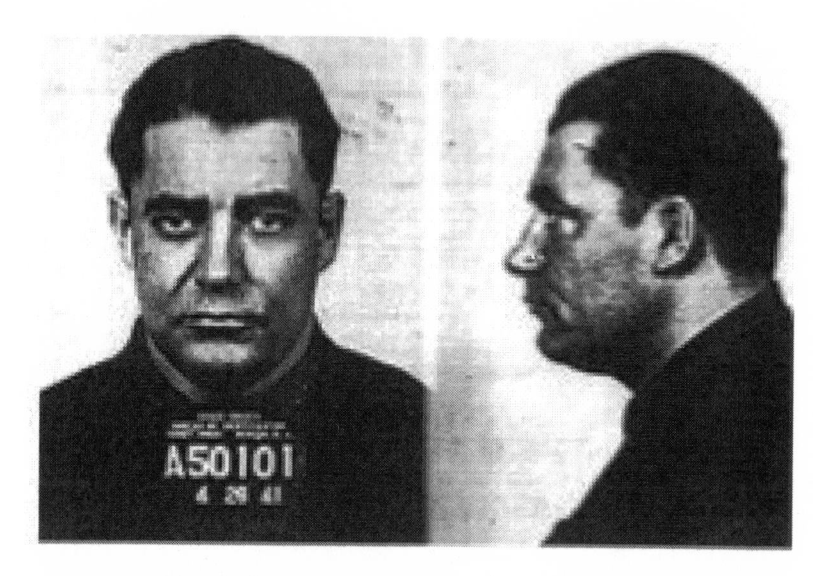

New York Police Department, April 28, 1941

Uncle Charlie Workman when he was arrested in 1941 for the murder of Dutch Schultz six years earlier. He was also known as "Handsome Charlie," although I don't know what his victims thought about that. I first met him twenty-three years later. I'm glad he loved Uncle George and my father. I also made him laugh a lot.

ARNOLD ROTHSTEIN, NEW YORK, THE 1920S

The convergence of the Jazz Age, the Roaring Twenties, and Prohibition was steroid to the pursuit of adventure and quick money. Two men embodied this New World for Uncle George, Ruby and their crew then in their early teens. Whenever possible they watched these men intently. So did many New Yorkers, not just aspiring criminals. Without television and with radio just becoming a household necessity, a sighting of either of them—how they dressed, where they were, who they were with, any shard of detail to fill out the story—was an event to share on the street.

Babe Ruth was one. He arrived in New York in 1920, the year Prohibition started. He had already been a baseball star in Boston. He was the first sports superstar in America, at a time when baseball, horse racing and boxing were the only sports that mattered.

Seven years earlier, in August 1914, the same month the first shots of the Great War (as World War I was known then) were fired in Europe, nineteen-year-old Ruth came to Boston from a Baltimore workhouse where he had lived the previous nine years. He had never seen a menu and never been on an elevator. He bought a bicycle with his first paycheck.

He became an immediate sensation in the sports world. Nobody had ever hit a baseball with such force before. He changed the game. He also attracted the attention of gamblers throughout the country.

By 1920 Babe Ruth, now on the New York Yankees, was a man of the night—a patron of the New York speakeasies that opened as soon as serving alcohol became illegal. His entrances to and exits from the many brothels in Manhattan were noted. Babe standing under a streetlight at midnight puffing on a cigar was an image Uncle George's crew prized—his carefree, easy money life was all they desired.

The other man dominating the 1920s for these boys and countless other street thugs and con men was not as well known as Babe Ruth, but his existence affected their lives more than could any baseball player: Arnold Rothstein.

Rothstein was a third-generation Jew—an uptown German Jew, at that. To many immigrant Jews in New York City this had great significance; the German Jews had settled in America generations earlier. They, like the newly arrived poorer Jews, also were not welcome in Protestant private schools, universities and country clubs. Many nevertheless became leaders in whatever commerce was open to them.

The German Jews founded investment houses with familiar names: Goldman, Loeb, Lehman. The department stores spreading over Midtown Manhattan (a merchandising innovation that began after the Civil War) were owned and operated by German Jews—Klein's, B. Altman's, Bloomingdale's, and Macy's founded by Isidor Straus. The new entertainment craze—silent movies—had names like Mayer, Goldwyn, and Harry Cohn on the screen.

* * *

The uptown German Jews financed social outreaches, including the Educational Alliance on the Lower East Side, for the newly arrived Yiddish-speaking, rag-wearing Jews. They intended to Americanize these Eastern Europeans who were the eternal stereotypes mocked in anti-Semitic newspaper cartoons in Europe and America.

But of all the uptown German Jews only Rothstein mattered to these young boys on the Lower East Side.

Despite Rothstein's refined upbringing the gambling halls and dealing making, legal or illegal, were his passions.[1]

Uncle Charlie had vivid recollections of Arnold Rothstein: "Everyone knew who he was. Even though he was from uptown he walked around Delancey Street like he owned it—the way we wanted to.[2] He was different. If someone was talking to him on a street corner that person became important and someone for us to know."

Rothstein cultivated an air of mystery. F. Scott Fitzgerald used Rothstein as his touchstone for Meyer Wolfsheim, the elusive, shady character in his novel *The Great Gatsby*.

In his early twenties Rothstein had been a protégé of Tom Foley, a sometimes sheriff, a member in good standing of the Tammany Hall corruption machine, and an owner of gambling halls all over the city. Rothstein became Foley's trusted adviser and opened his own gambling houses and saloons that, because of his new connections, were free from police harassment. Foley and Rothstein partnered in bail bonds and real estate companies. Soon nothing was out of Rothstein's grasp.

Rothstein bought a racetrack in New York and fixed races all over the country. People came to him to finance their ventures, legal or illegal—it didn't matter. He had the refined presence to dine with bankers and judges or stand at a green felt table and roll the dice in a classy uptown illegal gambling hall just as readily as he could put a knee down on a concrete alleyway and shoot craps.

Uncle George once stood outside a gambling joint on Delancey Street. He thought he might have been twelve years old. Arnold Rothstein stepped through the door onto the street. George later amused, imagined his star struck stare must have attracted Rothstein's attention. Rothstein motioned Uncle George to come toward him. He complied in shock. Rothstein gave Uncle George a few bills and told him to stuff them in his pocket. George did so.

"You know Nat's game over on Hester Street?" Rothstein asked the astonished Uncle George, who nodded. The crap game was a popular one, a lot of action into the night. It was in the garage of an abandoned warehouse. Nat let everyone know he had a gun and would shoot to kill whoever tried to take over his action.

"Give that to Nat," Rothstein said casually. George took off in the direction of Hester Street.

He pulled the cash out of his pocket and gave it to Nat.

"Mr. Rothstein told me to give this to you," he said as assertively as he could manage. Decades later Uncle George still remembered the thrill of mentioning himself and Arnold Rothstein in the same sentence.

* * *

Arnold Rothstein had become the undisputed King of the New York Underworld. Every grifter, gambler, conman, prostitute, politician, and police detective knew who "A. R." was. By the mid-1920s Rothstein was already a major importer of illegal booze.

Nobody knew how many ships, distilleries or trucks he owned, or where he operated. It didn't matter, he was the man to see. He made deals with gangsters and bankers with the simple terms jotted on the back of a napkin in a restaurant, a handshake in a barbershop, or whispered codes on a street corner. It was all matter-of-fact deal making.

But one venture raised Rothstein to prominence amongst every underworld character in America: the 1919 World Series.

That World Series, between the Chicago White Sox and the Cincinnati Reds, had been fixed. The White Sox players were successful in their attempt to lose the series—although they were so clumsy their plot was apparent to every newspaper reporter covering the games. It became a nationwide scandal. Newspapers identified Arnold Rothstein as the fixer. He testified and denied everything, of course. The players' written confessions were lost. Ultimately, they were acquitted of the criminal charges brought against them.

Nonetheless, in 1921 the new and first Commissioner of Baseball, Kenesaw Mountain Landis, banned them for life. Their careers were over.

It was never proven Arnold Rothstein had an involvement in the fix, but the years of newspaper coverage of the scandal gave him even greater street credibility.

To the young thieves it was a miracle they could see someone on the streets that may have actually fixed a World Series—the biggest sporting event of the year. Their esteem for Rothstein deepened even more when it was rumored that the conspirators came to Rothstein to finance the fix, but he turned them down. Then, knowing the fix would be in, he bet on the winning team and made a fortune without having to pay anyone off.

* * *

The gangsters Rothstein anointed were immediately given respect on the streets. He had an extraordinary eye for criminal talent: Meyer Lansky, Lucky Luciano, Ben "Bugsy" Siegel, Vito Genovese, Frank Costello, Waxey Gordon (no relation to Uncle George), Lepke Buchalter. It would later seem as if Rothstein had a specific purpose for each one of them. But above all it was about organization and making deals—deals with anyone who could deliver. Have dozens of partners in dozens of deals. If they were reliable, keep them close.

Why kill a rival when you can divide the proceeds with him?

At the same time, in the 1920s, Old World Sicilian criminals didn't take kindly to the idea of making deals with even non-Sicilian Italians, let alone with Jews and the Irish. They had their own corrupt officials in City Hall, but not to the extent of the New World gangsters working with Rothstein. It was inevitable that the Old and New would one day clash.

Ruby, Uncle George, Uncle Charlie, Sammy Kass, and Johnny Eder never imagined that within just a few years they too would be important players in this criminal network forming right before their eyes, and that, for the next sixty years, they would be at the center of what would be known as "organized crime"—a criminal organization that began on their streets on the Lower East Side and morphed into an industry that rivaled any other in size and political power in America.

---

1 Rothstein's father and grandfather had prospered at times and struggled at other times in New York's garment industry, but they were always respected men in the Jewish community. Arnold was born in 1882, forty years before the teenagers began hanging out in front of Bessie and Isaac Geik's tenement on Ludlow Street.

Rothstein should have been another generation of garment manufacturer or an attorney or doctor. His family would have supported those pursuits, except there was one barrier to this genteel future: there was nothing on which he wouldn't either bet or take anyone else's bet. Gambling and crime was the world that excited him.

2 Delancey Street is the main drag of the Lower East Side. The easternmost part of the wide street is the entrance and exit to the Williamsburg Bridge that spans the East River from Manhattan to Brooklyn.

Library of Congress, Prints and Photographs Division, NYWT&S Collection

Arnold Rothstein—the man who brought together the young Italian and Jewish hoodlums of the Lower East Side of the 1920s and created "organized crime." His simple message: Why kill each other when you can share the unimagined illegal wealth created by Prohibition—the dumbest law ever enacted anywhere? Rothstein should have been a successful businessman, but underneath his sophistication he was just another degenerate gambler (as we would say in New York).

5

THE CLEVELAND SYNDICATE, 1928

The Roaring Twenties bred new rackets and bigger payoffs for the criminal underworld, and in 1928 Uncle George, Ruby, Uncle Charlie and their crew came of age. While this world of unimagined wealth opened up to teenagers on the street, their families and synagogues were often horrified by the criminality of their young people.

Prostitution in Eastern Europe had been a scourge since the middle 1800s. Cities always attracted the hungry, the adventurous and the naïve from the countryside—the Jewish women of Eastern Europe were no exception. They fled country villages for Warsaw, Vilna and Odessa—big cities with large Jewish populations and thriving criminal elements. The women fled forced marriages, hopelessness, and strangling lives of tradition; some were socialists and revolutionaries hunted by the Russian police after the 1881 assassination of the Czar.

Smooth-talking men deceived young Jewish women—employing the same ruses used on American women at train stations in Detroit, Chicago and New York—with promises of exciting careers, but instead pimped them into white slavery.

By 1928, three generations of Jewish prostitutes worked the Lower East Side streets and speakeasies. To the disgust of the Yiddish language newspapers, the prostitutes, their Jewish pimps and the flophouse hotel owners participated in a shameful industry. The newspapers printed anguished letters from prostitutes unable to free themselves from their pimps.

Letters also described another crime devastating their community: drugs. Heroin, cocaine and opium were not limited to the opium houses of Chinatown, as stereotyped in silent movies and newsstand crime magazines of that era. The same Jewish and Italian criminals who smuggled booze also controlled the drug and prostitution underworld.

Nevertheless, there was also for immigrants who had fled the pogroms in Eastern Europe a pride in the Jewish gangsters who would fight off anti-Semitic attacks by the Irish and Germans, large ethnic groups in the inner cities at that time. That these men were to be both feared and admired was a contradiction in the Jewish community for the rest of the twentieth century.[1]

Some of these criminals later claimed moral conflicts with prostitution and drugs. Still others found the corruption of labor unions to be against their own family's history of socialism and workers' rights—yet nothing stopped them from extorting and strong-arming small business owners, running crooked gambling dens and even assassinating other refugees from the horrors of Europe—their own people.

My father Lou was thirteen years old when his life changed in one moment on Delancey and Essex Streets. Two of his older friends, Maurice and Pete, had focused on a well-dressed drunken man across the street—they waited to pounce on their target and dig into his pockets.

Lou felt the sharp slap across his head; his hat fell to the street. He turned to see his brother George and Uncle Charlie only inches from his face. Uncle George said, "Don't even think about it. We're the criminals, not you." Lou remembered Charlie smiling.

My father spent his life as close friends with the young men who later became the nucleus of organized crime, but he was never allowed into the rackets. He lacked the instincts and ruthlessness to survive even if he had wanted that lifestyle.

That same year George, Ruby, Charlie and Sammy Kass caught the attention of "Trigger" Mike Coppola and Sam "Red" Levine, two men who were already well known to Arnold Rothstein's emerging gangland leaders Meyer Lansky and Lucky Luciano. Trigger Mike and Red Levine were contemporaries of Lansky and Luciano but lacked their star power—some gangsters loved the streets too much.

"Trigger Mike" Coppola, born in Italy (probably in Sicily) in 1903 was by 1928 already well connected with the East Harlem Italian gangsters. He had the reputation of being the most sadistic of all of them. His violence was not limited to the streets—his wives were also targets. It was rumored that he killed his first wife days after she gave birth to their child. She supposedly had overheard him plotting the murder of an East Harlem political activist. His second wife moved to Rome to escape their marriage and his alleged abuse of her daughter by a previous marriage. She was found dead next to an empty bottle of sleeping pills on her nightstand.

Decades later Uncle Charlie and Johnny Eder remembered Trigger Mike. "He was the sickest bastard of all," Charlie said, "there was just something about him. He liked to shoot people."

Johnny Eder said, "Mike had the worst rep of all of them. Maybe that was because he was a little guy—maybe five feet four or five. He had to prove himself all the time. Yet he became one of the wealthiest mob guys ever."

The New York Jewish underworld respected Sam "Red" Levine for a unique characteristic; unlike other hitmen, Sam was religious. He wore a skullcap, a *yarmulke,* under his fedora. He "kept kosher"—there was only kosher food in his house—and he lived quietly with his family in Brooklyn. He was never seen in a Broadway speakeasy or brothel.

All the years I knew Red, he had a longtime girlfriend, Sylvia, who had an ardent attraction for mobsters. (Red still had a wife and family in Brooklyn, of course.) Sylvia, a friend and confidant of our mother Reba since their school days, was an Auntie Mame character to my sister, Iris, who viewed Sylvia's life with great curiosity when we were young teenagers.

Decades later, our mother reminisced that she would sometimes get dressed nicely and leave the Bronx to meet Sylvia in Manhattan for a drink. I was curious: "Two great-looking then forty-year-old women going into a bar in Manhattan? Men must have hit on you, right?"

"Are you kidding? We went to one of Red Levine's bars. Who would ever talk to Red's girlfriend or me? Nobody even came near us."

Over the years the myth emerged that Red Levine would never kill on Saturday—the Jewish Sabbath. Uncle George corrected that claim, saying, "If the price was right, Red would kill anyone on any day."

Red Levine was arrested in March of 1928 for felonious assault. His status increased immensely in the New York underworld because two gangland stars were also charged in the same assault: Meyer Lansky and Benjamin "Bugsy" Siegel. One version of the story is that the three drove their victim, John Barrett, a small-time criminal, who they suspected of cooperating with the police, to the outskirts of the city and kicked him out of the car. As Barrett ran into the darkness, they shot at him—moving target practice—and he was hospitalized with a bullet wound.

Then one of them laced a roasted chicken with poison and gave it to Barrett's wife for her husband. When Barrett discovered the donors were his intended assassins, he threw the chicken out of the hospital window.

Decades later I heard Uncle George say, "That whole story is bullshit. The poisoned chicken, the target practice. Barrett jumped out of the car and ran into the trees to hide. He caught a bullet. But like any good bullshit story that target practice one soon became the truth."

Sometime in early August 1928 Trigger Mike needed two hit men for a contract in Cleveland, the scene of violent gang wars for control of the immensely profitable booze shipments smuggled in from Canada. Some of the notorious Purple Gang of Detroit, including Morris "Moe" Dalitz, had moved their operations to Cleveland—and, as in so many other cities, bodies were found in cars parked on Cleveland's side streets, sprawled in alleyways, or with feet protruding from shallow graves in basements of abandoned houses.

This intended hit was a Jew who made himself hard to find except for Saturday religious services. Trigger Mike wanted Jews to do the job—ones who might have even been in a synagogue at least once or twice in their lives and who wouldn't attract attention—so he gave the job to Uncle George and Red Levine. The details of their trip to Cleveland are lost to history.

However, Dalitz, the leader of the Cleveland Syndicate, also known as the Cleveland Four, was to become the most influential person in George's criminal life.[1]

Red Levine told one of the oldest "Chinaman jokes" in the Jewish joke catalog. I laughed even though I had heard it before—and still do. "Morris and Harry go into a Chinese laundry. Harry argues with the Chinaman. They leave. Outside, Harry says, 'That fucking Jew bastard.' Morris says, 'What are you talking about, he's Chinese.' 'Yeah,' says Harry, 'they're the worst kind."

* * *

Morris "Moe" Dalitz, a Boston-born Jew, moved as a youth with his family to Detroit and began bootlegging at a young age. Michigan was a "dry" state two years before the rest of the United States. So, when Prohibition became a federal law in 1920, Moe and his gang had experience smuggling booze from Canada through Lake Huron and Lake Erie. When he arrived in Cleveland around 1928 his mob already controlled the waterways to Canada. Cleveland, also on the banks of the Great Lakes was, like Detroit, an "open" city, with a government as corrupt as any in North America.

Dalitz's flotillas on the Great Lakes, and soon waterways everywhere, were called "the Little Jewish Navy"—later they became "the Big Jewish Navy." They smuggled liquor from Canada and the best scotch from Great Britain.

Dalitz, according to some, by 1928 ranked as an equal with Meyer Lansky, Lucky Luciano and Frank Costello in the crime world. They remained trusted partners for decades after prohibition ended—primarily in gambling, both legal and illegal.

One difference separated Dalitz from the rest of what would soon be called the National Commission: He was, and had been for years, an owner and operator of legitimate family-run industrial laundry companies in Detroit and Cleveland—and later, in Las Vegas. Dalitz no doubt would have been a success in these operations without any mob connections. So would have the other members of the Cleveland Four—the four men who would guide the fortunes of the Cleveland Syndicate for the next five decades.[2]

When Moe Dalitz left Detroit, his brother Louis stayed behind to manage the family laundry businesses and also handle the ongoing rumrunning from Canada. His speakeasy customers in New York called him "Lou the Chinaman." What else? They weren't creative geniuses, after all. Any white guy in the laundry business was either "the Chinaman" or "the Chink."

Jimmy Fratianno, a Cleveland hoodlum and hitman, said decades later, "Ya see, how did these Jews get rich? Guys like Moe Dalitz, Sammy Tucker, Morris Kleinman—the ones that owned the Desert Inn. They had two or three gambling houses in Cleveland, right? Maybe they declare a million dollars at the end of the year. After seven, eight years you want to invest $5–10 million in something you can show that you reported it. In 1941 they bought the Beverly Club in Kentucky. They had money to show. The Italians couldn't do it. You give an Italian a million dollars, he'll put it in the cellar. He can't invest it."[3]

Of course, a lot of Italian gangsters also owned legitimate businesses, but it's always hard to resist a good story.

Fratianno became a government informant years later, when he thought he was being set up for a hit.

* * *

There was an unexpected outcome from Uncle George and Red Levine's mission in Cleveland: George caught the attention of Moe Dalitz. Dalitz had one of his mobsters arrange for George, on his way back to New York City, to take a suitcase of cash to Meyer Lansky's crew in Saratoga Springs in upstate New York. George could hardly believe his good fortune—barely eighteen years old and he was carrying a suitcase from one of the biggest rumrunners in America to Meyer Lansky, already a well-known figure in the criminal underworld.

Not only was he going to the Mecca of sophisticated gambling, but also it was August, the high season for Saratoga Springs, with its famous racetrack at the center of the action. To the gamblers and grifters on the Lower East Side, Saratoga Springs was the grand summer playground of the wealthy Protestants—the same ones who looked down upon the Jews, Italians and Irish.

Arnold Rothstein had been well known to the Saratoga Springs gambling crowd even before the Great War. Though Rothstein was a Jew, he had already owned a racetrack and knew the mentality of gamblers, and, to him, the WASPs (White Anglo-Saxon Protestants) were no different from any other gamblers.

The elegant mansions around the lake in Saratoga Springs had separate lavish retreats for gambling and prostitution. Despite all the illegal activities, everything transpired there with a sense of old American civility, unlike the hard-edged Manhattan "carpet joints" (the upscale speakeasies). In the lake houses—chefs prepared lavish menus, cool breezes drifted in from the lake, fine wines were poured, and spectacular floor shows set Saratoga Springs apart from other gambling spots in America.

Rothstein found that, just as in New York City, the police, judges and racing officials in this upscale resort town were willing to look the other way. Fixed races were not out of order and huge bets would never be turned down.

Even though the patrons of the racetracks and casinos were wealthy, Rothstein understood that the locals were working people, often struggling, so he made sure to spread money throughout the county. The lake houses bought produce from local farmers and cattle ranchers, especially those with close ties to the Republican and Democratic Party leaders. Rothstein kept every building contractor in the county busy and well rewarded. He never forgot that his people were from the Big City and that their welcome was, as would always be true, based on spreading the wealth among the locals.

Both Meyer Lansky and Arnold Rothstein understood the core of gambling: the odds. Each game—roulette, craps, blackjack—had immutable odds for every possible wager. Some dumb bets greatly favored the house; others gave the casino just a razor-thin margin.

In Saratoga Springs, Meyer Lansky recognized that these upscale casinos would be his future. He often recounted that when he was a child, every Friday his mother gave him a nickel to take to the neighborhood baker to warm the Sabbath dinner. One Friday Lansky lost the nickel to scammers in a craps game on the sidewalk. His parents severely punished him, and the family had a cold dinner. It was humiliating.

For the next few weeks he watched the games on the streets and realized that the men running the game had a shill—one of their crew who made a few winning bets and got the suckers to lay down their money. Lansky observed everyone's behavior and finally one day, at the last second, he put down a nickel along with the shill's bet. The men running the game couldn't protest or they would give away the con to their marks. Lansky left with ten cents and was determined to master all dice games. He learned a lot on the streets, but it wasn't until Saratoga Springs that his vision of the future of gambling—legal and illegal—became clear.

For Meyer and Arnold, the success of a casino depended entirely on volume: reeling in a large number of gamblers eager to throw money on the green felt tabletops. And, to have the gamblers stay loyal to a casino, the operators had to be honest, which wasn't the nature of criminals. Lansky demanded honesty from every employee; dishonesty in a casino, or even the rumor of it, would spread quickly in the gambling world. Gamblers could accept big losses as long as they were confident that they weren't being cheated.

Casino odds are etched in stone, but they are calculated over the long term. Ultimately the odds turn every winner into a loser. However, anything can happen on a given roll of the dice or turn of a roulette wheel. To let "the odds play out" the house needs a sizeable bankroll to pay off unexpected winners. Money has to be there for payouts—there are no excuses. That may have been the reason Uncle George carried money to Meyer Lansky's casino—the night before, a long-term loser may have, for once, become that short-term winner.

Uncle George said it best three decades later. My brother Bernard, a NYPD detective at the time, was at a crap table at the Stardust in Las Vegas. It was the Cleveland and Chicago mobs' hotel; by then Uncle George was an important part of that operation. Bernard felt a tap on his shoulder, he turned around, Uncle George asked him, "Do you think we built this place so you can win?"

Uncle George later remembered his first trip to Saratoga Springs. "We were just ghetto Jews and Italian peasants from the tenements. Saratoga Springs was a class of people we knew existed but were ashamed to be around. They had big money and they didn't have to flash it. I was more nervous going there because of the rich people than I was carrying money from Moe Dalitz to Meyer."

My sister Iris told me that Uncle George would write down a word he didn't understand and later look it up in his dictionary. He also traveled with a pocket-sized picture of his mother—our Grandma Bessie—that he had in a fold-up blue leather frame. I imagined that he propped the frame of dear old Mom on his hotel room nightstand above the drawer where he had the gun to be used for the next contract.

The courtliness of Saratoga Springs also served as an ideal for the Cleveland Four's casinos in Cleveland, the surrounding counties and later across the border in Kentucky—all with elected officials willing to look the other way. The Cleveland Four joined forces with the Mayfield Road Gang, the Italian Mafia that had been there for many years. They all saw the end of Prohibition, and they also knew that gambling was an enduring part of American life that they intended to take to a new level. Thus, the Cleveland Syndicate was born.

---

[1] The wavering between pride in, and shame of, the young criminals in the Jewish American communities no doubt existed in other ethnic groups as well. However, the extra dimension of constant anti-Semitic attacks made these contradictory feelings somewhat more pronounced.

The Yiddish press editorials often expressed the simple truth that these men did not have to be criminals to survive, despite the tenement poverty where they were raised.

It was often noted during Lepke's Murder Inc. reign of terror that he had four siblings: one brother was a college professor and rabbi, another a dentist, and the third a pharmacist; his older sister was a teacher, the head of the English department in her school.

[2] Because of their close association with Meyer Lansky and Charles "Lucky" Luciano, the four Jewish businessmen-gangsters became a visible element of organized crime in Cleveland, even after they joined with the Italian Mayfair Road mob. The Cleveland Four, the Cleveland Syndicate, and the Mayfair Road mob are often used interchangeably. For purposes of this story, I refer mostly to the Cleveland Syndicate or the Cleveland Four.

According to some researchers, the Cleveland Syndicate and the New York and Chicago mobs were the most powerful groups in organized crime for the next fifty years.

[3] Mike Wallace's interview with *The Last Mafioso* Jimmy «The Weasel" Fratianno in 1981

84

NAME : Michael COPPOLA

ALIASES : Trigger Mike, Mike Ross, Mike Russo, Mike Marino

DESCRIPTION : Born 7-20-1900 Salerno, Italy. 5'5", 155 lbs., brown eyes, black-grey hair, I&NS file A 10292316.

LOCALITIES FREQUENTED : Resides 4431 Alton Road, Miami Beach, Florida. Frequents Collins Avenue and 23rd St., Miami Beach, and makes occasional trips to East Harlem area in Manhattan.

FAMILY BACKGROUND : Parents: Giuseppe & Angelina (both dead), brothers: Ralph, John, Vincent, Louis, sisters: Mrs. Helen Multitillo, Mrs. Amelia Gallo, Mrs. Josephine Tufaro, Mrs. Mary Frediroso.

CRIMINAL ASSOCIATES : Joe Rao, Joe Stracci, Tom Lucchese, Frank Costello, Tony Strollo, Meyer Lansky, all of NYC, Joe Massei, Fred Felice, Patsy Erra, all of Miami Beach, Fla.

CRIMINAL HISTORY : FBI #677976, NYCPD-B #54988. Arrests since 1914 include burglary, felonious assault, homicide, and Federal Narcotic Laws.

BUSINESS : Believed to have interest in Midtown Social Club, 21st Street and Collins Ave., Miami Beach, Fla.

MODUS OPERANDI : Currently involved in gambling activities in Miami Beach. Has been a feared and powerful racketeer from East Harlem area NYC, and has engaged in narcotic smuggling and distributing with top Mafia associates.

Property of U. S. Govt – For Official Use Only
May not be disseminated or contents disclosed

After Dutch Schultz was murdered in 1935, "Trigger" Mike Coppola took over Schultz's numbers racket in Harlem and the Bronx. He became one of the wealthiest mobsters in New York. He retired to Miami in the early sixties and spent time with Uncle George playing cards and listening to Dean Martin and Frank Sinatra—who else?

New York City Police Department, September 9, 1935

Sam "Red" Levine, a religious Jew, always wore a yarmulke (skullcap) beneath his fedora—even when he was a Murder Inc. assassin. I spent many Sundays in his bar, The Spot, on Grand Street on the Lower East Side watching baseball games on a small black and white TV.

Sam "Red" Levine

Aliases: James Cromin Red Levine Joseph Brown William Hayes

Description: Born on March 28, 1903, in New York City; 5 feet 8 inches; brown eyes, red hair, ruddy complexion, stout build

Localities frequented: Residence: 30 Ocean Parkway, Brooklyn, NY; Bohrer's Trucking Co., 99 Sullivan Street; Farber's Bar, Suffolk Delancey Streets RB Trading Co., 11 West 42d Street, all in New York

Criminal associates: Louis Cohen, Harry Stromberg, Saul Gelb

Criminal history: Dates from 1921 and includes arrests for vagrancy, gambling, burglary, grand larceny, felonious assault, homicide, robbery.

Modus operandi: A dangerous criminal closely associated with narcotics. Uses violence and strong-arm methods to organization for distribution of large quantities of narcotics. Has interests and is an important member of the New York underworld on the East Side.

Agencies familiar with individual: US Bureau of Narcotics, New York Police Department, FBI No 255223, New York City Police Department No B-63122

New York City Police Department

THE CLEVELAND FOUR

Morris Kleinman

UNLV Libraries Special Collections

Louis Rothkopf

Special Collections, Michael Swartz Library, Cleveland State University

Moe Dalitz, Sam Tucker

The National Archives

The Cleveland Four were the brains behind one of the most successful organized crime syndicates in America from 1930 into the late 1970s. They were equal partners, although Moe Dalitz was the one they all looked to as their undisputed leader. Uncle George and Ruby were their trusted co-conspirators for decades.

NEW YORK CITY ELECTS THE PERFECT MAYOR

A new mayor took office in New York in 1926, and he was perfect for the Roaring Twenties—Jimmy Walker didn't just tolerate the speakeasies, he embraced them. He was ever the rakish man about town, and his simple truth was that corruption would be ignored, and at times encouraged—especially if his entourage could profit from it.

Mayor Walker also supported honest public works projects throughout the city. He established the Sanitation Department to rid the city of the piles of rodent-ridden trash, and he continued building out the transit system so that working people from the Bronx, Brooklyn and Queens could get into Manhattan rapidly.

The New York underworld began taking notice of Uncle George, Ruby, Uncle Charlie, Sammy Kass, and Jacob "Cuppy" Migden.[1] Ironically, Johnny Eder benefitted most from Mayor Walker's administration—and was the only one in the crew who never resorted to violence or extortion. He had grown from the teenage peddler of George and Ruby's stolen candelabras five years earlier to a fence with limitless sources of stolen goods and willing buyers.

One night Johnny met a well-dressed man in an uptown speakeasy. Years later he remembered that the man had a Patek Philippe watch on his wrist. Johnny knew its value as he had fenced a few of those stolen watches over the years.

"I was getting good quality jewelry from burglars and selling the swag (stolen items) to reliable jewelers. Everybody made money. We knew each other. So, I meet this guy, Vincent. He tells me he has some jewelry to unload. He says he bought it for his wife and they were getting divorced. He tells me he took it from her jewelry box before he left her. I heard that story before—it was usually just stolen like everything else."

Johnny then hits it off with Vincent and meets him a few times to buy pieces of his jewelry. Vincent, it turns out, is a relative of Mayor Walker and is knee deep in getting city contracts for whoever pays him off. Vincent introduces Johnny to City Hall politicians and contractors. Johnny quickly realizes they all have a racket—or something to sell. He becomes a popular guy around the city agencies. He goes to their weddings, communions and bar mitzvahs. They take him to Yankee Stadium or fights at Madison Square Garden with tickets they get from companies or underworld characters looking for some way to scam the city.

Johnny told me years later there were so many burglars and thieves throughout the city the police department set up a special "fence unit" targeting people just like him. He laughed thinking about it, "No matter what the police tried to do, Jimmy Walker's City Hall was the best place for a fence in New York. Who was going to bust you for stolen merchandise in an elected official's office? And you could always get a few favors out of them for the gangsters."

* * *

The underworld by then had another conquest in sight: gaining control of the city's dozens of trade union locals. Trade unions proved to be soft targets after decades of wars with the companies for recognition. Since the end of the Civil War, New York had been a center of union organizing and political unrest.

The Slugger Wars began at the turn of the twentieth century and endured until the end of the 1920s.[2] The unions paid for gangster protection on the picket lines, and businesses often paid the same thugs to be strikebreakers.

In the mid-1920s Arnold Rothstein brought the underworld leaders Lepke Buchalter and Meyer Lansky together. He asked: why work as strikebreakers for the companies? Why hire out thugs to the unions to protect the strikers? Why not gain control of the unions? Why not put our own business agents into the unions?

An early target was the Cutters Union, representing the most skilled workers in the Garment Center: the garment cutters. Its members cut fabric precisely to the clothing patterns—mistakes were costly, so a company's survival depended on their skills. They were at the core of production. If this union called a strike, then the garment industry in New York, and throughout America, would shut down in an instant.

The sky is the limit, Rothstein preached—control the union, put your own guys into no-show jobs, shake down the companies with threats of strikes, and keep your hands clean, no need to hit someone in the face with a lead pipe wrapped in a newspaper. Also, control of the unions meant control of the contractors and businesses. Then the mobsters could shake down any industry.

They succeeded beyond their wildest expectations.

Mob control of the unions lasted for the next sixty years. Every construction job in New York City was mob controlled—their "business agents" knew every pressure point with company owners. Corrupt unions completely locked up the New York waterfront. The docks were such cash cows for shakedowns and cargo thefts that there were few labor stoppages on East Coast waterfronts from 1919 through 1945.

* * *

The presidential election was held on November 6,1928. The Republican, Herbert Hoover, representing a Middle America that supported Prohibition, ran against Governor Al Smith, a New York Democrat who opposed Prohibition. Smith, also Roman Catholic, proved that America was not yet ready for a Catholic president. Hoover would win in a landslide.

Arnold Rothstein bet on a Hoover victory. He supposedly covered $200,000 in Al Smith bets—some reported it as $500,000. Either amount could be right; I learned that when criminals talked about money the amount might be raised or lowered to fit the drama of the story being recounted.

While the election-night results were not a surprise, something happened two days before that shocked the New York underworld: Arnold Rothstein was shot. He died on election night. He was forty-six years old.

He never lived to collect the bets on Herbert Hoover.

---

[1] Jacob "Cuppy" Migden later would be responsible for the biggest blunder in New York City organized crime history: he fingered the wrong target for a gangland murder. Tragically, an innocent businessman died in front of his apartment building in the Bronx. I'd always known Cuppy by that one act since my childhood—but let me not get ahead of the story.

[2] The Slugger Wars were street battles that went on for twenty-five years in New York City for control of labor unions. It was one of the entrances into the crime world for Uncle George, Uncle Charlie, Ruby and Sammy Kass. For many of these guys, no matter how wealthy or comfortable they became, street battles would always be in their DNA. They projected that resolve effortlessly all their lives.

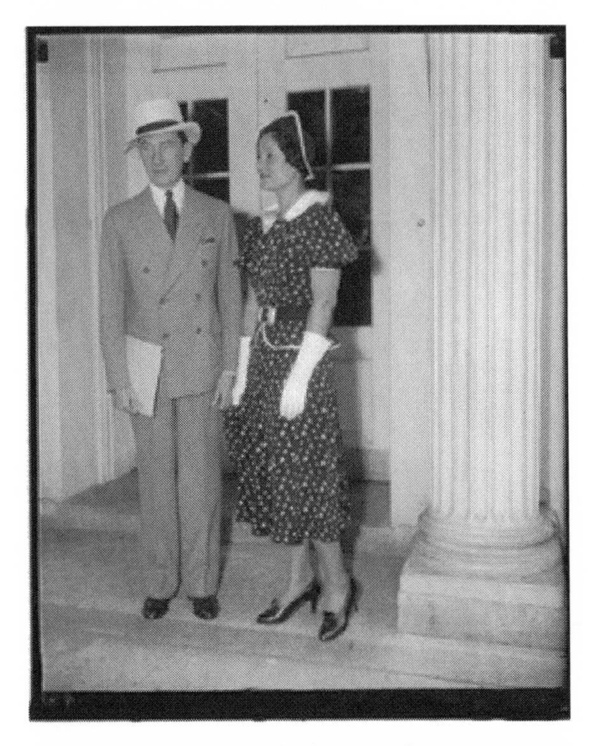

Library of Congress, Prints and Photographs Division, NYWT&S Collection

Mayor Walker with his wife in July 1937 visiting President Franklin D. Roosevelt at the White House.

The stylish Jimmy Walker had been mayor of New York City from 1926 to 1932. Known as Beau James, he embraced the speakeasies and ignored the widespread corruption in the city government—except when he could partake in it.

In September 1932 then Governor Roosevelt forced Walker to resign as mayor. Roosevelt was running for president and did not want Walker's corruption to hurt his chances. Walker had been unable to explain huge deposits in his personal bank account. Who would have imagined?

7

THE DEATH OF A. R.

"If Rothstein could die, then any of us could get killed. It didn't really change what we were doing, but it made us know that life could be very short."

— Sammy Kass, a career criminal and a friend of my parents since childhood

Later on, underworld grifters claimed they observed slippage in the way Arnold Rothstein carried himself in the last months of his life: larger than normal betting losses, overreactions to everyday business scrapes, appearing more sallow and preoccupied. It also just might have been the street hustlers' way of inserting themselves closer to this imposing character—a closeness they never really had when he was alive.

High stakes poker players could always find action at the Park Central Hotel in Midtown Manhattan. In September 1928 Rothstein had been at a card table for two days in one of the hotel's apartments with two men from California. Hands were dealt nonstop, with Rothstein losing and starting to unravel. The bystanders were shocked to see him erupting, throwing his cards down, mumbling—nobody had ever seen this before. These were the actions of common losers, never Rothstein.

Finally, Rothstein was outdrawn on the last card of the last hand after two days. He jumped out of his chair, cursing everyone. Rothstein's two opponents calmly totaled his losses: more than $300,000. He said he would pay in a few days. He left.

Days later he loudly told people around his table at the fashionable Lindy's Restaurant (and speakeasy) that he had been cheated and wouldn't pay off. Disbelief raced through the New York underworld—Rothstein reneging on a gambling debt. Unbelievable. Impossible. Weeks later gamblers urged him to close out the debt. He refused. "I was cheated," he said for everyone to hear.

On November 4, in high spirits, Rothstein again held court at Lindy's, taking action on the presidential election in two days. He was called to the phone. He left, telling patrons he was going to the Park Central Hotel, the scene of that marathon card game two months earlier.

A half hour later he lay slumped on the ground in the service entrance of the hotel, holding his stomach in an effort to stop the blood gushing from bullet wounds. He died two days later without naming his murderers.

As soon as Rothstein died, his widespread rackets were taken over by his protégés. Lepke Buchalter took control of the Garment Center and the corrupt unions. Meyer Lansky and Lucky Luciano moved in on the gambling joints that Rothstein had operated just the week before.[1] This would be the modus operandi of organized crime for the next sixty years: a boss dies and there is quick succession into his rackets, sometimes peacefully, sometimes not so peacefully.

---

1 Charles "Lucky" Luciano was born Salvatore Lucania in 1897 in Sicily. His name is the most recognizable of Mafia bosses of the 20th century. There are various accounts of his name change and the popular adoption of the nickname "Lucky." We'll just refer to him as Lucky Luciano.

COMING OF AGE, 1929

After Rothstein's murder, Ruby, Uncles George and Charlie, and their crew settled into the New York underworld that was anything but settled. Power struggles erupted and new battlefronts emerged. The younger gangsters, Lansky, Luciano and Siegel, who had been tutored by Rothstein, still had to deal with the Old World Italians, Joe Masseria and Salvatore Maranzano, who were killing off each other's men to maintain control over their rackets.

When Prohibition began in 1920, Joe Masseria, a Sicilian-born gangster, started distributing illegal liquor from curbside on Broome Street, not far from NYPD headquarters, making no attempt to disguise the operation from public view. One afternoon in the middle of crowded Grand Street, Masseria personally executed a gangland rival—he had a gun permit marked "unlimited" by a friendly judge. His go-to hitman and bodyguard, the ruthless twenty-four-year-old Charles "Lucky" Luciano, was responsible for many of the ensuing rubouts of Masseria's rivals and informants. Yet Luciano also had a connection with the Rothstein crowd—he knew that was how American crime needed to be conducted, not Masseria's old Sicilian way.

At the same time, Mussolini was determined to smash the Mafia in Sicily. In 1925 he sent a massive military force to occupy the island. Many of the criminals fled to the United States. One exile, Salvatore Maranzano, intent on ruling New York's crime world, made known his disgust of the younger Sicilians' willingness to do business with Jews. He and Masseria went to war on the streets of New York for the next six years, the body count increasing with each passing year.

"While those Italians were killing each other off, we were making fortunes in gambling, rumrunning and a dozen other things," Sammy Kass told me many decades later. "Those guys were already dinosaurs in the underworld. Everyone knew it was a matter of time before something happened. And it did."

Sammy Kass' lifelong crime mates Uncle George and Ruby moved up in the underworld. Trigger Mike Coppola operated an upscale casino and speakeasy near the West Side docks in Midtown Manhattan, not far from the Broadway theaters. The exterior was an old red brick warehouse that gave no hint of the action inside. There was no marquee announcing the club's name or its existence. It was "Danny's" to its clientele. (The name had changed several times during Prohibition.) Trigger Mike gave the casino a name so cab drivers would know where to go instead of "that brick warehouse over by the docks." There of course was no Danny.

Cabdrivers in New York knew where the action was in every borough—it was their job. They were the social media of that era. They rarely pulled away from the curb at Danny's after dropping off a gambler without the casino's doorman throwing a few bucks onto the front seat.

Trigger Mike put George and Ruby in as managers.

Both were still teenagers.

The "smart society set" often patronized Danny's— high stakes players, arriving in tuxedos and evening gowns. Ruby also had a professional interest in Danny's—the women wore dazzling jewelry. They were, as Ruby said decades later, "ostentatious." He sometimes befriended customers while his newfound crew of burglars would follow them home and case their buildings for days, or weeks if necessary. Danny's was not the only speakeasy or gambling casino whose patrons found empty jewelry boxes in rummaged-through apartments days after a boozy night of partying.

The occasional marks for burglaries weren't the only victims of these gambling joints. There were always far more losers at the tables than winners. Rothstein and Lansky understood if a gambler is confident the game is not crooked, they will come back certain that they can beat the house—that they just had "a bad run of luck." After they busted out again and again and were penniless, they turned to the loan sharks cruising every gambling hall.

The interest rate was "six for five"—borrow $500 and a week later the debt is $600— 20% interest per week! Often a sad sack gambler would borrow $500 and the next week could only pay the $100 "vig"—*vigorish*, the interest—and the week after he still couldn't pay more than $100. Often the $500 could never be paid and the borrower would forever be obligated for the $100 interest—each and every week.

Exorbitant interest rates most often put the borrower underwater, which required a force of collectors, often the same thugs who provided muscle for the decades-old labor disputes. Fear of physical violence was a much stronger inducement to repay at least the interest than a bad credit score would ever be generations later.

Even these busted out gamblers had to have someone or something to vouch for them. Did they have something valuable to pawn? Did they own a business? Were they lawyers or dentists who couldn't skip town and had good cash flow? After all, losing gamblers are everywhere—dentists as well as truck drivers, judges and schoolteachers.

The gambler might have lost the month's rent or his wife's savings for that new household wonder, the refrigerator; or the wealthier loser might have just watched his child's college tuition disappear at a roulette wheel. They couldn't go home with their pockets turned inside out. They were desperate and now captives of their new business partners: loan sharks.

In March 1929 Ruby was arrested for burglary, and a few months later for assault and robbery. The burglary happened after a young couple flashed impressive jewelry around Danny's. Ruby befriended them, and the outcome was a knock on their door by two pistol-bearing callers who made off with the jewels they had unwisely displayed in Danny's—and a few other fine pieces, no doubt. Ruby was at the wheel of the getaway car. A police car showed up just as the men were furtively leaving the building. They were all arrested—and to make it worse, the victims recognized Ruby as one of the casino managers. Another arrest for assault quickly followed. It brought heat on Danny's.

Then in the summer of 1929 Ruby was arrested once again—a turning point for Ruby and George. The charge was illegal entry. The judge, noting Ruby's recent arrests, sentenced him to three years. The details are lost to time, but a clerk at the jail mixed up Ruby's transfer papers and somehow they became discharge papers. He strolled out of jail onto the street and the awaiting Uncles George and Charlie.

The confusion with Ruby's papers was the work of Johnny Eder, the fence of high quality jewelry, who by this time had become a favorite in Mayor Walker's corrupt City Hall. Johnny knew a Department of Correction commissioner who was always looking for a quick buck. Johnny offered him a year's salary in cash to find a way to get Ruby out quickly—there would only be a few days before Ruby would be transferred to an upstate prison and taken out of reach.

The next day the commissioner told Johnny Eder to have someone pick up Ruby at a certain time. It worked fine—he disappeared off the streets. The commissioner got his year's salary bonus, and the jail clerk who mixed up Ruby's paperwork also was rewarded: he jumped at Johnny Eder's higher paying job offer—where else but at Danny's.

Trigger Mike Coppola ordered George and Ruby to avoid Danny's. George had already been away for a month, since he'd had a battle in the club with a gangster from Italian Harlem. The gangster had threatened to return and kill George—but worse than that, his uptown Italian mobster connections were heavyweights and likely to retaliate, if for no other reason than that would be their primal response.

Trigger Mike made it known on the street that George and Ruby would no longer be found at Danny's. Mike knew the Italian Harlem mob and would make peace with them, but George and Ruby would be wise to lay low. They stayed with our Uncle Harvey, George's older brother, at his apartment in Brooklyn. New York became less attractive to them. Uncle Charlie and a few others set them on a new course—one that would take them to Cleveland.

Author's family album

Cleveland, 1940. Uncle George on the left with his first wife, Anne, (she passed away a few years later), and Ruby Kolod on the right with his wife, Esther. By 1940 Uncle George and Ruby were veteran illegal gambling casino operators with the Cleveland Syndicate.

In the 1950s they would both be part of the criminal interests in the Desert Inn and Stardust casinos in Las Vegas. Uncle George took "the skim" from the Stardust Hotel to silent partners all over the country. On occasion, so did Frank Sinatra and the great one time heavyweight champion, Jack Dempsey.

A NEW ORDER

While George and Ruby moved up in the New York underworld, Meyer Lansky had his honeymoon in Atlantic City. It was May 1929. Arnold Rothstein had died a few months earlier—it was time for his protégés to take over. Frank Costello, Bugsy Siegel, Lepke Buchalter, Lucky Luciano and Meyer Lansky sent invitations to crime bosses to meet at the seashore city to toast Meyer's marriage and to set out a course for organized crime that none of them would have expected would last the next half-century.

Al Capone from Chicago, Abner "Longy" Zwillman and Waxey Gordon from New Jersey, Santo Trafficante from Tampa, and more than twenty others. They walked on the beach, met in small groups in the bars and boardwalk restaurants, and had formal meetings and dinners—similar to summit gatherings of world leaders before and ever since.

Crime was becoming more organized with each passing year—looking more like the steel, electrical, and railroad monopolies of the 1880s. Organized crime was already bigger than any legitimate industry. It was no longer neighborhood toughs killing each other in broad daylight, Efficiency, stealth and "sit downs" among the bosses instead of machine guns when a deal went bad would be the New Order: a nationwide syndicate, with families controlling their own territories.

But first there was the matter of the Old World Italians, Maranzano and Masseria. They left bodies all over the city in their vendetta. They had to be dealt with before this younger generation's vision of a crime monopoly could become reality.

Most important for this history would be the representatives from Cleveland at the Atlantic City crime summit: Moe Dalitz, and two of his three lifetime partners, Louis Rothkopf and Morris Kleinman. Representing Cleveland's Italian Mayfield Road Gang was Charles "Chuck" Polizzi. They understood that the center of power of this national syndicate would be New York. Time and again the Cleveland Syndicate demonstrated their understanding of crime politics and always anticipated the shifting winds that could blow from any direction, at any time.

They also recognized the approaching end of Prohibition and that the future was gambling. And they welcomed two underworld figures, Uncle George and Ruby, who were still in their teens but already had gambling experience and were sponsored by the new powers in New York City.

George Geik became George Gordon, and Ruben Koloditsky became Ruby Kolod. They would never look back.

10

HENRY FORD

Jews in America needed little reminder of the sea of resentment that existed outside the well-defined boundaries of their communities. The Yiddish language newspapers printed the daily indignations, and worse, experienced by its readers.

Henry Ford, the most vocal anti-Semite in twentieth-century America, regularly questioned the Jews' patriotism and whether they could ever be part of the nation's Christian culture. Before the Great War, he introduced the assembly-line production for the Model T automobile and set the country onto new roads and highways. He changed America forever and his importance rendered him an even greater threat to the Jews.

In 1919 he took over publication of the *Dearborn Independent*, a struggling community newspaper. The next year he began a series of opinion pieces that later became the contents of a four-volume set of books, *The International Jew: The World's Problem*.

The dozens of Ford's articles included, "Does Jewish Power Control the World Press?" "Germany's Reaction Against the Jew," "Jewish Copper Kings Reap Rich War-Profits," and "Jewish Jazz Becomes Our National Music." By 1926 the publication had 900,000 subscribers. Ford's articles were spinoffs of a turn-of-the-century Russian anti-Semitic hoax, *The Protocols of the Elders of Zion*.

Henry Ford stoked the widespread belief that the "international banking community" had incited the Great War—this had long been white nationalism's enduring code for an international Jewish conspiracy.

The Jews were easy targets in the Detroit of 1920—the heart of the Ford Empire. The Purple Gang had already been rumrunning from Canada for two years and the city had begun its descent into the corruption and violence that all America would soon experience. This identifiably Jewish gang made Ford's anti-Semitic connection between crime and Judaism all the more believable.

As Adolph Hitler began his ascent in Germany, spreading his rabid anti-Semitism, the Nazis acclaimed Henry Ford as a successful American industrialist who shared Hitler's racial views, giving their movement a priceless legitimacy. Ford, the only American mentioned in Hitler's 1925 autobiography *Mein Kampf*, was celebrated in Nazi circles even during World War II. Hitler had a large photograph of Ford on the wall of his Munich inner office.

Nonetheless, the one truth Nazi sympathizers in Detroit learned early on was that the Purple Gang and other Jewish groups could, and did, take to the streets and were eager to battle the anti-Semites. Ford was also an active foe of the trade union organizing that was gaining strength in automobile manufacturing plants. The presence of the Purple Gang working as paid union heavies battling the car plant security forces, whose ranks were often Nazi sympathizers, gave Ford more fodder for his anti-Semitic articles.

That these Jews relished fighting the so-called Aryans in the streets did not fit the prevailing Ford or Nazi narrative that Jews were just sneaky bankers engineering their cultural domination of Christian society.

Moe Dalitz understood that anti-Semites like Henry Ford presented a danger to Jews everywhere. Dalitz's crews in Detroit and Cleveland always wanted to fight the Nazis. Uncle George laughed recalling Dalitz's brother "Louie the Chinaman's" joke, "If one of our guys had to attach a stick of dynamite to the starter of a car we hoped it would be a Ford and that a few fucking Nazis would be in it."

11

A SENSATIONAL MURDER, 1930

The Cleveland Italian and Jewish mobsters began the new decade closer to each other than these two ethnic groups were anywhere else. They also worked with trusted Irish gangsters. They understood that cooperation and staying in the background were keys to their success—and to their survival.

An ethnic twist to the Italian-Jewish underworld in Cleveland had been a shadowy secret. Al and Charles (Chuck) Polizzi, two of the leaders of the Italian Mayfield Road Gang, were also the closest to the Jewish mobsters, especially Chuck. But were Chuck and Al brothers? Or cousins? Even under oath at a trial, Al couldn't verbalize their relationship. He had never thought about it. He wasn't sure.

Charles Polizzi was not a Polizzi at all.

He had come to America from Eastern Europe with his parents, who were Jewish refugees from the pogroms, as were so many other immigrants. His parents died young, and Charles was orphaned. The Polizzi family adopted him when Al himself was a young boy. Chuck was raised as an Italian.

Uncle George once told his close friend Chuck Polizzi, when the tally of one criminal enterprise or another didn't add up, "If you're really a Jew, count like one."

Al became Chuck's older brother, and together they were dominant figures in the Cleveland underworld. To add another layer to this ethnic twist, the next-door neighbors of the Polizzi family were Yiddish-speaking immigrants. Al claimed to have learned to speak Yiddish from them. He was very proud of this language skill, peculiar as it was for an Italian gangster.

Years later Ruby laughed at the story. "Al was so proud that he spoke Yiddish. We never wanted him to know he was just putting words together. My mother wouldn't have understood a damn thing he said. But he tried."

It was here in Cleveland that stand-alone casinos with fine food and entertainment were destined to be at the core of the Cleveland Four's empire. The Mounds Club, owned by one of their associates, Tom McGinty, opened in 1930. The Flamingo and the Harvard Club opened soon after, and others in nearby counties. Uncle George and Ruby managed them, along with the growing Cleveland Syndicate criminal roster. Their presence insured there would be no takeover attempts by other gangs, and they could oversee the collection of debts the clientele always incurred.

Moe Dalitz traded pieces of the Ohio casinos for interests in the gambling action in New York and in Miami, a new crime frontier under the control of Meyer Lansky. Another clever deal also put Dalitz's syndicate at the center of Lansky's move to set up gambling, free of United States laws—just ninety miles away in Havana, Cuba.

This was the new direction for organized crime—trading interests in their assets with each other—and the Cleveland Syndicate had a lot of assets to barter. It was portfolio diversification as would be practiced by every mutual fund manager fifty years later.

George and Ruby arrived in Cleveland a year before a murder captivated the city. It was, along with the ensuing trial, a sensational news story for the next several years. In 1929, a well-known former

Cleveland city councilman, William Potter, had been charged, along with two others, with embezzling $33,000 from the city in phony real estate transactions. He was acquitted, but then immediately charged with perjury.

Investigators assumed that the corruption running deep in the city administration was tied to criminal elements—and that William Potter might have quite a story to tell. He was penniless and unable to raise funds to support his family. He was likely to flip on whatever criminal enterprise was at the core of the real estate scam.

On the night of February 3, 1931, Potter was shot dead in a rented apartment. A woman living in the building identified Hyman (Hymie) Martin, a rumrunner from Pittsburgh, as the man leaving the apartment. The superintendent identified Martin as the man who had rented the apartment.

Martin fled. Apprehended soon after in Pittsburgh, he was returned to Cleveland for the trial. Dramatic reenactments of the murder scene, a parade of shady witnesses, and front-page newspaper coverage created a sensation in Cleveland. After a number of votes the jury found Martin guilty. He was sentenced to life in prison.

A few months later an FBI memo identified Moe Dalitz and one of his partners, Louis Rothkopf, as having been at the apartment building the same day the murder was committed. The report also implicated a third partner, Morris Kleinman, as the mastermind of the Potter murder. None of them were available for police interviews—they had left town.

Eleven months later an Ohio Court of Appeals overturned Martin's conviction on curious grounds, including that the prosecution had engaged in "abusive, unjust and inflammatory personal vituperations." Once the involvement of the Cleveland Syndicate in the murder became known it seemed reasonable to assume that the appeals court received fair compensation for their odd ruling. After all, overturning a murder conviction because the prosecution used "inflammatory language" must have been amusing to those who orchestrated the outcome.

Martin went to trial a second time. Witnesses recanted their earlier testimony or were unavailable, and the defense indignantly claimed that prosecution witnesses were on the government payroll. Martin was acquitted of the murder charge after just one hour of deliberation. He disappeared from public sight.

Martin soon appeared in Miami managing the Cleveland Syndicate's Florida gambling interests. Decades later, in 1965, a *Miami Herald* investigation of the extremely profitable *bolita* (a Latino version of the numbers racket) and other illegal gaming in Florida featured Uncle George and Hymie Martin as the main operators.[1]

Uncle George had been Hymie Martin's boss for the Cleveland Syndicate since he beat the Potter murder charge and relocated to Florida. Uncle George and one of the Cleveland Four, Morris Kleinman, both entered Miami hospitals to avoid testifying at the ensuing government inquiry.

But it was a pair of murders in New York City in the same year that would define organized crime for the next fifty years.

---

[1] The Miami Herald investigative series is quoted in the Cleveland Plains Dealer, Sept 9.1965 *Pettibone Boss Ex-Boss is Key 'Hymie' Man*

Kent State University Special Collections

March 26, 1931—Hymie Martin center in dark suit, apprehensive. On trial for the murder of William Potter, Martin was found guilty. The Appellate Court judges overturned the conviction. At the second trial the jurors found Martin not guilty. He quickly disappeared.

Martin soon reappeared managing the Cleveland Syndicates' new illegal gambling interests in Florida. In 1965 a Miami Herald investigative series revealed Uncle George had been overseeing Hymie Martin's gambling operations for the Syndicate for three decades. Hymie did well for himself taking the heat for the murder.

12

MASSERIA AND MARANZANO

Impeding the new bosses Luciano and Lansky's organization of crime was the ongoing street war between the old-timers: "Joe the Boss" Masseria and Salvatore Maranzano. New York City newspapers branded it the Castellammare War, after a town in Sicily.

The abrupt ending to that war has been recounted many times and is unnecessary to revisit but for a few sidebars of interest to our story.

Masseria, doubting Luciano's loyalty, arranged for his assassination. Luciano discovered he was a target. In April 1931, he took Joe the Boss for lunch at a favorite Italian restaurant in Coney Island. Luciano excused himself to go to the bathroom. Several gunmen entered—it was the last plate of scungilli Masseria ever dug his fork into.

Soon after, Maranzano made the mistake of declaring himself "boss of all bosses." In September 1931 Maranzano summoned Luciano to a meeting in his Midtown Manhattan office. He had contracted Irish-born hitman Vincent "Mad Dog" Coll to whack him. Once again Luciano learned about the setup—one of the many reasons he was "Lucky."

Luciano's associates had to act quickly. Meyer Lansky prepared for the Maranzano finale. He hired a crew of Jewish gunmen who would be unknown to the Sicilians likely to congregate around Maranzano. They learned how to dress and act like government agents. To Lansky and the gunmen, besides it being just business, taking out Maranzano would also be payback for his contempt for the Jews in organized crime.

The "government agents" entered Maranzano's office demanding tax documents. Three of them occupied Maranzano's men while Red Levine—the religious Jewish hitman—and another gunman went into the inner office. They shot Maranzano and Red Levine slit his throat, or stabbed him in his heart, depending on the storyteller. On their way out of the building the assassins walked past Mad Dog Coll, who had entered the lobby intending to fulfill his assignment to kill Luciano, who of course, was a no-show for the event. Coll turned around and left the building with his now dead employer's killers. It was, after all, just business.[1]

More than two decades later I was in Red Levine's grungy bar, The Spot, on Grand Street on the Lower East Side, with my father and sister, Iris—Lou's way of taking his kids out on a sunny Sunday afternoon. I was probably eleven years old. The smell of stale beer in any bar will always transport me back to The Spot.

Even at that young age I knew it was "a flop house" bar, not like the French Romanian on Delancey Street, another mob hang out a few blocks away, that had real tablecloths and waiters in tuxedos, no matter how threadbare they might have been.

Red held court, reminiscing with local, old-time wise guys. It was taken for granted in those circles that Red was the main character in the seminal Maranzano assassination but I never heard anything more certain to report here.[2]

What I do know is that by the time I was eleven or twelve years old I had already become comfortable with Red's gruff but often light-hearted presence as well as his fearsome reputation—just as I had with Uncle George, Sammy Kass and the others.

Anyway, back to the account at hand.

With the old-timers Masseria and Maranzano dispatched to another dimension, Luciano hosted a meeting in Chicago. Just as at the Atlantic City crime convention two years earlier, mob bosses from every city gathered again.

These men now managed greater cash flow and resources than any American corporation—with a control over local law enforcement and politicians unprecedented in American history.

The Depression was then two years into its decade-long economic tailspin. Throughout history the survivors of economic catastrophes and those who grow even stronger from them are those with the most resources to begin with—and so it would be for this Depression. Whoever had cash also had the ability to buy even more assets at bargain prices. Organized crime would be well positioned for the Depression.

So, the leaders, Meyer Lansky and Lucky Luciano, again asked the questions whose answers had by now become obvious: Why continue Old World vendettas and tribal feuds? Why not make deals and honor them? Why not divide up territories among themselves? Why not earn together when new opportunities are presented?

Newly created crime families divided territories and formed a National Commission of bosses that would render final rulings when disputes arose. And disputes were inevitable, as the weaving of interests and agreements became the pattern of their enterprise.

Lucky Luciano would be the leader. He wisely chose not to repeat Maranzano's mistake: He rejected the title of "boss of bosses." Why be a target of younger gunmen like he had been only a few years earlier? Why upset the other bosses who had big egos? There was untold wealth on the table from the illegal and increasingly legitimate businesses throughout the country. Let cooler heads among them resolve the disputes that arise from criminal activity on the streets. Let the National Commission "sit downs" operate like civil courts—cases are heard, damages are compensated, and everyone goes back to their rackets a few dollars richer or poorer.[3]

The new crime bosses understood there would always be betrayals, informants, *schtunad* (dumb) loners who couldn't adapt to the new corporate mindset, and some who just couldn't help stealing from their own crime families. For those eventualities they set up a hit squad located in New York—another indication that New York was the power center of this new crime empire.

Lepke Buchalter and Albert Anastasia organized the assassination branch. One of the first men drafted onto this team was Uncle Charlie who had, by this time, distinguished himself in the underworld. He was a natural. So were Sammy Kass and Red Levine. In a few years, as organized crime grew even larger, more hits needed to be contracted and more willing assassins were put on the payroll.

It wasn't until Abe "Kid Twist" Reles—the gentleman who exited through the sixth-floor window of the cheap Coney Island hotel years several years later in 1941—revealed the existence of the hired killer collective that the name Murder Inc. first appeared in the *World-Telegram*, a New York daily newspaper.[4] The name captured the public's fascination, and the killers were romanticized in cheap novels, in Hollywood B movies and, later, in amusingly inaccurate television recreations of their crimes.

Sammy Kass, a for-hire gunman at the outset of Murder Inc. who worked for Waxey Gordon, still another of Arnold Rothstein's protégés, casually told me in the late 1980s how Murder, Inc. was so effective.[5] Of all the relatives and close family friends I spoke with over the years about organized crime, Sammy Kass had the most plainspoken, often witty, reflections of all.

"What made the Combination (the name used by its members before Murder, Inc. was popularized) different was that the gunmen worked all over the country, not just in New York. If a connected guy in Kansas City had a problem with someone who owed him money, or an informer, or whoever it was, they could hire guys from New York to do the job. The guys to be hit would never see them coming."

Sammy described an operation: "Maybe two guys would go out on a train to Kansas City or Detroit. Maybe together. Maybe separately. Someone would meet them at the train station and take them to different hotels. They would have a meet in a warehouse with some of the guys who were in on the contract. Maybe they even looked at mugshots of the marks that the police on the payroll gave them. Anyway, they would plan it and know the routines of the guys they were going to take out. They were real professional. Someone would pick them up in a stolen car." Sammy noted that he stole cars in New York for robberies and, he guessed, murders when he was a teenager.

"They would do the job sometimes in broad daylight on a street, sometimes in an ambush at night. However, it was planned. It didn't matter—it always got done. After the job they would be taken to a farmhouse or somewhere safe. Then they might get on a train separately back to New York. If they got stopped, they always had a reason to be there and they had locals swear their story was true. Maybe they would say they were salesmen or buying a restaurant owned by a local guy—whatever story. It didn't matter, they never got stopped. They looked like everyone else at the train station."

There was no television, no cell phones, and no cameras in hotel lobbies, garages, outside of restaurants, or at the train stations. A witness just saw an average-looking white guy in a suit and fedora driving away.

"All the police had to show them were mugshots of local bums. The New York guys were long gone by that time." Sammy nodded his appreciation of the efficiency of this national enterprise.

---

[1] Mad Dog Coll himself met an untimely end less than a year later while on the phone trying to shake down a far better connected criminal, Owney Madden, the one-time owner of the Cotton Club in Harlem. A version of Coll's demise is that Madden had the call traced and alerted the killers who brought the telephone conversation to an abrupt end.

[2] Sylvia Lorber, Red Levine's longtime girl friend, and our mother's close confidant, sometimes remarked after Red passed away that "those guys said far more than they should have but they were great fun to be with."

[3] In all the years the National Commission sat in judgment you can bet there was never a single lawsuit by one mob faction against the other for trademark infringement or breach of contract as in Corporate America. Huge criminal defense retainers—the cost of doing their distinctive business—displaced the usual corporate legal department budget.

[4] The premise of Murder Inc. existed throughout history. Uncle George and Red Levine's 1928 trip to Cleveland as unidentifiable gunmen was an example—assassins from a few towns away who would never be seen again. This tactic was employed by criminals hundreds of years earlier.

[5] Sammy Kass's family name was Kassop. He had two brothers, Ben and Harry. Ben was close to my family after he was released from Sing Sing following a well-publicized bust with his brother Sammy and one-time crime boss, Waxey Gordon, in 1951. The other brother Harry was a physician. His two criminal brothers put him through medical school. Dr. Kassop was our family doctor for my entire childhood.

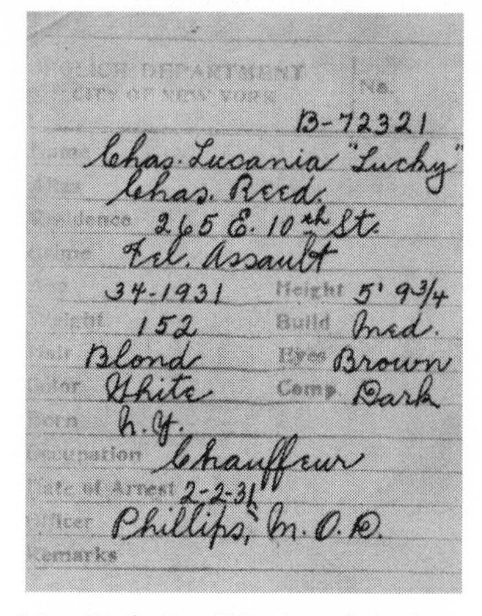

POLICE DEPARTMENT
CITY OF NEW YORK
No. B-72321
Chas. Lucania "Lucky"
Chas. Reed
Residence 265 E. 10th St.
Fel. Assault
34-1931 Height 5' 9¾
152 Build Med.
Blond Eyes Brown
White Comp Dark
N.Y.
Occupation Chauffeur
Date of Arrest 2-2-31
Officer Phillips, M.O.D.
Remarks

New York City Municipal Archives

Charles "Lucky" Luciano. February 2, 1931—it would be a productive year for Lucky. He participated in the murder of the two bosses, Masseria and Maranzano, and he also became "the boss of bosses" (although he never sought that title for himself).

Not bad for someone who described himself as a "chauffeur" when he was arrested.

He was thirty-three years old in this photo.

13

THE WAR OF THE JEWS

The new National Commission had to address another urgent matter; the two Italian old-timers, Masseria and Maranzano, had just been taken out, now two Jewish gang leaders, powerful ones, had to be taken off the streets.

One was Irving Wexler—known throughout the criminal underworld as Waxey Gordon. Like Masseria and Maranzano, Gordon was fifteen years older than Luciano, Lansky, Bugsy Siegel and the other gangsters now establishing the corporate structure of crime. Gordon had little interest in playing nice and certainly didn't think he had to take orders from these younger guys.

When Luciano needed to eliminate the two Italian gang leaders to save himself Lansky had his back. Now it was Luciano's turn to back up Lansky in what the underworld called "The War of the Jews." Lansky and Luciano understood ethnic politics—Lansky stayed in the background while Luciano took out the Italians (with the help of a few Jewish gunmen). Luciano would now stay in the background as Lansky orchestrated the fate of Jewish gang leaders who could bring them all down.

Sammy Kass was close to the story. "Waxey's bookkeeper Goruch was scared to death of taking a fall. You knew he would rat out the whole operation. They had him in jail so nobody could get to him. So this lawyer, a commissioner of something in Elizabeth, turns up in the middle of the night at the jail. The lawyer was in hock to Waxey for tens of thousands of dollars. He puts on a show for the police—claims to be this guy's attorney. He gets Goruch bailed out for $500—in the middle of the night. Who knows how much he gave the police? Nobody was around. As soon as this guy steps onto the sidewalk he was as good as dead" (one of Sammy's favorite expressions).

Waxey Gordon grew up in the turn-of-the-century Lower East Side. He was a pickpocket and multi-tasking young street criminal—as they all had been. He had a sturdy, solid physique and nasty disposition—ideal qualities for a hired street thug, or "schlammer," as the Jews at that time would say.

By the mid-1920s Gordon was a major importer of illegal booze into the New York area. He was also a close associate of Arnold Rothstein, as were Lansky and Luciano. Gordon never accepted Lansky and Luciano's rise in the ranks; he saw them as young upstarts. During the next few years, he would often accuse Lansky of masterminding hijackings of his trucks and shootings of his crews. He was probably right on both counts.

In 1925 a captain of a Gordon rumrunning boat believed he had been shortchanged. He informed the government about the arrival of another boat carrying an even larger stash of liquor. The Feds intercepted the ship, raided Gordon's New York operations, and arrested his crew. Gordon was arrested later.

The captain, the star witness against Gordon, was found dead in a well-guarded New York hotel room. The coroner ruled it a suicide and Gordon and his associates walked free—but his booze smuggling organization was crushed. He opened a beer brewery in New Jersey and soon controlled the largest bootlegging and distribution network in the New York area.

Gordon attracted unneeded attention: He was named "New York's Public Enemy #1" in 1930 by a local newspaper. By that time, his and Lansky's personal war intensified—with the usual rising body count.

The government targeted Gordon's operations with a strategy that had just proven successful in Chicago. Al Capone had been convicted of tax evasion—not murder, not extortion, but tax evasion. Paper trails do a lot of the work in federal tax evasion prosecutions—a simple truth that was becoming clear to both the government and the underworld.

The Feds transferred their large team of accountants and investigators, the core of the Capone prosecution, to New York. Luciano and Lansky's spies within the Gordon beer distilling empire produced piles of incriminating documents to support the government's case.

One minor figure in the Waxey Gordon crime family would take on a big role as the investigation unfolded. Samuel Goruch, a lowly bookkeeper in one of Gordon's offices, had opened a number of bank accounts in different names through which large sums of money had been laundered. When his role was uncovered, he went into hiding. Federal agents located him and in 1931 he was held in jail for contempt—and also for safekeeping.

Sammy shrugged his shoulders and pointed his palms up to the ceiling, a centuries-old gesture of my people. "Nobody ever heard from him again. You can bet he never saw the sunrise. But no matter what they did, it didn't matter. Waxey was his own worst enemy, He testified at his trial and made no sense. Everything he said was bullshit. The jury took about an hour to find him guilty. The judge gave him ten years."

* * *

The Waxey Gordon prosecutor was thirty-year-old Thomas Dewey trying his first major organized crime case. He would soon become the single most effective prosecutor against organized crime throughout the 1930s. He later became governor of New York. Dewey ran for President of the United States in 1944 and again in 1948, when he was narrowly beaten by then President Harry Truman.

With Gordon in jail and his empire divided up among the Lansky-Luciano organization, another Jewish mobster had to be dealt with. This character was even more dangerous to the new National Commission than Gordon—Arthur Flegenheimer, known on the streets as Dutch Schultz.

Much has been written about Schultz and how he ran afoul of the National Commission. Of greater interest to this chronicle is how Schultz crossed paths with the Cleveland Syndicate—and it didn't work out well for the Dutchman.

But first I should note that among all of these events one was of far greater consequence to my life—a sixteen-year-old who would later be my father found a job. It was 1931—the Great Depression was grinding into the soul of America. The future "Big Lou" was hired for a week's work as a clerk for a music publishing company. It was a job that would last for twenty-nine years. His friends gave him the nickname "Bim," the name of a character in one of the many popular syndicated newspaper comic strips—the only one with a legitimate day job.

Dad filled orders for sheet music. The company was on 52nd Street—a Midtown Manhattan street alive with jazz clubs. Because of the nightlife, 52nd Street also attracted organized crime figures. By 1931, as his older brother George rose in the Cleveland Syndicate hierarchy, Lou, even though just a company clerk, became a confidant and lifelong friend to New York's organized crime figures; but he always remained to them a "civilian." More about that later.

Vincent "Mad Dog" Coll, a onetime gunman on Schultz's payroll, had been hired by Maranzano to be Lucky Luciano's assassin.

Coll thought that he should be a partner with the notoriously cheap and overly paranoid Schultz. The Dutchman turned him down. In 1930 Coll left Schultz's crew and formed his own. He quickly gave credibility to the prevailing derisive Jewish-Italian view of Irish mobsters by kidnapping a few mob figures' family members. This alone destined him for an early departure from this Earthly Dimension.

Coll and Schultz devolved into open warfare. During one attempted kidnapping, four young children were accidentally shot. One of them died. Coll was blamed for the murder. Mayor Jimmy Walker gave him the name "Mad Dog."

Schultz and Owney Madden, another major NYC underworld figure, each put a $50,000 bounty on Coll. The end came suddenly in February 1932. Coll was in a telephone booth in a drug store on 8th Avenue and 23rd Street, supposedly threatening Owney Madden with a kidnapping of a relative if he didn't pay Coll a $50,000 ransom. Madden kept him on the phone while the call was traced. Another more plausible story, at least to some, is that

Schultz's guys tracked Coll to the nearby hotel where he was living and then to the drugstore phone booth. Either way the call was rudely interrupted.

Three men pulled up in a car. One stayed in the car. One stood outside. The third entered the store and unloaded the contents of a machine gun into the phone booth. Fifteen bullets were later counted in Coll's body. But here at this moment is the source of one of the most enduring jokes in all my years of listening to these accounts.

Turning to leave the drugstore the gunman made eye contact with the frightened-to-death pharmacist, who no doubt thought that he, as a witness, was also destined for a sudden ending. Instead, the gunman says, "If he wakes up give him an aspirin."[1]

I read many retellings of Mad Dog Coll's last telephone chat. Never once was the killer's medical advice to the pharmacist ever mentioned. I shared my curiosity with my brother Bernard, who despite (or maybe because of) his law enforcement status, was treated like a kindred spirit by underworld characters.

Bernard laughed. "Years later one of Schultz's guys worked for Uncle George in Cleveland. He told the story many times. It became one of their jokes. Who knows if it's true?"

* * *

A few years earlier a racket that had been off the radar of organized crime became a victim of its own success. It had long been left to independent operators in Black, Italian and Latino neighborhoods.

But in the late 1920s, with the end of Prohibition in sight, "the numbers" racket aroused the interest of America's inner cities' underworld.

---

[1] Abraham "Bo" Weinberg, Dutch Schultz's most called upon gunman, was likely Coll's assassin. However, neither Schultz's high regard for Weinberg as a gunman nor his alleged witty comment to the pharmacist spared Weinberg a grim ending a few years later when Schultz had good reason to question his loyalty.

The underworld gossip had it that Weinberg's feet were encased in concrete and then he was dumped still alive into the East River. Whether that is true or not will never be verified—but Weinberg was never seen again; that needs no verification.

Matty Zimmerman/AP/Shutterstock

The one-time major racketeer of the 1920s and '30s, Waxey Gordon (far left) busted in July 1951 on the Upper East Side of Manhattan in a drug sting. With him are the Kassop brothers, Sammy Kass (second from right) and one of my favorites of all of these people I am writing about, Benny Kassop (far right with his head in his hand).

The hapless looking guy in the white shirt next to Waxey Gordon is the driver that fateful night, Arthur "Fat Artie" Repola. In June 1965 Repola was ambushed in the Bronx in a gangland murder attempt. He died ten days later.

In addition to going to Sing Sing for a few years, Benny lost the affections of Sylvia Lorber, the lifelong friend of my mother and of my sister, Iris. Sylvia turned her interest to Sam "Red" Levine, with whom she spent the rest of his life (while he still maintained his family in Brooklyn).

Author's family album

Reba and Lou, our parents are in the front seat. Sylvia Lorber and Benny (Kass) Kassop are in the back, circa 1947. This was a happier time than in the previous photo, where Benny is hiding his face right after being busted in one of the most publicized New York City arrests in 1951.

Dutch Schultz 1931 mugshot

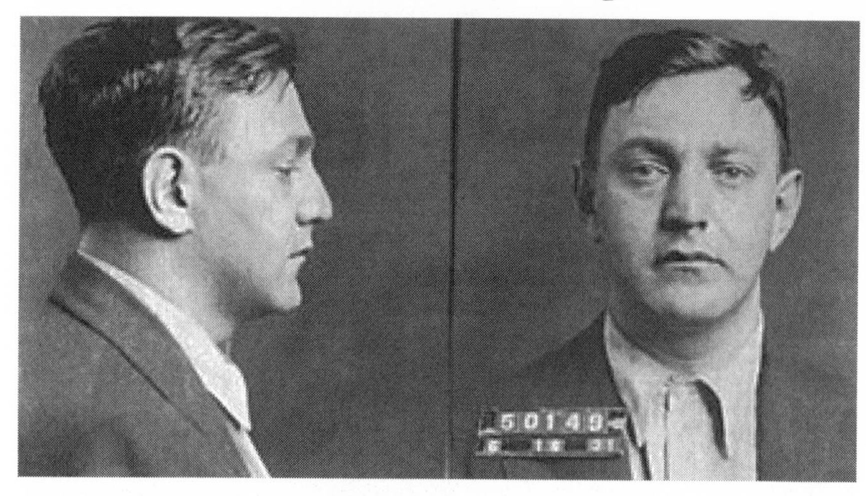

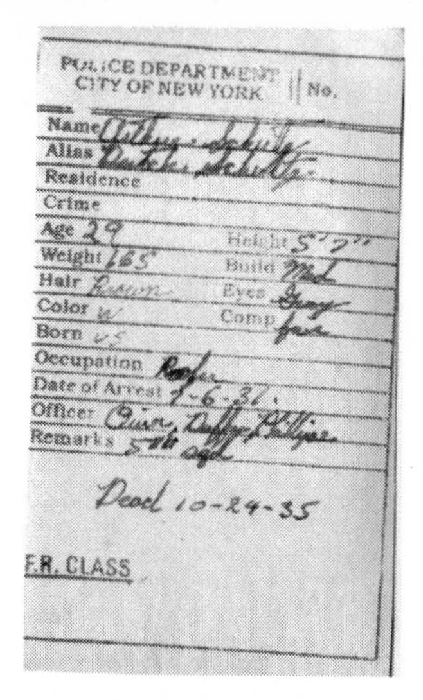

POLICE DEPARTMENT
CITY OF NEW YORK | No.

Name Arthur Schultz
Alias Dutch Schultz
Residence
Crime
Age 29 Height 5'7"
Weight 165 Build Med
Hair Brown Eyes Gray
Color W Comp fair
Born U.S.
Occupation [illegible]
Date of Arrest [illegible]-6-31.
Officer [illegible]
Remarks [illegible]

Dead 10-24-35

F.R. CLASS

Burton Turkus Papers, Special Collections, Lloyd Sealy Library, John Jay College of Criminal Justice/CUNY

Dutch Schultz was a bootlegger, speakeasy owner, labor racketeer, bouncer and killer, with his turf mainly in the Bronx and later Harlem.

However, no gangster could be more unfit for the emerging corporate criminal world than Schultz. Crazed violence, betrayals and warfare even within his own gang accompanied him throughout his rise in the New York underworld. Nonetheless he had a seat at the table of the crime leaders in the late 1920s and into the 1930s.

THE NUMBERS RACKET

The numbers racket has a long history in American culture.[1] At the turn of the twentieth century it thrived in Italian, Latino and African American neighborhoods. Its premise is simple.

A player picks three numbers, which can be random numbers, their home address, their child's schoolroom or birthdate, or even from dream books (nonsense, but a fascinating art form for me when I was a teenager in the Bronx).

Dream books have been popular inspirations for choosing a number since the early twentieth century. They were (and still are) cheaply produced books with cover art often of cartoonish people of color wearing elaborate Middle Eastern head wrappings seated in front of crystal balls. Sold at newsstands, beauty parlors, and corner candy stores, the books coupled fantasies, everyday objects, and disjointed fragments of dreams with corresponding numbers. Duke Ellington might be "8," sex with the downstairs neighbor's wife a "2," a cigar a "3", producing 823.

Dream books were the most creative merchandising ploy in any racket. Players in tenement buildings talking with their neighbors about revelations in the dream books created even more devoted "numbers" players.

Uncle George's older sister, Aunt Sarah, visited me in the hospital in the Bronx when I was a teenager. Auntie immediately found a pay phone and called her runner to play my room number for the next day. That was the science of number selection. I played "652" every day —for reasons I no longer remember—when I was a loader at the Pepsi-Cola Bottling Company in Long Island City, across the East River from the United Nations.

The numbers racket had nothing in common with the illegal casinos in Cleveland or the Miami of the 1930s. No two gambling enterprises could be more different. The casinos catered to upper class sensibilities—evening gowns and tuxedos, fine dining, loans ("markers") to the high rollers, limousine service, lavish floorshows and live music.

Meanwhile, numbers could be played for a quarter, a dollar, a dime, even a penny. The cash flow to the numbers operators was enormous because of the small payoffs for winners. Picking three random numbers in sequence has a 999-to-1 probability of occurring. The actual payoff for winners was only 600-to-1.

The "runners" taking the action were everywhere—in barbershops, on street corners, and in every tavern. On a warm Sunday morning a mom and dad walking to church might stop to give a runner fifty cents or a dollar for the next week's play. A runner would walk up to the fifth floor of a tenement to collect a quarter from a shut-in.

On my street in the Bronx, Milton "took the numbers" at the top of the staircase to the 170th Street subway station—he was there every day. He knew all his customers' names and the numbers they usually played. He kept it all in his head. They all did. Milton sent his two children to college just from his daily numbers' collections—his only job. In many neighborhoods "the numbers" was the biggest employer.

The runners received a percentage of their collections and expected a ten percent tip from the winners. They delivered their mountains of coins and bills to collectors who managed ten or fifteen runners.[2] The collectors would total the day's take and give it to "the bankers" (the mobsters controlling the action) who would take care of the police and politicians out of their huge cash flow and also pay off the rare winners.

The number for the day was easy to find in the evening newspapers. On summer nights men gathered around the newsstands smoking cigarettes and cheap cigars waiting for the evening edition to arrive. There were different sources for determining the winning number, depending on the numbers bank.

Often the number was embedded in the horse racing results—a combination of betting payouts for different races. I remember "the Brooklyn number" was the total mutuel handle at whatever major racetrack was having its season—Hialeah, Gulfstream, Aqueduct, Del Mar.[3] The total mutuel handle was the amount of money bet on all races at the track that day. The winning number was the last three digits. With a total mutuel handle of $1,389,652 the number for the day would be 652. Finally, I can now see in print the number I played for so long and never "hit."

Anyone with a few thousand dollars could start a numbers bank. Throughout the 1920s African American and Latino bankers cleared millions of dollars every year—in dimes, nickels and quarters. Sometimes a bank busted out if an operator embezzled the day's take and disappeared, or if a number that had a lot of action hit big—the flight number of a plane crash would always get played the next day.

A three-digit play that threatened the existence of numbers banks was 359, the last three digits of Marcus Garvey's federal penitentiary inmate ID. Garvey the founder of the "Back to Africa" movement had a massive following in African American communities in the mid-1920s. He established the Black Star Shipping Company that was intended to eventually transport African Americans back to Africa. He was convicted of mail fraud involving company stock and spent two years in the Atlanta federal penitentiary.

* * *

The huge action generated by this nickel-and-dime racket attracted unwanted attention. In 1928 New York, Jimmy Hines, a corrupt city official, tipped off his long-time patron Dutch Schultz that the numbers operating in the African American and Latino neighborhoods out of sight of organized crime had been generating millions of dollars every year.

Schultz went to work immediately—by 1930 he had forced many of the bankers to take him on as a partner. Others he intimidated out of business. Some disappeared. Characters such as Bumpy Johnson and Stephanie St. Clair, a tough-minded Caribbean woman, together ran a multi-million-dollar numbers bank. They fought Schultz's takeover as best they could—but the results were predictable.

White organized crime, with its paid off law enforcement allies, conspired to dominate the racket. African American and Latino numbers banks were raided; the runners were arrested, intimidated and entrapped. Those who mounted a spirited defense of their banks disappeared or were murdered. The numbers racket had become what would later be called in more genteel Wall Street circles—a hostile takeover target.

By 1935 Schultz cleared $10 to $20 million a year from the numbers rackets.

---

[1] The numbers had other names: the "Italian numbers," and "the policy," so named from the belief that it was cheap insurance for a possible "big hit" in the future (makes no sense to me!).

[2] Settling up the daily take from the numbers was often a neighborhood affair. There were men and women living by themselves in small apartments throughout the Bronx—I'm sure the same was true throughout the city. Many had long associations with the mob, such as women whose late husbands might have been low-level criminals, or men living quietly after a prison sentence. Numbers collectors would rent their apartments as out-of-the way "offices" for a few hours each afternoon after the last horse races were run.

Mrs. Lewis lived across the hall from us in apartment 25. At about 3:00 pm she would leave when two or three men arrived—she visited neighbors, my mother especially. We all knew the men and what they were doing.

Mrs. Lewis left a pot of coffee brewing, with plates and cups set out on her kitchen table. More than once she gave me money: "Alan, could you run down to the bakery and pick up a nice coffee cake for me?"

[3] "Mutuel" as in *parimutuel*, the betting system at racetracks. I thought I should clarify it so the reader does not take "mutuel" to be a misspelling, as I did when I first saw it on racing forms.

15

CONEY ISLAND RACE TRACK

"Only queers wear silk shirts"
– Dutch Schultz 1935

Schultz probably didn't have as much disgust for gays as he did for anyone who would pay $15.00 for a silk shirt. Proud of his $2.00 shirts, Schultz never minded the rumpled, always cheap suits he wore, or the slovenly look he projected throughout his life. He was an oddity among the mob bosses who had accumulated huge fortunes, often while still in their early twenties. Their expensive wardrobes validated their hard-won success. A newspaper reporter described Schultz's appearance as that of a "vagrant." Not a single other mob boss of that era would come close to that description.

As soon as Waxey Gordon was sentenced to ten years in federal prison, the Feds and New York State focused on Dutch Schultz, also a good bet to be a tax evader. At the end of 1931 Dutch took himself off the streets and stayed in hiding for two years. His absence attracted other high-ranking gangsters to his lucrative operations. In 1934 he surrendered. Once the Feds indicted Schultz, the underworld was sure that he would go down with a long prison sentence. Nobody thought he would beat the case.

Lepke Buchalter moved in on Schultz's labor union racketeering in the Bronx and Manhattan. Trigger Mike Coppola saw the numbers as open for takeover and started drawing Harlem bankers into his own operation.

Then the unexpected happened. Schultz, with help from his clever lawyers and a determined public relations campaign in the small upstate New York farm town where his second trial was held was acquitted of all charges. He had fit in comfortably with the town folks, donating to charities and churches, and charming the small jury pool; even his cheap suits fit the style of the locals more than if he had arrived in the expensive suits of the typical New York City gangster.

The irate judge's condemnation of the not guilty verdict didn't matter. Schultz was free to regain control of his rackets. However, Lepke, Trigger Mike and the others were not amenable to walking away from those healthy cash flows and had other ideas.

Determined to convict Schultz, New York Governor Lehman drafted Thomas Dewey, the young federal prosecutor of Waxey Gordon, to be the special state prosecutor. Since the Gordon conviction, Dewey had returned to private practice but took on the new assignment. Schultz would be Dewey's main target. Schultz became more untethered than he had ever been.

As the often-told story goes, Schultz wanted the National Commission's approval to assassinate Dewey. Meyer Lansky, Luciano and the others knew this would be the end of organized crime—killing a special prosecutor would turn the complacent public against them. Prohibition had never been taken seriously and gambling was not a crime to most people. The underworld had made hundreds of millions for the past fifteen years from their well-cultivated rackets—so why risk the public turning against them by allowing the disheveled, increasingly erratic Dutch Schultz to kill Dewey?

Lansky and Luciano, and the other bosses, could see the moves on the always-changing chessboard. Organized crime had become a national operation, as was Murder, Inc. Gamblers, hit men and other criminals were crossing state lines every day. They were violating federal laws, not just laws that local police and politicians ignored for the right payoff.

In 1935, at the urging of its director, the Bureau of Investigation had just been given a new name: the Federal Bureau of Investigation. The director, a young J. Edgar Hoover, had been courting newspaper coverage for himself more than for his agency, which gave him celebrity status. He was content capturing dime-store bandits and small-town bank robbers. He understood that it was easier to apprehend lone wolf stickup guys in the Midwest than lawyered up Yiddish- and Italian-speaking organized criminals in the Big City.

So why, reasoned the National Commission, turn the Feds into their pursuers across state lines by killing a prosecutor?

An increasingly commanding voice in organized crime also exerted pressure to get rid of Dutch Schultz, by imprisonment or assassination—the Cleveland Syndicate. Its role in Dutch Schultz's murder was never widely known. I was lucky enough to have Sam Schrader as my next-door neighbor for several years in Manhattan.

* * *

Sam Schrader began his long criminal career working for the Cincinnati-based bootlegger George Remus.[1] After Remus' bootlegging empire crashed in the mid-1920s the Cleveland Syndicate recruited Sam Schrader into their "Little Jewish Navy," smuggling booze from Canada to Cleveland and Detroit. Later, when Prohibition ended, Dalitz, as would any competent corporate manager, moved his key personnel from smuggling to other operations. Schrader started working in the illegal casinos by then managed by Uncle George and Ruby Kolod.

Decades later Sam Schrader, my brother Bernard and I were among the first occupants of Southbridge Towers in Lower Manhattan, just south of the Brooklyn Bridge, next to the Fulton Fish Market. The three of us often would go to the recently opened World Trade Center for coffee in the morning. Sam loved Chinese food, and since Chinatown was just a few short blocks north of us, that too was a regular destination. A few times Uncle Charlie met us there. He had been released from Trenton State Prison several years earlier. He joked that while in prison he missed his family the most, then it was Chinese food.

Sam Schrader related the following story: Dutch Schultz couldn't bear anyone hitting the number. It didn't matter to him that the payoffs were small compared to the huge cash flow the racket generated. He saw it all as "his money" and took it personally when players actually won. There was no convincing him that winners were great for business— a winner would tell everyone in the neighborhood.

So Schultz set about to fix the daily winning number. An Irish mobster, Bill Dwyer, owned the Coney Island Race Track in Cincinnati. The track had been closed for several years and reopened in 1933—by then there was legal betting at Ohio racetracks. Schultz made a deal with Dwyer and became the operator of the racetrack.

The racetrack proved to be a goldmine for Schultz, not just because of his take from the racetrack betting but for a less obvious reason—Schultz used the total mutuel handle from his Coney Island Race Track as the daily number, and there was no way he wasn't going to fix it to limit payouts.

He hired Otto "Abbadabba" Berman, a reputed math genius, to fix the betting totals at the track. Berman would receive a call from New York with numbers that were heavily played and he made certain they didn't hit. For this Berman was supposedly paid $10,000 a week, a huge sum in 1935, made even larger considering Schultz's reluctance to part with any money at all.

According to Sam Schrader, the bookkeepers at the racetrack later revealed that it was a simple operation to change the betting totals. All Berman need do was change a digit and nobody was any wiser. The sophisticated Cleveland Syndicate believed most mob guys had caveman intellects and that Berman easily dazzled and confused Schultz and the other criminals with formulas or whatever he improvised to make himself an irreplaceable part of the operation.

Schultz needed large sums of money for his years of legal defense bills, and he became even more erratic, shortchanging his bankers and numbers runners. They rebelled openly—his control was slipping.

The Cleveland Syndicate approached Berman with a deal for Schultz. They wanted a piece of the Coney Island Race Track and some of the numbers racket in New York.

They had leverage Schultz would understand; the Cleveland Syndicate owned Ohio politics—Schultz was from another world. The racetrack was in their backyard. There are many moving parts to the operation of a racetrack. Using the blueprint of labor racketeering, the Cleveland Syndicate could easily make it impossible for the track to function.

What would happen if the race caller didn't show up? Or if the cashiers at the betting windows would go on strike? What about fire regulations? What about the safety of the horses? Harassing the bettors? There were infinite possibilities, and none of them were good for Schultz.

Sam Tucker, one of the Cleveland Four, met with Berman.[3] The 1935 Coney Island Race Track season ended on October 22. Berman would be traveling the next day to Newark to meet Schultz. Tucker wanted him to take back a simple offer; the Cleveland Syndicate would now be Schultz's partner in the racetrack.

Sam Schrader believed it was a ploy by the Cleveland and New York mobs to keep Schultz unaware that he was already destined for assassination. It was always possible Schultz might act first against the New York bosses, as Luciano had done when he took out Maranzano and Masseria four years earlier after he discovered he was their target. So, if the Syndicate kept the Schultz crew talking they would be less likely to reach for their guns.

The day after the racetrack closed for the season, Berman went back to Newark. The same night he was in the Palace Chop House when Uncle Charlie entered with Mendy Weiss. Berman would be one of the other three assassinated with Schultz.

---

1 I don't want to interrupt the Dutch Schultz drama with an account of George Remus' rise and fall. Suffice it to say, my family criminals and their associates had an elementary school education. Remus, though, was well educated—a pharmacist turned lawyer, turned wildly successful bootlegger. However, he lacked the street smarts to not taunt the Feds, which was his downfall.

2 A retired numbers runner told me that if someone in Harlem had a big hit the runner would give a Cadillac salesman the winner's home address so they could try to sell the winner an overpriced car. I don't know if it's true or just another racist urban legend.

3 Sam Tucker was one of the Cleveland Four, along with Moe Dalitz, Morris Kleinman and Lou Rothkopf. They were all from immigrant families and often spoke Yiddish to keep references in conversations private. From the number of "Sams" and "Samuels" in this story I would guess that it was a popular name in Jewish families in the first decade of the twentieth century.

Library of Congress, Prints and Photographs Division, NYWT&S Collection

Arthur Flegenheimer, better known as Dutch Schultz. Uncle Charlie shot him in a barroom toilet in 1935. There were three other soon-to-be dead bodies before Charlie and his sidekick left the bar.

Schultz had few admirers in the NYC underworld; he was a paranoid mob boss who rarely inspired loyalty from his criminal associates.

16

UNCLE CHARLIE KILLS DUTCH SCHULTZ

Uncle Charlie and Mendy Weiss rolled up to the Palace Chop House in a car driven by a gangster wannabe, Piggy Schechter. The two gunmen told Piggy, unknown to the Schultz crew, to see how many men were in the back room Schultz used as his office. Piggy returned; there were four men in the back, he said.

Uncle Charlie and Mendy entered with guns drawn. They motioned for the bartender to get down—he gratefully complied. They went to the back room and saw only three men. Charlie knew Schultz and didn't see him, so he went to the nearby bathroom. The order of events is unclear, but they are also unimportant, as the result would be the same—four dead men.

Charlie went into the bathroom and saw Schultz urinating. He shot twice, with one bullet striking the Dutchman below the heart and exiting through his lower back. Uncle Charlie joined Mendy in shooting the other three. Otto "Abbadabba" Berman, the accountant, fell to the floor immediately. He died four hours later. The other two, both mortally wounded, returned the fire, not hitting Charlie or Mendy Weiss.

Mendy, seeing the job finished ran out to the car. Schultz stumbled toward a table, sat down, and passed out. Uncle Charlie had other ideas: he went through Schultz's pocket, looking for cash, in either the bathroom or after Schultz's face landed on the table.

Dutch Schultz would die the next day.

According to Uncle George, Charlie insisted that picking through his victim's pockets was always the right thing to do. Uncle Charlie reasoned, "If I don't take the cash, the next person with his hand in the dead guy's pocket is gonna be a detective. Why leave it for that bum? He gets a paycheck." It seemed like common sense to him.

Mendy, knowing Uncle Charlie couldn't resist looking for cash, ordered Piggy to drive back to New York. The job was done. Charlie was left behind. Charlie walked back to New York City.[1] He also had $8,000 that he had pulled out of one of Schultz's pockets. (That's what he later told Uncle George; but as I said, dollar amounts tend to fluctuate according to the storyteller.) The cash bonus didn't soothe Charlie's fury that Mendy left him.

Uncle Charlie complained to Lepke, who ordered a meeting with Mendy Weiss. Lepke urged them both to forget it—the job was done, Schultz was dead, let it go. He sent Charlie to Miami to cool off. Charlie complained to Lucky Luciano, who told him to shut up; there was nothing more to say. Uncle George recalled meeting Charlie in one of Meyer Lansky's Hallandale casinos; he couldn't stop talking about "being left behind."

Because both Charlie and Mendy Weiss were such upstanding, reliable assassins, Lepke had to blame someone for leaving a valued hit man stranded in a bar with four dead bodies. Of course, that someone would be the hapless Piggy, whose hoped-for career as a criminal came to a quick end. He was soon after found tortured and shot, with his body burned.

For Uncle Charlie the assassination didn't work out as well as he might have hoped—the negative outcome was his own fault. He just couldn't help violating Rule #1: Keep your mouth shut. Some of this aftermath is embedded in mob lore.

At a party in Brooklyn attended mostly by Murder Inc. assassins, Charlie recounted how Mendy left him behind with Schultz and the other three expiring bodies. Unfortunately for Uncle Charlie, the party was in Abe "Kid Twist" Reles' apartment. A few years later Reles would remember every detail of Charlie's recitation when he informed on his fellow assassins.

My brother Bernard, an accomplished planter of illegal bugs and wiretaps for the NYPD in the late 1960s, could only imagine the thrill of getting a clean recording of Murder Inc.'s most feared assassins at a party in Brooklyn.

While Uncle Charlie's grievance with Mendy Weiss festered, the Cleveland Four took a one-third ownership in the Coney Island Race Track. It had gone bankrupt soon after Dutch pissed into a urinal for the last time. The total purchase price was $1,000.Thus the Cleveland Four's individual buy-in for one-third of the operation was all of $86.33 each.[2]

It was just one of the pieces of the Schultz criminal empire that fell into his rivals' hands. Lepke, who had already established himself as the tight-fisted manipulator of New York City trade unions, took over Schultz's unions.

The numbers rackets had been the real cash machine for Schultz for the two years before his death, having generated millions of dollars for his crew. Trigger Mike Coppola, never seen as a wily businessman, but rather as a violent killer, became the undisputed boss of the Harlem and Bronx numbers. He was to control this racket for the next thirty years.

Trigger Mike traded pieces of the Harlem numbers racket for a stake in the Cleveland Syndicate's successful Ohio casinos—and it was Trigger Mike's former underling, Uncle George, who represented the Syndicate's interests in Mike's Harlem numbers racket. Mike then traded off another piece of the numbers with another longtime ally,

Meyer Lansky, for an interest in the growing Miami rackets. All of these racketeers had still another conquest in sight: Cuba, just ninety miles off the Florida coast.

By the mid-1930s Meyer Lansky was the mob's man in Havana. He had already paid off Fulgencio Batista, the Army Chief of Staff in Cuba, the military and political power on the island. The setup seemed too good to be true—an independent country open to gambling under the control of American organized crime, with a corrupt military chief as their full partner. Lansky had already given Batista $500,000 as a tribute from the Cleveland Syndicate and other crime families. The future looked very promising.

The Cleveland Syndicate had still another prize conquest in sight—and it was in their backyard.

---

1 For those as curious as I as to how long the walk back to New York City might have been for Charlie, it probably took about eight to ten hours—not a lot for a physically fit, twenty five year old man no doubt on an adrenaline rush after leaving four dying men in a tavern.

Why didn't he just take a taxi back to Brooklyn? That was a joke I shared with my brother on occasion. Maybe it's mentioned in other accounts of this well known murderous undertaking.

2 *Mr. Mob: The Life and Crimes of Moe Dalitz* by Michael Newton (Jefferson, NC: McFarland & Company, 2009), P. 77-78.

Each of the Cleveland Four later received $31,153.18 when the racetrack was sold in 1948— a 374% profit on their individual 1936 $83.33 investment.

17

NEWPORT AND COVINGTON, KENTUCKY

New Orleans, Memphis, Natchez and other cities alongside the Mississippi and Ohio Rivers had always been havens for river pirates, floating whorehouses, and sawdust-floored "bust out" gambling joints, where craps were played with loaded dice, roulette wheels fixed with magnets, and prostitutes slipped knockout drops into the cheap booze they enticed their marks to buy. A patron would rarely leave town with even a dime.

Newport, Kentucky, was no exception. Since the Civil War the citizens of Cincinnati, just across the Ohio River, had known it as "Sin City." Bad roads and twisting mountains separated Newport from the rest of Kentucky, allowing its corrupt local government to operate in isolation. Next to Newport the city of Covington, Kentucky, separated by the Licking River, enjoyed the same isolation that allowed its equally dishonest gaming industry to also flourish.

Once they took possession of the Coney Island Race Track and renamed it River Downs Racetrack, the Cleveland Syndicate made their next move; taking over the rackets in Newport and Covington, Kentucky. They employed the same ground game as organized crime used to take over the numbers rackets in inner cities just a few years earlier—this time targeting the small, independent casino owners who ran the "bust out" joints. The operators would be easy to isolate and intimidate, then the mob would buy them out and upgrade the casinos to attract higher rollers.

They first bought a casino, the Arrowhead Club in Cincinnati, but already had their target in Newport lined up. It was the Beverly Club—the classiest carpet joint in the area. It was equal to the prosperous casinos the Cleveland Syndicate owned in Ohio. The young Frank Sinatra appeared at the Beverly Club and a parade of celebrities had passed through.

Best of all, it was owned by Peter Schmidt, an independent operator who the Cleveland Syndicate thought would be open to a buyout. Schmidt, like Sam Schrader, had been part of George Remus' operations in Cincinnati. Once Remus'criminal empire vanished, Schmidt moved across the river and built the Beverly Club.

Sam Tucker had represented the Cleveland Syndicate in the Coney Island Race Track offer to Dutch Schultz; now he negotiated with Schmidt. Tucker took Sam Schrader with him. Schmidt refused to give over control to the Cleveland mob. Sam Schrader was surprised.

"It was a good offer," Sam said thirty-five years later. "Schmidt by that time was a local. We weren't. We wanted someone to run the place who knew the politicians and who to pay off. We offered him a lot of cash up front and a piece of the weekly take, and he could stay on and manage the joint. It was a sweet deal for Schmidt. He said he would think about it. I went to see him a few days later. He wouldn't take it."

On February 3, 1936, The Beverly Club burned to the ground. The six-year-old niece of the caretaker died in the blaze. The arsonist was never found. Most likely the hopeful buyers of the Club had lit it up.

Tucker and Schrader went back to Schmidt with another offer; they would buy him out completely. He still wasn't interested. Instead, he renovated the building and reopened it, more luxurious than ever. With its oak paneling, crystal chandeliers and an elegantly designed interior with thick blue carpeting, it was the blueprint for the Las Vegas casinos of the 1950s. Schmidt renamed it the Beverly Hills Country Club. He had an extravagant opening in April 1937 attended by local politicians, government officials from the surrounding states, and the usual freeloading celebrities and press corps.

The now grander casino whetted the Syndicate's interest even more. To show their determination, they employed the persuasive techniques they had learned over the years. In the summer of 1937 a group of machine-gun-toting bandits held up the Beverly Hills Country Club, terrorizing the patrons. Of course, the robbers were never captured. Vandalism and threats to the employees occurred regularly, including "ding donging": men urinating on the carpets in the most visible part of the casino.

Finally, Schmidt agreed to sell out to the Cleveland Syndicate. "He got less than we offered the year before," Schrader said. "He was lucky to be alive. Back in those days the pleasant negotiations only went on for a short time. Everyone knew it was a losing battle. He wound up building a bowling alley in Newport. I saw him there a few times. George Remus showed up also. Schmidt and Remus deserved each other—they both thought they were smarter than everyone else, and both got screwed."

The mob soon built another elegant location, the Lookout House in Covington. Sinatra (always attracted to mob-run enterprises), Nat King Cole, and Dean Martin and Jerry Lewis performed in the posh nightclub. Covington and Newport, Kentucky, prospered as gambling and entertainment destinations in the Midwest until the end of the 1940s, when the Cleveland Syndicate turned their attention to their greatest prize—Las Vegas.

18

NAZIS ON THE STREETS

"The Nazi bastards saluted American flags in Madison Square Garden. They had them up on the stage with swastika flags and a huge painting of George Washington. They sang 'The Star-Spangled Banner' and then they sieg heiled the swastika, and swore allegiance to Hitler."

–Johnny Eder, 1989

The night of February 20, 1939 dramatically bared the existence of Nazis on Main Street America. A German American Bund (an American Nazi organization) rally filled Madison Square Garden with 20,000 supporters. Mayor Fiorello LaGuardia, whose mother was Jewish, insisted the Nazis had the right to free speech.

Newsreel footage of the Nuremberg rallies and the violent attacks on Jewish shopkeepers had been seen in movie theaters—Americans already knew of the growing Nazi police state in Germany. The police estimated that 100,000 anti-Fascist protesters filled the streets around Madison Square Garden that night.

Mayor LaGuardia wisely provided 1,500 policemen to keep order.

Fritz Julius Kuhn, the German-born leader of the Bund, Jew baited from the podium, called President Roosevelt "Rosenfeld," denounced Jews as "communists," and called George Washington "the first American fascist." Kuhn had taken photos with Hitler on a recent trip to Germany. It was his intention to be the American führer when the Nazis dominated the world. Not surprisingly, one of his first jobs in America was on the assembly line in Nazi sympathizer Henry Ford's auto plant in Detroit.

Hitler's supporters held rallies in German neighborhoods in big cities all over America. There were Nazi youth camps and countryside retreats in New Jersey and Long Island. Jewish leaders feared the rise in America of the anti-Semitism they had fled a generation earlier.

Four years before the Madison Square Garden Nazi rally, Stephen Wise, a well-known rabbi, and Judge Nathan Perlman approached Meyer Lansky. They wanted Jewish men to fight the Nazis in the streets. It was crucial that the anti-Semites never think Jews wouldn't fight back. They offered to raise money to finance anti-fascist fighters. Money didn't interest Lansky; he was already the highest-ranking member of the National Commission, America's largest cash-flow business.

But Judge Perlman's hint that the police would look the other way as long as none of the Nazis died did interest Lansky. Lansky agreed—Nazis wouldn't die but every other imaginable physical pain would be dispensed. He also asked Perlman and Wise to use their considerable influence to insure that none of his street fighters would be subjected to negative publicity in the press.

Lansky's seasoned street thugs trained others who had no connection to organized crime but wanted a piece of the Nazis to avenge the treatment of their families in Europe. Jews with baseball bats, lead pipes, and brass knuckles attacked Bund rallies at will. The Nazis, despite their brown shirt uniforms, swastikas and blowhard bravado, were never eager to fight these Jews in the streets.

Sometimes an anti-Nazi would infiltrate a rally and throw a stink bomb into the front of the meeting hall.[1] The intense smell would drive the Nazis out the doors and into a gauntlet of men armed with pipes and baseball bats. The outcome was always the same: broken bones and skulls.

My twenty-one-year-old father was one of the "civilians" outside a Nazi rally in Queens. A man wearing a swastika armband, fleeing the stench, ran straight into him and Red Levine. Red hit him in the face with a lead pipe. The Nazi fell to the ground. Dad remembers Red leaning over and picking the guy's head up by his blood-soaked hair. Leaning into the poor bastard's face, Red took off his fedora, exposing his yarmulke.

"Look at me, you Nazi bastard. I'm a fucking Jew. Now you know we can hurt you. I'd kill you but it's against the rules."

Red Levine laughed at the idea that he was "following Meyer's rules" and bounced the barely conscious Nazi's head off the concrete sidewalk.

* * *

The Nazi rallies were advertised in German language newspapers as meetings with less inflammatory names: the German American Businessmen's Association, the Hamburg Men's Group, etc. The Nazi training camps in the countryside were also identified in these newspapers. Maybe they thought there was not a single Jew in New York City who could read German.

Harold and Frank, two young Jewish refugees from Germany, worked at one of Trigger Mike Coppolla's numbers banks in the Bronx. They were also eager members of the brigades Lansky had assembled to fight the Nazis. They read about a Bund rally to be held at Camp Siegfried (yeah, that was its name!!) in Yaphank, a small backwater town on Long Island, sixty miles from Manhattan.

There were even trains running from Midtown Manhattan to Yaphank. Harold and Frank couldn't resist a personal visit. A few days later they were on the train shoulder to shoulder with other Camp Siegfried bound passengers—many wearing brown shirts, carrying swastika flags, and singing marching songs. Harold and Frank walked into the camp with a throng of ecstatic Nazis.

They were stunned—it was a prosperous community, with log cabins in neat rows, hundreds of people walking around in brown shirts, marching grounds, a swimming pool, classrooms and streets named after Hitler, Goebbels and Goering. Harold and Frank couldn't believe that the Nazis from a Germany they had just fled were now sitting around picnic tables only one hour out of New York City.

Fortune shines on the bold, as the saying goes—and these two young Jews going to a Nazi summer camp for an afternoon outing qualified as bold. They listened to someone talking Nazi crap for a few minutes. They chatted with Sidney, a man standing next to them. Then Sidney offered to drive them back to New York. He lived in Yorkville, a German neighborhood (back in the 1930s, anyway), on the Upper East Side of Manhattan.

The brothers accepted Sidney's offer. They told him they lived in Brooklyn. They listened to his anti-Semitic rant for a while, then Harold asked Sidney to pull over by a phone booth next to a closed gas station. Harold called their boss Sol "Blubber" Bloom in Williamsburg, a neighborhood in Brooklyn. He told Blubber about the Nazi camp and Sidney's nasty Jew talk. Blubber told Harold to "throw da bum in the trunk and bring him over." Williamsburg was also the home of growing numbers of Hassidic Jews; Orthodox Jewish men wearing long black coats, oversized fur hats and long *payes* (sideburns).

Harold and Frank grabbed the terrified Sidney. They ripped off his clothing and tied his hands and feet with strips of his pants. They jammed a rag into Sidney's mouth and threw his nude body into the trunk. In Williamsburg Sol "Blubber" Bloom was waiting with a baseball bat, along with a crowd of Yiddish-speaking men. Harold pulled the nude Sidney out of the trunk—he had shit himself, especially after hearing these crazed Jews. Frank yelled out in Yiddish, "Who wants this Nazi bastard's swastika?" He threw the cloth armband into the crowd encircling the car. Harold and Frank hailed a taxicab and went home.

Sidney, the hapless Nazi, was beaten senseless and thrown back into the trunk sobbing. Blubber drove Sidney's car up to 86th Street, the heart of Yorktown, the German neighborhood. He stopped a man. "Here," he said, giving the man the car keys. "There's a fucken Nazi in the trunk. I think he's still alive." Blubber took a taxi back to Williamsburg.

That episode was still one more longstanding joke in the wise guy bars, like Red Levine's The Spot. Red remembered, as I can only describe as fondly, "There would have been a lot of Nazi bodies around Manhattan if Meyer had allowed it. As it worked out, the Nazis were scared shitless of fighting the Jews. They knew it. We knew it."

* * *

Fritz Julius Kuhn, the rabble-rousing Jew baiter in Madison Square Garden that memorable night, became a marked man in New York when, several months later, Germany invaded Poland and the world was on its way to World War II. No longer tolerant of Nazi free speech, Mayor LaGuardia wanted Kuhn in jail, whatever it took.

New York State indicted Kuhn for embezzlement of Bund funds. It was a bullshit charge, but nobody cared. In December 1939 Kuhn was sentenced to two-and-a-half to five years in prison and stripped of his US citizenship. After Kuhn's release from prison the Feds held him as a foreign agent until the war's end. Deported back to Germany, Kuhn was charged with war crimes and spent the rest of his life in and out of German jails.

Jews later recalled that, despite the American Nazis' allegiance to Hitler and their public support of his views of world domination, few were rounded up during the war. Yet, on the West Coast Japanese Americans, most of them American citizens who had never even once expressed support for the Japanese government, were nonetheless rounded up and sent to desolate internment camps in the deserts of the Southwest for the remainder of the war.

---

[1] Stink bomb: a bottle with a mixture of household chemicals: ammonia, hydrogen sulfide, vinegar, and matchstick heads. After a few days or weeks of fermentation the combination produces an unbearable stench, sometimes described as "rotten eggs" or "an open sewer with rotting dead bodies."

The stink bomb was an essential weapon for extortionists in the 1920s and '30s. A teenager working for the mob would throw a glass bottle off a wall or through a window of a movie theater, clothing manufacturer or jewelry store. Racks of clothing in a manufacturer's warehouse, or the seats in a movie theater, never lose the ghastly odor, which damp weather only intensifies.

The stink bomb tended to bring the extortion target to the negotiating table very quickly.

New York City Municipal Archives

A Nazi picnic at Camp Siegfried, 60 miles from Manhattan, in 1938.

The Nazis posed for this photo, one of many taken by undercover NYPD detectives —part of the Alien Squad. Maybe one of these jack offs was Sidney, the Nazi tied up nude in the trunk of his car, with Sol "Blubber" Bloom driving him around NYC. Anyway, who'd want to go to a Nazi picnic with no beer on the table?

101

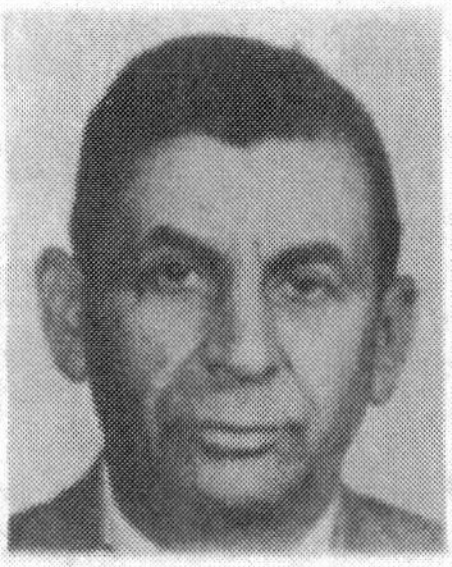

NAME : Meyer LANSKY

ALIASES : Born Meyer Suchowlansky, bugs Meyer, Morris Lieberman

DESCRIPTION : Born 7-4-02 Grodno, Poland, Jewish, 5'5", 145 lbs, brown eyes, grey brown hair. Naturalized Brooklyn, NY, 9-27-1928.

LOCALITIES FREQUENTED : Resides 612 Hibiscus Drive, Hallandale, Fla. Frequents Gold Coast Lounge, Hollywood, Florida, Miami, NY, & Las Vegas.

FAMILY BACKGROUND : Divorced from Anna Citron; children from first marriage; Bernard, Sandra, Paul; second wife: Thelma Schwartz; mother: Fenke (deceased); brother: Jack.

CRIMINAL ASSOCIATES : Lucky Luciano, Giuseppe Doto, Francisco Saveria, Anthony Accardo, Santo Trafficante, Jr., Jack Lansky.

CRIMINAL HISTORY : FBI #791783. NYCPD #B70258. Record dates from 1918 and includes arrests for petty larceny, felonious assault, bootlegging, gambling, narcotics.

BUSINESS : Has interests in Havana Riviera, Capri Hotel and Sans Souci Gambling Casino, all in Havana, Cuba, & Flamingo Hotel, Las Vegas, Nevada.

MODUS OPERANDI : One of the top non-Italian associates of the Mafia. Controls gambling in partnership with leading Mafiosi. Finances large scale narcotic smuggling and other illicit ventures.

Property of U. S. Govt — For Official Use Only
May not be disseminated or contents disclosed
Without permission of Commissioner of Narcotics

19

THEY GOT THE WRONG MAN

The 1930s were an unimagined success for organized crime. The gangsters who couldn't see the benefit of an organized corporate structure—Maranzano, Masseria, Schultz and Waxey Gordon—were dispatched from the streets. Some were sent up for long prison sentences, but for most, the easier way—permanent elimination. However, one event dramatically affected the future of Murder, Inc.—the assassination department of the National Commission.

It was a Murder, Inc. fuck up—what should have been just one more efficient mob hit. Instead, it went terribly wrong. It occurred about 8:00 a.m. on July 25, 1939, in a comfortable middle-class neighborhood in the Bronx, just as people were leaving their apartment buildings and walking to the nearby Tremont Avenue D train platform.

Irving Penn, a music-publishing executive, left his apartment building at 250 East 178th Street never thinking that the occupants of the car bearing down on him were intent on killing him. But kill him they did.

Jacob "Cuppy" Migden had spent the past several weeks casing Penn's building, clocking his arrivals and departures. It was a job designated to lower-level hoods; the ones who pulled the triggers wouldn't be standing around for days in front of a marked man's apartment building. Cuppy pointed Penn out to the triggerman, Dandy Jack Parisi, who blasted away from the car window with deadly accuracy.

But Irving Penn wasn't the intended target of the hit. It was instead Philip Orlovsky, the onetime union racketeering partner of Lepke Buchalter. Orlovsky had been informing on Lepke to Tom Dewey, the special prosecutor and nemesis of New York City's organized crime figures. Other informants had just been eliminated in a frantic effort to leave nobody to testify against Lepke—now it was Orlovsky's turn to pay the price.

However, fate intervened that day. Orlovsky had an appointment with his barber and left the building earlier. Penn, bearing a similar stocky body type as Orlovsky, walked into the hit.

The Penn murder turned public opinion against organized crime overnight. It was a front-page story in every city newspaper for weeks. Mob boss Ben "Bugsy" Siegel had once said, flippantly, "We only kill each other." It was a belief held by many regular citizens, and so a benign attitude existed towards organized crime that had, after all, provided illegal booze for years, and took bets and numbers from ordinary citizens. That changed the day Penn fell to the sidewalk.

To add to the public relations nightmare for organized crime were Irving Penn's last words, as reported by a detective: "I don't have an enemy in the world."

* * *

Pressure on law enforcement to find the Penn killers intensified. Detectives finally identified the getaway driver, Seymour "Blue Jaw" Magoon. Magoon informed on Parisi and Cuppy. Cuppy had already left town and had plastic surgery to alter his identifiable face (see his 1931 bad hair day mugshots). He was captured in St. Louis and brought back to New York City. He pled guilty to a lesser charge and spent five years in Sing Sing.

Later, in the early 1970s, Cuppy Migden operated a small women's cosmetics store on 37th Street in the Garment Center, a few doors from our father's new business, a trucking company. The store was a front for a loansharking and bookie operation. Cuppy and his partner, a jeweler/gambler/fence, Robbie Margolies, were life-long friends of my parents. I often stopped there to visit them. I rarely saw a woman shopping for cosmetics in the store.

I sometimes wondered how did these two criminals know the difference between the fragrances they were supposedly selling? My sister told me years later that occasionally our mother and Robbie's wife, Sonia, visited the store to mentor them about their products. I doubt either of them would remember a single detail from those lessons.

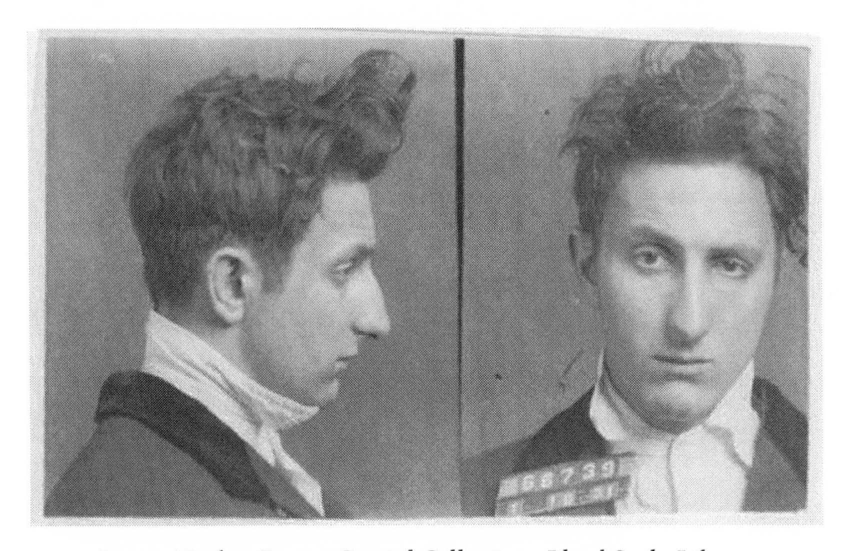

Burton Turkus Papers, Special Collections, Lloyd Sealy Library, John Jay College of Criminal Justice/CUNY

Jacob "Cuppy" Migden grew up with Uncles George and Charlie and became one of the Murder Inc. crew. He definitely was having a bad hair day in this 1931 mugshot—eight years before fingering Irving Penn, an innocent businessman who was shot and killed instead of the intended target: a former partner of Lepke now informing on the mob. The public outcry pressured the district attorney to bring an end to Murder, Inc.

Author's family album

My mother (left) with Jacob "Cuppy" Migden next to her. My father is on the far right.

After the bungled Irving Penn mistaken assassination, Cuppy had plastic surgery and went into hiding. He still got caught and did time in Sing Sing. Years later, Cuppy and another family friend, Robby Margolies, operated a small cosmetic store in the Garment Center. It was mostly a front for loansharking and sports betting. I used to stop by to say hello—I've never noticed so many men in a women's cosmetics store before or since.

Courtesy of the Avi Bash Collection

Charles Workman and his wife, Catherine, on an idyllic vacation, probably in Florida in the late 1930s. Uncle Charlie no doubt thought that, like all the other Murder, Inc. hits, the Dutch Schultz murder had been just another job—after all these contract assassins operated with impunity for years. That would change very quickly once Abe Reles started talking.

KID TWIST

"You ain't got no corroboration"[1]
– Abe Reles, March 1940

For the mob the 1930s ended with the innocent Irving Penn dying on a Bronx sidewalk, and the new decade would begin with a shocked public first realizing the enormity of the criminal enterprise responsible for his death—a nationwide cartel with its own killing machine.

On January 1, 1940, William O'Dwyer, recently a Brooklyn judge and before that a policeman and laborer, was elected Kings County (Brooklyn) District Attorney. Born in Ireland and wise to the streets, O'Dwyer had greater ambition; he was determined to be the mayor of New York City. Crime was an issue he understood.

O'Dwyer appointed twenty-eight-year-old Burton Turkus as his assistant district attorney. He gave Turkus the mandate to eradicate what they both thought were just warring hoodlum groups in Brooklyn. Brooklyn detectives had open cases on countless homicides in the borough throughout the 1930s. They had little hope of solving even one of them. They so rarely did.

Since the Penn murder only six months earlier the police had been given their marching orders to roust criminals wherever they were found street corners, candy stores, dingy poolrooms and storefront social clubs. For New York City detectives, "rousting" meant just one thing;

they needn't be too gentlemanly when bringing someone to the station house—and they weren't.

Uncle Charlie reflected years later. "We could see big changes once O'Dwyer became the Brooklyn D.A. I lived in Brooklyn—most of us did (referring to the Murder Inc. hired gunmen.) We knew every detective. They gave us a lot of room. It was a kind of respect. But when they had to come down on a gangster, they did it. Everyone knew how it worked."

He laughed recalling once while standing on a Brooklyn street corner two detectives jumped out of their car, ignored him, and instead smacked around a small time hoodlum a few feet away. "They had respect for us," was Uncle Charlie's prideful conclusion.

Both Turkus and O'Dwyer knew that arresting criminals for vagrancy was a poor substitute for solving the murders on newspaper front pages. The gangsters would quickly be bailed out and on the streets again. Given the underworld ethic of silence, it didn't seem that it would ever be possible to charge them with anything more serious than vagrancy.

But just as soon as the new decade began, everything changed overnight.

A few days into January 1940, District Attorney O'Dwyer received a letter on stationery from Rikers Island, the New York City prison. It was a short note. Harry Rudolph wanted to talk to the Brooklyn DA about a murder in East New York (a Brooklyn neighborhood). Rudolph, a career criminal (weren't they all?), was being held as a material witness to another crime. The police already knew Rudolph—he was an informant, considered unreliable, even crazy by experienced detectives. Nonetheless, Turkus wanted to hear him out—what did they have to lose?

Rudolph told Turkus that he hated the Brownsville mob because they killed his friend, Red Alpert, one of the many bodies carted off the streets of Brooklyn over the previous decade. Rudolph claimed to be present when Alpert was killed. Who did it? Rudolph identified Abe "Kid Twist" Reles, Buggsy Goldstein and Dukey Maffetore as the assassins.

This was stunning—someone, no matter how unreliable, was naming the killers. Reles and Goldstein were not just any killers; they had long police records for every violent crime and were well known and feared on the streets.

O'Dwyer immediately had the grand jury indict the three suspects for murder in the first degree. He ordered the police to pick them up. They couldn't be found at their usual hangouts, so Captain William Sullivan, chief of the Twelfth Detective District, put the word out on the Brooklyn streets that the three of them should be in his office 8:00 am the next day. (They did things like that back then.)

Buggsy and Abe Reles arrived at Sullivan's office on time.[2] Both had been arrested for vagrancy a few days before and this seemed to be just more harassment. The police rounded up Dukey later in the afternoon. O'Dwyer charged all three with murder in the first degree. The court held them without bail.

It was February 2, 1940—the last day any of them would ever be on the streets again.

So now the District Attorney had three gangsters indicted for murder and only one unreliable witness, Harry Rudolph—an inmate on Rikers Island, a paid informant, no less. This would not be a winning case for the prosecution.

Johnny Eder, the fence and lifelong family friend who had made inroads into Mayor Walker's City Hall twelve years earlier, by now had become a confidant of every city government official—he knew everybody in the Brooklyn DA's office.

He recalled the months after the three hoodlums were arrested and told my father and me about it decades later. My father had heard this account many times before.

> *"O'Dwyer was a smart guy. He knew how gangsters operated. DAs could manage what stories were given to the newspapers, so O'Dwyer put on a show. He arrested the wife of someone they were trying to flip. She had a little baby at home. The guy got so scared about his wife in jail he gave up whoever he could. O'Dwyer made it seem like everyone was informing on everyone else. There were rumors all over Brooklyn. Every hitman was trying to remember who knew what about him. After all, murder carried the death sentence in New York back then.*
>
> *"We found out later a lot of it was just bluffs. The DA really needed someone who knew the big picture, someone near the top who could rat out everyone else—not just one of the drivers of a stolen getaway car or a guy who may have ice-picked someone once. It was a gamble and it worked."*

In March 1940 Mrs. Abe Reles walked into the Brooklyn DA's office and said, "My husband wants to talk to you."[3]

* * *

On March 23, 1940, Abe Reles started negotiating with District Attorney O'Dwyer—but it wasn't going to be easy. Reles was the template for "hardened criminal." He had been arrested dozens of times, and implicated in numerous murders, extortions, and beatings in broad daylight, yet, more often than not, he walked out of court, freed many times by the same judges. He had never given a statement to any law enforcement agent. It was difficult for the DA's office to imagine that this swaggering killer would ever talk.

O'Dwyer and Turkus faced a feral killer who insisted on walking free in exchange for his testimony. There would be no plea deal for reduced charges. Free. The DA couldn't just let Reles on the streets after he confessed to dozens of murders. But the other prosecutors believed Reles could implicate every criminal who had been untouchable just the day before.

The Criminal Code of the State of New York Article 399 stated, "A conviction could not be had upon the testimony of an accomplice, unless he is corroborated by such other evidence as tends to connect the defendant with the commission of the crime."

Corroboration—it was crucial to the prosecution of a crime, Reles knew that as well as anyone in the DA's office. He let them know they "got no corroboration" for any murders he might have been involved in, but that he "was the guy who could tell you where to get it."[4] Those details could convince a jury that, even if he was a contemptible killer, he knew "where the bodies were"—in this case, literally.

O'Dwyer proposed a deal: immunity for any murders Reles revealed to the grand jury, but he could be prosecuted for anything he didn't tell them—provided they could get corroboration. Reles agreed.

Why did Reles step forward? He might have thought that being the first to inform would give him the best deal. No doubt he was shaken by the rumors of informers O'Dwyer leaked to the press. His wife also said,

"I want to save my husband from the electric chair. My baby is coming in June."[5]

Nobody in the DA's office expected Reles' torrent of details of countless murders. They were stunned by his recall of mob hits ten years earlier. Stenographers filled dozens of pads with his non-stop monologues. He delighted in his dramatic recounting as well as the shock on the faces of his interrogators. When he finally took a deep breath a few weeks later, he had presented specifics of dozens of murders.

Now the investigators understood these were not random murders by street gangs fighting over neighborhood turf. Instead, a specialized group of men committed the murders, under the control of Lepke and Albert Anastasia. Reles called it "the Combination."

The grisly daily revelations and newspaper headlines shocked New York City and all of America. A newspaper reporter quickly labeled the Combination "Murder Inc.," the name that forever after described these killers.

As soon as Reles' confessions were known on the streets, other gunmen came forward with a variation of "I wanna see someone from Brooklyn." To silence potential informers, crime bosses ordered a search-and-destroy operation against all possible witnesses to any murder. The body count increased with a number of "insurance" murders—anyone the mobsters thought might be willing to talk. The DA, concerned for Reles and the other informers' safety, moved them to the Half Moon Hotel in Coney Island. It was transformed into a high security jail, with steel doors, 24/7 heavily armed police guards, and security checkpoints.

Corroboration—an elusive goal a few months earlier, was now abundant. Just a few months later, in June 1940, O'Dwyer filed murder indictments in Brooklyn. Courts in Manhattan and other jurisdictions filed criminal charges as well. Guilty verdicts, plea deals, long sentences and soon executions in Sing Sing followed quickly.

Murder Inc. was no more.

Burton Turkus[1] describes a "pleasant young fellow" brought into his office soon after Reles began talking. Turkus thought he was a defense attorney. The visitor was poised, emotionless and alert. It was Uncle Charlie. Turkus already knew that Charles Workman was one of the top mob gunmen who had just been identified by Reles as Schultz's killer. For the next thirteen months, brought in for questioning for several hours a day, Uncle Charlie sat quietly, saying nothing to Turkus—all the while immaculately dressed and unruffled.

Charlie had been his own worst enemy at Reles' party of mob hitmen years earlier (it may have been a New Year's Eve) when he complained about Mendy Weiss leaving him in the bar after Schultz was killed. Reles heard Charlie's every word. To seal Charlie's fate, another hitman, Allie "Tick Tock" Tannenbaum, was also at the party. Tannenbaum, once considered (as was Reles) to be a stone-cold killer who would never talk to the police, became an informer in May 1940, just two months after Reles.

Uncle Charlie was extradited to New Jersey—the jurisdiction of the multiple Schultz gang murders. Once he knew both Reles and Tannenbaum would testify against him, Charlie had run out of options. On June 10, 1941, to avoid a death sentence, he pleaded " no contest" and received a life sentence.

Five months later, on November 12, 1941, Abe Reles was found considerably rumpled up on the sun deck of the Half Moon Hotel in Coney Island. Wise guys later claimed that the sun deck was within sight of the Fun House—a walk through amusement of distorting mirrors, shaking floors, scary mannequins etc.—but I think that was just a private joke among them.

Harry Rudolph, the small-time criminal whose letter to O'Dwyer started the extraordinary chain of events that broke Murder, Inc., never testified. He died of reportedly natural causes on Rikers Island six months after talking to the DA.

The biggest catch of the Reles testimony was Louis "Lepke" Buchalter—the mob boss with a seat on the National Commission. Ironically, Lepke, the man who headed Murder Inc. and had ordered countless murders, as well as controlled dozens of corrupted trade unions, was convicted of the murder of a Brooklyn candy store owner, Joseph Rosen.[6] *Again, Reles and Tannenbaum were the star witnesses against him.*

On December 2, 1941, Lepke was sentenced to death in the electric chair at Sing Sing.

Five days later Japan attacked Pearl Harbor.

---

1 Burton B. Turkus and Sid Felder, *Murder Inc.* (Boston: Da Capo Press, 1951), 61.

2 "Buggsy" with two "g's" for Goldstein, "Bugsy" with one "g" for Siegel—this author offers no explanation except to note that neither homicidal maniac ever wrote his nickname down himself—that was left to the journalists of the era.

3 Turkus, *Murder Inc.*, 59.

4 Ibid., 62.

5 Ibid., 59.

6 Joseph Rosen, the candy store owner, once had been a Garment Center trucker. Lepke forced him out of business. The embittered Rosen was seen by Lepke as a threat to testify against him. He ordered Rosen to leave the city. Rosen didn't leave and instead ended up dead on the floor of his Brooklyn candy store.

Los Angeles Public Library Digital Collection

Author's note: defects in original photo

Allie "Tick Tock" Tannenbaum, on the left, and Abe "Kid Twist" Reles were arrested in 1940 in Hollywood. Both were Murder, Inc. assassins. The usually more sullen Tannenbaum flashes a big smile for the camera. What the heck—it's just another murder charge.

They informed on Uncle Charlie, who pled guilty to the Dutch Schultz murder to avoid a death sentence. Unlike Reles and the other informants, Tannenbaum, against all odds, lived a relatively long life. He died of natural causes in 1976 at the age of seventy.

Library of Congress, Prints and Photographs Division, NYWT&S Collection

Louis "Lepke" Buchalter is sentenced to death December 2, 1941—five days before the attack on Pearl Harbor. He looks as unfazed as if he had been found guilty of littering instead of murder. Decades later, Uncle Charlie lamented how "guys now show up in court for lightweight sentences in wheelchairs, oxygen tanks and hospital beds."

Library of Congress, Prints and Photographs Division, NYWT&S Collection

Louis Capone on the left (no relation to Al Capone) and, on the right, Mendy Weiss, Uncle Charlie's fellow assassin of the Dutch Schultz crew.

This is one of the more identifiable crime photos of that era, and for me the most curious of all. Only a few days earlier Judge Taylor had pronounced the death sentence for both of them, as well as for Lepke, for the murder of Joseph Rosen, a Brooklyn candy store owner.

Weiss and Capone are casually taking a train ride to Sing Sing's death row, where their electrocution was to be carried out within one month. No handcuffs, no orange jump suits, no restraints, and no hooded guards with automatic weapons—just a few laughs and a New York Times neatly folded in Mendy Weiss' lap. (They were executed twenty-seven months later.)

21

WORLD WAR II

The 1940s started with Europe at war and America declaring war on December 8, 1941, the day after the attack on Pearl Harbor. President Roosevelt tasked government agencies with overseeing both the diversion of materials away from the public and into war production and, at the same time, controlling prices that were certain to rise for the fewer available consumer goods. The Office of Price Administration (OPA) set price controls over countless consumer items, but ultimately its success relied on public support—the patriotic will of the people.

President Roosevelt moved the country to a rationing system in March 1942.[1] Tires were immediately rationed, since the supply of natural rubber, a crucial war material, from Southeast Asia had been cut off as soon as the Japanese occupied those countries. Soon after, food coupons for sugar were issued, followed by coffee, meat, canned fish, cheese and, eventually, a lengthy list of products.

Halting rationing system abuses fell to the enforcement agents of the Office of Price Administration (the OPA). The agents did not always find enthusiastic support on Main Street. They were unlikely to search cupboards for hoarded sugar or monitor transactions at store cash registers. Arresting a woman gathering sugar and flour for her daughter's birthday cake or a roast for Sunday dinner would not win support for the rationing system, or for the war. These were, after all, the wives, sisters and mothers of men lost at Pearl Harbor or stationed at far away bases training for the D-Day invasion.

Wherever black markets exist there are, inevitably, criminals—as well as just ordinary citizens trying to squeeze a buck out of a difficult situation. And so it was with the wartime rationing system. Ranchers falsified records of their slaughtered cattle to divert meat to the black market, and farmers didn't deliver all their tomato harvest to the price-regulated market for the same reason, but one of the most successful exploiters of the rationing system was well known in the New York underworld—not too surprising.

Carlo Gambino, born in Sicily in 1902, came to the United States as a nineteen- year-old. He immediately married into one of the New York crime families. Gambino became a soldier for Joe Masseria, the old school mob boss, who had that ill-advised lunch with Lucky Luciano in 1931.Gambino made a fortune during Prohibition distilling and smuggling booze, loan sharking, extortion and protection—a Prohibition-era resume similar to all the other characters in this narrative.[2]

Gasoline rationing started soon after America entered the war. Although the oilfields in Texas, Oklahoma and Louisiana provided sufficient supply to the American market, the oil tankers moving through the Gulf of Mexico and up the East Coast were prime targets for German submarines. Rationing gasoline to just three gallons per week was also intended to reduce tire wear. The speed limit was lowered to 35 MPH for the same reason.

Windshield stickers, coupons and booklets allowed different allotments and exemptions for different kinds of tractor transports and commercial trucking, among others. Gambino's crews targeted every kind of gas ration certificate.

Gambino's burglars emptied the improvised OPA offices of stickers, coupons, and books that he then sold to eager buyers throughout the Northeast. His crew fenced rationing stamps from small-time thieves and OPA employees looking for a few extra bucks. The stamps and coupons were hastily printed by the OPA and easy to counterfeit, which Gambino did as well. He cornered the market and supplied other mobs with stolen and counterfeit stamps. He made millions in those few short war years.

In the post-war years Gambino again proved his street smarts and business sense. He not only managed to survive the battles for control of the NYC underworld in the 1940s and '50s, but also emerged as Don Carlo, the last of the "boss of bosses"—a title he retained until his death in 1976.

After the war, Don Carlo used the millions he'd made in booze and gas rationing scams to move into legitimate businesses, ones that would do even better with organized crime backing. Garment Center trucking, with the mob's control of the essential Teamsters Union, rendered that business closed to anyone without mob approval. That had been a reality from the 1920s, when organized crime gained control of the Garment Center unions.

Don Carlo's two sons, Thomas and Joseph, owned Consolidated Carriers, which, due to their father's clout, was the largest trucker in the Garment Center. One of Consolidated's shipping points was next door to my father's trucking company on West 37th Street. (My father became a Garment Center trucker in the mid-1960s with the sponsorship of Uncle George and New York based organized crime figures soon to enter this story.)

Tommy and Joseph Gambino, and my father would often stand on the 37th Street sidewalk talking. The Gambino sons treated my father with great respect and were classy business executives. Thomas was a graduate of Manhattan College, a Roman Catholic college in Riverdale in the Bronx. Nobody would ever guess from his manner that he was also, by the 1970s, a ranking member of his father's crime family.

My father recounted one afternoon in the early 1970s when he stood in front of his storefront talking to Tommy Gambino. A limousine double-parked on the narrow street in front of them. Don Carlo Gambino emerged and walked to the sidewalk, followed by a bodyguard. A slight man with a porkpie fedora tilted back on his head, Don Carlo's most noticeable feature was a pronounced Roman nose—it filled his face. Nobody would have taken him for the Boss of Bosses.

Tommy said, "I'll see you later Lou. Dad is here." He turned and walked inside.

Don Carlo followed him, then stopped suddenly and turned toward my father. He walked up close, patted Lou on his cheek and said, "I hear you're doing a good job, sonny; keep up the good work." Then he turned and followed his son inside. My father smiled fondly when he told the story, and shrugged his shoulders.

But I'm jumping ahead.

In 1942, Uncle Charlie Workman, then thirty-four years old and facing life in prison, volunteered for a suicide squad to attack Japan. His request was denied.

When the war started, Charles "Lucky" Luciano was serving a thirty- to fifty-year sentence for compulsory prostitution. Thomas Dewey, the New York State special prosecutor, the target of Dutch Schultz's ill-fated assassination plot, had been the prosecutor at Luciano's trial.

Meyer Lansky tried to enlist in the Army but was rejected because of his age (he was forty). During the war Luciano gave his approval for the mob-controlled unions to aid the Department of the Navy's drive to rid the docks of enemy spies and saboteurs. Lansky assumed the role as Luciano's emissary to the mob bosses.[3] *Soon after the war ended, Luciano's sentence was commuted and he was immediately deported back to Italy. Lucky's life-long co-conspirator Lansky was of course at the center of the legal maneuvering.*

Uncle George registered for the draft in October 1941. Army psychiatrists diagnosed him as "a psychopathic personality." He was rejected. The reasons cited for his rejection included his arrest record and "bad judgment."[4]

Louis "Lepke" Buchalter was executed on January 21, 1944, at Sing Sing prison, along with the two Murder Inc. hit men, Emmanuel "Mendy" Weiss and Louis Capone. Lepke was forty-seven years old.

Moe Dalitz, age forty-two, was exempt from the draft. Nonetheless, he enlisted and joined the Army as a private on June 29, 1942. His experience with industrial laundries since the 1920s was invaluable to the war effort. He received a commission as second lieutenant in December 1942 and was assigned to the quartermaster corps on

Governor's Island, in New York City's harbor, supervising the vast military laundry services.

Having lived the good life, Moe found the upscale Savoy Plaza Hotel on 59th Street much more to his tastes than the barracks on Governor's Island. For the rest of his government service his unofficial residence was a hotel suite overlooking Central Park.

Dalitz was a music lover, especially of jazz, popular music and the great Broadway shows of the era. He had booked the popular bands and singers in his Ohio and Kentucky casinos. Now these acts performed a short walk from his hotel, on 52nd Street—the street where my father worked for Robbins, Miller & Feist, the music publisher. My father always knew which artists would be appearing in the nightclubs lining the street.

Cab Calloway, Duke Ellington, Billie Holliday, Bing Crosby, and Frank Sinatra, along with musicians and performers from the nearby Broadway shows, were likely to be on stage or at a table. It was "Swing Street."

Moe befriended my father, and they met to club hop. They were an unlikely pair: Moe Dalitz, one of America's most influential organized crime figures, and Lou Geik, by then an office manager, with a wife and two children (my sister Iris came later) in a one-bedroom apartment in the Bronx.

Moe Dalitz sometimes invited Jimmy Van Heusen, one of America's great songwriters, to join them. My father knew his music, as well as that of the Gershwins, Cole Porter, Sammy Kahn and the other composers of the Great American Songbook. My father's knowledge of the street endeared him to both Van Heusen and Moe Dalitz.[5] The three enjoyed each other's company, and that of the other Broadway characters they collected along the way.

One afternoon Moe Dalitz called my dad at his office. He asked Dad to come to the Savoy Plaza after work. My father remembered it as a beautiful spring day in 1943. He walked up Fifth Avenue to the hotel.

Dalitz opened the door. Meyer Lansky and Uncle George were seated around the coffee table. They motioned Dad to join them. They had a mission for him. Dad was a "civilian" and trusted by everyone in the room.

Uncle Charlie was in a New Jersey prison, and might be there for the rest of his life. His wife and family needed financial support.[6] My father had no arrest record and was a lifelong friend of the Workman family. He would be one of the people delivering cash to Charlie's wife. Having a gangster visit the family might one day jeopardize Charlie's future parole possibilities. There was no reason to take a chance.

My father delivered cash whenever asked for the next twenty-three years.

[1] Rationing continued until the end of the war. Ultimately, almost every product was rationed. Families received ration books, coupons and stamps. Some of these had expiration dates so that hoarding would be discouraged.

[2] Gambino had a reputation for being the wiliest of all crime figures. He maneuvered his way to the winning side in every street war between competing families. In 1937 he was arrested for tax evasion of proceeds from a huge, million-gallon distillery in Pennsylvania. He served twenty-two months in the Lewisburg federal penitentiary. He was released in time to find a new opportunity—to exploit the wartime rationing system.

[3] After the war there was speculation as to whether Luciano had really aided the United States intelligence agencies. In September 1954 William Harland, New York State Commissioner of Investigation, issued a report that detailed Luciano's invaluable assistance to the United States in the moment of the country's greatest danger.

Organized crime supported naval intelligence during the war. That support was later pivotal for the success of the Zionist War of Independence in 1948. See the next chapter for that story. (Harland Report, Tomas E. Dewey Papers, University of Rochester Department of Rare Books and Special Collections.)

[4] "Bad judgment"? Uncle George? Someone who had remained alive and prosperous throughout the previous decade—the most violent criminal decade in American history— was unlikely to have "bad judgment." An F.B.I report indicated that Uncle George had his military rejection in 1944 but I tend to go with the *Mr. Mob* date of 1941. Presumably he had "bad judgment" on either date.

[5] Jimmy Van Heusen won his first of four Academy Awards for Best Song in 1944—*Swinging on a Star* from the movie *Going My Way*.

[6] Organized crime had an efficient Social Security system of its own. Families of dead or imprisoned mobsters were often given generous and regular cash payments. It gave pause to a gangster who might want to inform, knowing there would be no support for his family if he did.

460

NAME : Carlo GAMBINO

ALIASES : Carlo Gambrino, Carlo Gambrieno, Don Carlo

DESCRIPTION : Born 8-24-02 Palermo, Sicily, an alien, 5'7", 200 lbs., brown eyes, black-grey hair.

LOCALITIES FREQUENTED : Resides 2230 Ocean Parkway, Brooklyn, N. Y. Frequents Carroll Paper Products Co; and Bensonhurst section of Brooklyn; also Italian section of East Bronx, and Miami, Fla.

FAMILY BACKGROUND : Married to his 1st Cousin Vincenza Castellana, son Tom married to Frances Lucchese (daughter of Tom Lucchese), father: Thomas, mother: Felicia Castellana, brother: Paolo, sister: Mrs. Giuseppina Giammona.

CRIMINAL ASSOCIATES : Lucky Luciano and Santo Sorge (deportees), Tom Lucchese, Hugo Rossi, Paolo Gambino (brother), Jack Scarpulla, Meyer Lansky, Scalice brothers, all of New York City.

CRIMINAL HISTORY : FBI #334450, NYCPD-B #128760. Arrests from 1930 include larceny, federal liquor laws, and violation I&NS laws.

BUSINESS : Owns Carroll Paper Products Company, Brooklyn. Is a member of S.G.S. Associates, a labor consultant firm in Manhattan.

MODUS OPERANDI : Attended Apalachin Mafia meeting 1957 as one of the Mafia leaders from NYC. One of the most powerful Mafia leaders in the U. S. With his brother Paolo has been involved in large scale narcotic and alien smuggling.

THE MOUNDS CLUB HEIST

The war years affirmed the simple truth that gambling and prostitution are timeless. Despite the Depression and World War II, organized crime never lacked for a healthy cash flow.

Wartime rationing hardly affected the Cleveland Syndicate's casinos; their patrons ate and drank well —Midwestern farmers and ranchers were paid top dollar for their black market produce. Nonetheless, while many locals welcomed the casinos, since the early 1930s there had always been strong opposition to their presence. The attacks came from different directions—farmer organizations, religious groups, business associations, crusading reporters and even a few elected officials.

Despite the reformers, illegal Ohio casinos thrived into the late 1940s. Throughout the years, patrons, and especially the long-suffering wives of gamblers, sued the casinos. Court documents described shattering losses—children's college tuition, life savings, family businesses. Lawsuits were filed regularly for real or imagined accidents suffered in limousines and private cars taking the plaintiffs to the casinos, and for slip-and-fall accidents on the properties. The casinos quickly settled out of court—civil suits were a cost of doing business.

By the end of the war, local law enforcement had been pacified by the casinos and well rewarded for their feigned inability to even locate the casinos named in criminal or civil complaints. Rarely did they see the hundreds of slot machines in their county, and often they reported no evidence of liquor or gambling at any establishment.

In 1935, Eliot Ness nationally famous for his role in Al Capone's tax-evasion conviction became Safety Director for Cleveland.[1] His arrival elated the citizens' groups fighting the casinos in their backyard and the rampant police corruption. Their hopes were short lived.

Sam Schrader, the mobster who had told me about the Dutch Schultz Coney Island racetrack "negotiations," had been with the Cleveland Syndicate throughout Ness' long run as Safety Director. "Ness couldn't succeed no matter how much he tried. The police departments let the casinos know his every move. Two police chiefs' sons worked in one of the casinos. It was a pain in the ass because we had to work hard to make the police look like they were doing something. A few captains or inspectors would get fired or be asked to resign. It was all for the newspapers so that the reformers would think something was changing. One captain, I think his name was Peterson, wanted to retire anyway. One of our guys on the city council had him resign and he moved with his wife and kid to Miami. He got a job as head of security in a casino your Uncle George and Hymie Martin had something to do with."

Ness believed only Italians populated organized crime—not an uncommon belief at the time, or even much later. So, much to the amusement of the Jewish mobsters, Ness only targeted the Mayfield Road Italian guys, who were partners with the Jews in the Cleveland Syndicate. It didn't matter anyway; he never did any damage to the rackets in Cleveland.

According to Uncle George, "Ness had a drinking problem and a big ego. He thought it would be easier to go after the colored guys in the numbers than the white guys who were mob connected. But the police also protected the colored guys. Ness went crazy when he found out that the police inspector, who was his most trusted guy, had been part of the numbers game for fifteen years. I forget his name."

The years of keeping the reformers at arm's length took a dramatic turn on September 29, 1947. Overnight it became clear the extent to which the police had protected the casinos in their counties.

* * *

> "The case is too big, too complicated and too damn confusing for an immediate solution."
>
> *James Maloney, Lake County Sheriff (1937–1948), just hours after the machine-gun-carrying masked men robbed the Mounds Club*

Even the barest facts of the robbery were disputed—were there eight men with machine guns, or were there ten, or fourteen? How did they gain entrance? Did they overpower the guards or go unchallenged through an open door in the kitchen? Was the kitchen door left open intentionally, or was it opened to let air into the hot kitchen? Was it an inside job? Were they Army veterans? Who would be crazy enough to target this mob-connected nightclub?

The masked, army-fatigue-wearing men came in just as the midnight show began. The audience, with its focus on the performers, the popular vaudeville act, Peter Lind Hayes and Mary Healy, paid no attention as the gunmen took their positions. That changed quickly when one of them unloaded rounds from a machine gun into the ceiling. That was an attention-getter.

The gunmen led the more than two hundred patrons into a smaller area, their cash and jewelry taken. A few bandits forced the manager to open the safe; others had the kitchen staff lay on the ground. The robbers called each other by numbers, never names—they were disciplined. An hour later they were gone.

The take was between $250,000 and $500,000, depending on who was doing the counting. Gambling started again soon after the robbers disappeared into the woods surrounding the club, stealing a patron's car.

The bigger mystery followed within hours.

News of the robbery circulated quickly throughout the county. Lake County Sheriff James Maloney came to the Mounds Club with other law enforcement personnel early in the morning. An employee behind the locked door asked the sheriff if he had a search warrant. He didn't and was not allowed access to the crime scene. The befuddled sheriff seemed unsure whether he could enter without a search warrant. Newspapers pointed out derisively that of course Sheriff Maloney could have entered the club if he had reason to believe a crime had been committed. It was well-established law. He chose not to enter, which wasn't a surprise as he had long claimed ignorance of the club's existence throughout his eleven years as country sheriff.

It was nine hours before county law enforcement entered the club.

The local newspapers called it "The Crime of the Century." It was obvious that the Lake County Sheriff's department actively hindered the investigation. The embarrassed governor vowed a cleanup of illegal gambling in the state. The heat was on in Ohio.

After the robbery, the Mounds Club owners concentrated on protecting the registry book with its five thousand names, including officials who had always denied the existence of the club. One detective investigating the heist claimed he didn't see evidence of gambling—the tables, he noted, were set up for dining, with cloths spread out over them. He maintained there was no reason for the Mounds Club to have a state-issued liquor license, as the club did not appear to sell liquor—despite the centrally located bar.

To nobody's surprise, the police never caught the robbers.

Sam Schrader described how the months after the robbery unfolded:

The sheriff was over eighty years old, never a bright guy. Perfect for the job. I don't think any casino people saw him even once in the eleven years he was sheriff. He was on the payroll, and I think his son worked for George and Ruby somewhere. The deputy sheriff was seventy-five years old. Nobody even knew there was a deputy sheriff.

Moe [Dalitz] and the others never wanted the stickup guys to be caught by the police. There would have been years of trials, investigations, and newspaper stories. Every cop in the county, and in Cleveland, would have his name in the paper. The reform people would be all over us. We'd never be able to operate again. They just wanted the stickup guys to disappear.

The sheriff had no idea what to say. He was smart enough to keep the Cleveland Police away from the club. They had real investigators and a crime lab—all that stuff. He was going to retire in a couple of months anyway. Even though the Cleveland police had been our guys for decades—we just wanted fewer people involved.

The sheriff had someone dig the bullets out of the wall and he kept them away from the Cleveland cops. I forget what they did with the book with the names of all the customers. That would have been dynamite if a newspaper got its hands on it.

We got a laugh out of the sheriff saying he suspected the Cleveland Syndicate was behind the robbery—or guys from Detroit. We owned the club. We didn't need to rob it.

We wanted to find the guys so that the robbery would be forgotten—no long trials or anything—and we could get back to business. So, Moe pretty much deputized the whole Cleveland police department—they were on the payroll anyway. He promised to buy a house in one of the nice neighborhoods for the cop who led us to the stickup guys. The police knew we didn't mess around—money was no object.

Expiration dates were already stamped on the stickup men's foreheads: it was just a matter of time. The casino owners assumed that at least one of them had worked at the club—robbers casing the club would not know the locations of the always off-limits counting rooms and offices. These guys knew the layout too well. Their discipline carrying out the operation made it a good guess they were probably veterans, together during the war—which had ended only two years earlier.

The Cleveland Syndicate bet on the loser criminal mentality to lead them to their prey—someone was going to flash more money than they should have; someone was going to impress a woman who would rat him out as soon as he did her wrong. It was an old story.

Uncle George and the other casino operators' detectives worked the prostitutes in Cleveland. They let the women know that whoever led them to the stickup guys could count on a huge cash payoff from the club owners.

However it happened, a few weeks after the heist, Tess, a call girl who worked the hotels, came into the station one afternoon with a diamond ring one of her regular customers had given her the night before.[2] He had called her to his hotel room. She told the detectives he was a guy who couldn't afford that ring. His name was Raymond. She guessed from his boots and how he talked that he was a war veteran. She had seen Raymond a few times with a blond-haired guy who was also her customer.

"Our guys told the detectives not to bother having the club patrons identify the ring—they didn't want anyone involved anymore," Sam continued. "We were going to bluff this guy Raymond."

However they set it up with Tess, the detectives rounded up Raymond and his blond-haired friend at the same time. They told Raymond that they identified the ring as part of the Mounds Club heist. He swore a burglar had given it to him to pay back a debt and then left town. The detectives knew he was lying and that they may have gotten lucky.

They took Raymond and his friend to a farmhouse one of the Syndicate guys owned outside Cleveland. It had been used before as an out-of-the way place where a little extra persuasion could be used to get information from a poor soul. Raymond gave up the leader as he sobbed and begged for his life.

The leader had been Raymond's sergeant in the infantry during the war. Some of the other stickup guys were from Raymond's army unit, too, but he didn't know the rest. One thief gave up another. The police were then able to find the driver's licenses of a few of them in the motor vehicles department records. The ones who lived in Cleveland were as good as dead—as Sammy Kass would say. The Cleveland Syndicate only had to call their crime partners in other states to round up the doomed stickup guys one at a time. Some may have escaped—who knows?

Five months after the Mounds Club heist most of the stickup men disappeared. The Cleveland Syndicate didn't even try to locate the money or the jewelry. They just wanted everything to go back to how it was before the heist.[3]

But that was no longer possible. The curtain had been lifted on decades of illegal gambling, prostitution and corruption. The heat had been turned on, and the incoming governor made shutting down illegal gambling in the state a personal goal.

The Syndicate's days in Ohio were drawing to a close but, as had happened so many times before, even greater opportunities appeared elsewhere—Las Vegas and Cuba both offered something unheard of—legal gambling.

---

[1] The Syndicate treated Eliot Ness's time in Cleveland with derision. His ace Cleveland police investigator, Lieutenant Ernest Molnar, was a longtime spy for the numbers bankers—apparently everybody knew this except Ness. Ultimately, Molnar was fired and charged with several counts of bribery. He was convicted and sentenced to sixty-six years in prison. He served four years and disappeared from view.

Eliot Ness' law enforcement career ended in 1944. His personal life was in turmoil, mostly due to his drinking and bad business choices. He died in 1957 of a massive heart attack—two years before *The Untouchables,* the mostly fictionalized account of his career, aired on television for the first time. Most adults I knew at the time of the TV series thought Ness was "a bum." He died penniless.

[2] Sam Schrader remembered the names "Tess" and "Raymond" but without certainty. No doubt the names of these actors in the drama were unimportant to the casino operators.

[3] There are other accounts of the manhunt for the Mounds Club stick up guys. Official investigations continued for a few years with the case never being solved. An excellent account of the investigations is in *Tommy's Place—Welcome to the World Famous Mounds Club* Frank Monastra 2020. Monastra is a longtime observer of and writer about Cleveland organized crime.

23

THE HOTEL FOURTEEN

On July 1, 1945, David Ben-Gurion stepped onto the sidewalk in front of the Hotel Fourteen at 14 East 60th Street in Manhattan. He turned to his left. Central Park was right in front of him, on the other side of Fifth Avenue. It was a steamy New York summer day.

Ben-Gurion had experienced his share of fateful encounters in his life, with the assurance of still many more to come, but he knew this day would be as dramatic as any he could ever imagine.

Then Chairman of the Jewish Agency for Palestine—he later would be recognized as the founder of the State of Israel and become Israel's first prime minister—Ben-Gurion had come to New York City to gain support for the partition of Palestine, one part of which would be a free Jewish state.

He walked past a low iron gate that opened to a few steps leading down to a basement metal door. There would have been no reason for him to take notice—there was nothing remarkable about the gate, the steps, or the door. Yet meetings behind that door, unknown to Ben-Gurion, would play a role in the foundation and survival of the still nonexistent Jewish state.

He walked uptown to the penthouse apartment of Rudolf Sonneborn, an industrialist who had invited influential Jewish business leaders to this secret meeting. Sonneborn intended to gather desperately needed financial and political support for a free Jewish state in Palestine.

Ben-Gurion understood this meeting would decide the fate of the Jewish people's quest for a homeland. The clock was running out on a positive outcome. The full weight of his peoples' future rested upon his words that very day.

The war in Europe had ended two months earlier. Now Ben-Gurion needed immigrants to populate the Jewish armed forces that would inevitably confront the vastly larger Arab forces. His objective was for two million Jews to emigrate from Europe to Palestine.[1] He would also need American financial support for the purchase of military equipment. However, support for either goal would violate the United States Neutrality Act prohibiting arm sales and financial support to "belligerent nations."

The British, while observing the worldwide blockade of aid to the Jewish forces in Palestine, nonetheless armed the Arab nations with modern fighter aircraft. Both the British and American governments consistently communicated their support for the Arabs, no doubt because of their control of the vast oil fields of the Middle East.

The Hotel Fourteen was not a random choice for Ben-Gurion's stay in New York. The Haganah, the Jewish paramilitary force, had its New York office in the same hotel. They were the Zionist unit tasked with creating a worldwide underground for supplies and fundraising for the Palestine war effort.

Also not coincidentally, the famous nightclub, the Copacabana, a showcase for America's top entertainers and a mob hangout, occupied the ground floor of the building. Frank Costello, a ranking member of the National Commission, owned the Copacabana.

It is unlikely this man, David Ben-Gurion, born in Poland, and having lived in Palestine since before World War I, had any understanding of the importance American organized crime would play in the creation of the Jewish state. He was soon to learn, and to quickly embrace, this reality.

The metal door at the bottom of the steps Ben-Gurion had just walked past led to the cavernous kitchen of the Copacabana, which over the next four years would serve as one of many meeting places for the New York underworld, rogue former wartime US intelligence agents, and Haganah operatives, all coordinating illegal matériel shipments to the Zionists in Palestine.[2]

They were no strangers to each other, nor were they strangers to the newly elected mayor of New York City, William O'Dwyer, who only five years earlier while Brooklyn District Attorney, had brought Murder, Inc. to an end. O'Dwyer, with his wartime service as a member of the Allied Commission for Italy, had developed contacts in the Italian government that would prove to be of great support to the underground Zionist operations in America and Europe.

They had all collaborated in Europe and New York, and together played a heroic and patriotic role in the war effort. Now this unlikely alliance had a new mission— to support the Zionist War of Independence.

How naval intelligence, organized crime, trade unions, government officials and business operators joined forces in the early days of World War II deserves a short detour.

* * *

Four years earlier, as soon as America had entered the war in December 1941, naval intelligence had a desperate dilemma; German submarines were attacking Allied shipping unchallenged and with great precision along the entire length of the East Coast. Essential war materials for Great Britain, then under relentless air attacks by the Nazi Luftwaffe (Air Force), went down with the ships and thousands of merchant seamen, sometimes within sight of America's coastline. It was the most desperate time of the war for the Allies.

Citizens groups along the coast watched for submarine landings of German saboteurs. To prevent nighttime shipping from being silhouetted and made easy targets for German torpedoes, blackouts were enforced along the Atlantic coast.

But US naval intelligence was troubled—how did these German submarines remain so far from their home bases for so long? Were Nazi sympathizers under the guise of commercial fishermen refueling the submarines? How were they being supplied? Didn't the submarines need distilled water for their large batteries? Were there active Nazi spy rings on the docks?

Government agents remembered the 20,000 Nazi sympathizers who attended the infamous rally in Madison Square Garden only three years earlier. Those people were still walking the streets of East Coast cities—along with thousands more who had marched in Nazi parades before the war started. Where were they now?

The intelligence agencies' attempts to infiltrate the docks had all failed. Midwestern, blond, well-educated intelligence agents weren't exactly a good fit in longshoremen's bars and pool halls along the waterfronts. Also, tightlipped dockworkers were unlikely to ever say anything to strangers.

Organized crime controlled the docks along the East Coast. It was a gold mine of extortion, thievery, contract murders, no-show jobs, and anything else mobsters could improvise. There had hardly been a work slowdown or strike on the docks in decades—it was just too lucrative for the mobs.

Navy intelligence couldn't procure union cards for their undercover operatives—nobody trusted the government, especially the union business agents. Everyone on the docks would quickly be alerted to the agents' presence.

Naval intelligence instead focused on a powerful organized crime figure: Joseph "Socks" Lanza.

In the early 1920s, the nineteen-year-old thug and fish worker, Lanza, formed the United States Seafood Workers' Union. From his base of operation at the Fulton Fish Market just south of the Brooklyn Bridge, he soon controlled the entire East Coast seafood industry. Every fish stall owner at the market and every seafood distributor, local or national, paid him tribute. There was not a single fishing fleet that did not answer to him. He never netted less than $1 million a year for the next forty years.

Naval intelligence knew Lanza could be the link they needed for access to the fishing fleets. But could they convince an organized crime figure to engage in counter espionage work? They approached Lanza's attorney, who soon reported that Lanza would assist the government, but there was a problem; he was on trial for conspiracy and extortion.

How could Lanza encourage his people to work with the government? That would make him look like an informant, as if he were making a deal for leniency. He needed someone to vouch that he was using his power to help his country in its moment of need. Lanza knew who that person was—Lucky Luciano.

Luciano's word was still law in America's underworld, even though he was stuck away in a prison on the Canadian border serving a thirty- to fifty-year sentence for compulsory prostitution.

Who could reach out to get Luciano's approval for Lanza's counter espionage work? Luciano's attorney had not seen his client since he had been incarcerated a few years earlier, but he knew that Meyer Lansky had Luciano's complete confidence.

The attorney urged naval intelligence to contact Lansky. Lansky understood the gravity of the moment and convinced Luciano to give Lanza his blessing. Lansky let every mob boss know of Luciano's approval. It was a done deal.

Intelligence agents soon roamed the Atlantic coast on Lanza fishing fleets. Lanza made certain that everyone in the commercial fishing world eliminated—in any way they had to—anyone who might be a security threat.

Naval intelligence called their collaboration with organized crime Operation Underworld —not too creative, but then it was wartime, after all. To expand their undercover operations to the docks and throughout the city, mob-controlled union support was necessary—Luciano's influence would be even more crucial.

Luciano had opened the door for Lanza, who at the beginning was pivotal to the task; but now it was Luciano calling the shots. He brought mob bosses and lower-level family members into the growing undercover operation.

Agents became union elevator operators and maintenance workers in targeted office buildings. Black bag teams (government trained burglars) could then have easy entry into foreign consul's offices and suspected business fronts for enemy countries—safes, filing cabinets, and trashcans were all fair game.

Soon naval intelligence had personnel working as waiters and bartenders in nightclubs. Dockworkers were ordered to be vigilant and report suspicious drunken talk in the seedy waterfront bars where they gathered after work.

In January 1943, Lanza's conviction on the conspiracy and extortion charges disrupted Operation Underworld. He was sentenced to seven to ten years.

That same month, the Allied military forces began preparing for the invasion of Europe; the landings would be in Sicily. The Sicily invasion was scheduled for July 1943, just six months later.

However, there was one problem that had weighed on Allied capabilities since the beginning of the war; on-the-ground intelligence had been ignored by the military. It just never fit into the prewar view of the fraternity-boy intelligence agencies. For them, intelligence was a pursuit done while holding cocktail glasses in upscale bars.

Luciano spread his net out even further. He ordered mob leaders to bring Sicilian-born Americans into naval intelligence's posh midtown hotel headquarters. Old timers and recent arrivals examined large maps and reviewed every topographical detail. The immigrants brought in family photographs, especially of the ports, channels and coastline—every scrap of information added value to the big picture.

Sicilian businesses on the East Coast still had their Old World contacts. Their decades of importing prized Italian olive oil, cheeses and—for a few of the criminals—morphine base for heroin, made them valuable intelligence sources. The Sicilians identified friends and family on the island who could be counted upon to aid the Allies after the invasion.

The Sicilian Mafia hated Mussolini since he invaded the island in 1925 and arrested and killed anyone suspected of being in the Mafia. Many gang members fled to America from Sicily in the 1920s. The local mobsters on the island, and throughout Italy, would be receptive to the Allied forces.

It was a massive undertaking, and only Luciano's stamp of approval made it work. Throughout the operation it was Lansky who brought the orders to every mobster who then followed Luciano's lead.

The July 1943 invasion of Sicily and then of mainland Italy was as brutal as any experienced during the war. Military intelligence officers were deeply relieved by the local population's willingness to work with them. The name Luciano proved to be as great a currency in Italy as it still was on Mulberry Street on the Lower East Side.

Rome was liberated in June 1944. Soon after, both the Allied forces and the grateful Italian citizenry and Mafiosi welcomed another anti-fascist force to their side; the Palestinian-born Jewish Brigade that had fought alongside the British through North Africa and now in Italy.

By the end of the war, US naval intelligence was indebted to Lansky, the New York underworld, and the Jewish Brigade's valiant wartime achievements. This indebtedness would prove to be invaluable to the Zionist War of Independence—its preparations began as soon as the war ended.

Back to David Ben Gurion's fateful summer day alongside Central Park.

* * *

David Ben-Gurion entered Rudolph Sonneborn's living room, crowded with men who on that day would decide the fate of the Jewish people. It was that simple.

The questions came quickly, as Sonneborn's guests spoke over each other. My father once described these impassioned tribal encounters as "two Jews, three opinions."

"Would the arms we finance ever be used in the United States?" "Would they ever be used against the United States?" "Why didn't the Jews fight the Nazis more than they did?" "How do you know they can fight now?"

Ben-Gurion knew they could fight because they already had, as partisans in every Nazi-occupied country in Europe. Then there was the Jewish Brigade, the Palestinian Jews who fought alongside the British across

North Africa and into Italy. When the war ended a few months earlier, the Jewish Brigade then set out to find still-terrorized Jewish displaced persons throughout Europe. They smuggled death camp survivors to Mediterranean ports, especially along the long Italian coast, evading the British blockade of Palestine to deliver them to their Promised Land.

The Jewish displaced persons streamed into Italy after the war. Italy was a sanctuary for them. Dozens of ships carried them to Palestine. The British government pressured the Italian government to close down the ports to slow the migration to Palestine. The Italians would have none of it—they had resisted the Nazis' attempts to round up Jews, and they would surely not collaborate with the British demands either. (Note: my Greek Jewish mother always admired the Italians for their brave support of their Jewish neighbors during the Nazi occupation and then after the war helping the Jews to secret transit points along the Italian coast—the beginning of their perilous Mediterranean crossing to Palestine. "Talk about stand-up people. Those Italians stood up to the Nazis," she said.)

"If they fought alongside the British during the war, why are the British turning on them now and preventing them from going to Palestine?" one of Sonneborn's guests asked Ben-Gurion.

"Because the British are bastards, and like all colonial powers they turn against their subjects who support them in their wars. Didn't they do that to the loyal Irish who took heavy losses in World War I? And access to Arab oil is always more important to them than the lives of Jews." I can't say those were Ben-Gurion's exact words, but it was a common understanding among Jews then and forever after.

Some of Sonneborn's guests expressed shame that they had been unaware of the Holocaust until the war was over. "Is there another way for the Jews to have a state without a war?" No, Ben-Gurion answered honestly—as soon as the British leave Palestine, the Jews would declare a state and the Arabs would attack. It was unavoidable.

"When would that happen?" Two or three years, Ben-Gurion correctly estimated.

"Where would the armaments come from?"

"Every country would be flush with military surplus," Ben-Gurion said. America already had vast stockpiles of equipment that could be bought and somehow smuggled through the blockade. Millions of dollars would be needed.

Ben-Gurion reminded them that violation of the Neutrality Act was a federal offense and heavy jail sentences were likely regardless of the current support for the Holocaust survivors. Nobody could predict what public sentiment would be in a year or two. This was their moment in history, he said—there would never be another chance. The fate of the Jewish state was in their hands alone.

Ben-Gurion's audience understood the gravity of that moment. They all agreed to risk their freedom, reputations and wealth for this cause. Ben-Gurion told them they "should consider themselves the American arm of the underground Haganah."

The men knew they could supply equipment and funds, but their greatest allies would have to be the New York City dockworkers and those along the East Coast. Organized crime controlled the docks, and its support would be crucial.

The mob-controlled unions quickly signaled their support for the blockade-breaking conspiracy. Word went out along the East Coast docks. The large numbers of Irish dockworkers needed no prompting to screw the British. An enemy of the Brits was a friend to the Irish—Nazis excluded, of course. Support for shipments of equipment destined for the Jewish army was underway.

* * *

Soon a tangled worldwide network of shell companies and phony bank accounts emerged, enabling the transfer of funds, shipments of military equipment, and smuggling of concentration camp survivors and military personnel into Palestine.

William O'Dwyer had been elected mayor of New York City in 1945. The dock bosses, organized crime and the Haganah could not have asked for a more engaged ally than the mayor. He let the large New York City Irish community know they were all participants in the fight for the Jewish state.

Johnny Eder, a City Hall regular for the past seventeen years, had by the end of the war become one of the mob's go-to men in city government. According to Johnny:

> *"Mayor O'Dwyer never let us down. I was with him when he called Irish police commanders and his people in the customs offices. He was a one-man show. He hated the Brits. Bill had been a cop on the beat and a laborer. He spoke the workers' language. He told me once, 'Johnny lad, I'm more of a damn Jew than you these days.'*
>
> *"A lot of people never knew that the mayor had been a general in Italy during the invasion. He was on a military commission to rebuild the country. He had influential contacts in the Italian government and mob guys over there. Between him and the intelligence guys and Luciano's people, they worked miracles for the Haganah in Italy.*
>
> *"Some of us met the Haganah agents in the kitchen of the Copacabana. They had their offices upstairs. It was a natural. Nobody could overhear us with all the noise in the kitchen.*

"There were always a few of Frank Costello's guys standing around the door—especially when the shows were on. It wasn't like someone unfamiliar was gonna wander through the basement door by accident."

It was no coincidence that Johnny mentioned the meetings in the kitchen of the Copacabana. We were standing in front of the bandstand in the Copacabana with my sister Iris forty years later. Johnny, never a nightclub patron, had probably not been back to the Copacabana since those days he came in through the basement door.

On this evening Johnny came in through the front door—we were celebrating our parents' fiftieth anniversary. "Fat" Tony Salerno, a well-known mob figure in the 1980s, and his Jewish sidekick Sammy Kass arranged the event. Tony even showed up for awhile. Where else would this anniversary celebration be held but at the Copacabana?

Johnny continued:

> *"Customs agents and dock bosses had to know when military equipment came through destined for the Jews. It was a precision operation. A lot was sent to Italy and some to, of all places, Czechoslovakia, one of the few countries in Europe supporting the Jews. A lot of volunteers—ex military guys—came from all over the world.*
>
> *"Most of the Irish dockworkers and customs agents didn't take money for looking the other way when a shipment came through. One of them said, "No charge on this Jewish stuff."*

Johnny remembered dockworkers loading military equipment going to Egypt or other Arab countries onto ships with other destinations, including Uruguay or South Africa; any place else was good enough.[3]

By May 1948 the Haganah knew that without pilots and aircraft to counter Arab air superiority, their struggle would be doomed. US planes were available on the military surplus market for a few thousand dollars apiece, but because of the embargo they were off limits.

Fighter aircraft were available in Czechoslovakia, but for $180,000 each—an exorbitant price, especially for planes with such doubtful flight readiness. Nonetheless, Ben-Gurion's orders were to buy the Czech planes immediately. The Haganah needed $1,000,000 the next day. Mobsters and legitimate businessmen made feverish phone calls and secured the financing.[4] The planes were purchased in what proved to be the very last moment that could save the Israeli military from defeat.

Johnny remembered some wise guys speculating about the ultimate destination of their fundraising and illegal arms shipments. "It did occur to us that clever Jews might be making the Palestine war more dramatic than it was. How would we know if someone had his hand in the collection plate? Most of us had been in the crime world all our lives so we weren't the most trustful people around. We did learn later that those Czech planes and all that equipment did save the Israelis. We were relieved to know it was such a close call and that we made a difference."

* * *

In 1946 the Haganah desperately canvassed American Jewish communities for pilots with combat experience. Raising money for aircraft purchases would be an easier matter than finding pilots dedicated to an Israeli nation—or so they thought.

Synagogues and community centers identified possible recruits from the returning veterans. A Haganah operative approached Louis Lenart. Lenart, a World War II Marine Corps fighter pilot in the South Pacific, had flown dozens of missions bombing Japanese positions on Okinawa while the battle for that strategic island raged. As soon as the Okinawa airbase was secured, he flew air raids on the Japanese mainland until the end of the war.

Lenart was also a refugee from anti-Semitism in Hungary and had lost many family members during the Holocaust. He would do anything for the survival of a homeland for Europe's remaining Jews.

Lou Lenart had the perfect resume.

The Haganah recruited Lenart and sent him to a secret base in Italy. He flew transport planes to Palestine, carrying contraband military equipment to the forces besieged by the neighboring Arab states.

Lou Lenart recalled:

"Italy was different than I expected. We found out that Jewish and Italian gangsters in New York made sure we were taken care of. I grew up in Wilkes-Barre, Pennsylvania, fighting all the anti-Semitic kids there—I knew nothing about New York gangsters. I never heard of Lucky Luciano. But everyone around the Italian ports knew his name. He was living in Naples and made sure we had everything we needed.[5]

"We were flying out of secret airfields, bringing Jews and equipment to Palestine. We had ships leaving all the time. The British were really pissed off. They sabotaged a few ships and pressured the Italians to turn us in so we couldn't keep sending people to Palestine.

"But the Italians weren't going to listen to the British. Tons of equipment and thousands of our people got to Palestine. We owe the Italians a lot."

* * *

When Ben-Gurion ordered the Haganah to buy the Nazi fighters in Czechoslovakia, Lou Lenart and other pilots flew there for training. One of those pilots was the young Ezer Weizman.[6] He'd been a member of the British Royal Air Force, but had no combat experience. Weizman would later become the Commander of the Israeli Air Force and the President of the State of Israel. He and Lou remained close friends for the rest of their lives.[7]

The Haganah purchased a version of the ME-109—the Messerschmitt—the backbone of the Luftwaffe's fighter force. The Czechs had outfitted these planes with engines and parts from other German aircraft, making them hard to maneuver. Lenart, the most experienced pilot in the group, passed the preliminary test. Weizman and a few others passed a few days later. They began what they thought would be extensive training in formation flying, dive-bombing and air-to-air combat.

The irony was never lost on these young men that Jews were now flying Nazi aircraft to secure Israel as a free state for the Jews.

Lou Lenart recalled:

"On May 14, 1948, we heard David Ben-Gurion's radio broadcast declaring an independent State of Israel. Ben-Gurion also said that the daily attacks by the Egyptian Air Force were taking their toll. We returned immediately to fight for Israel. We didn't have time to finish training. The ME-109 fighters were taken apart and flown to Palestine in transport aircraft.

"We put the planes together at night so that the Egyptian planes wouldn't see us. Only two weeks later, on May 29, we heard that Egyptian ground forces were only twenty-six miles from Tel Aviv. Some of our demolition guys had blown

up a bridge that stalled the Egyptian advance. It would have finished Israel as a state."

The Egyptian infantry would have to be decimated by these few untested Czech planes. There were no other options. The next morning Lou Lenart led the other three pilots on a surprise attack on the Egyptian armed column. (The Egyptians were unaware of Israeli aircraft, let alone an Israeli Air Force.) The air attack succeeded beyond any expectation. An intercepted message from the Egyptian commander to headquarters in Cairo stated, "We had been heavily attacked by the enemy and are now scattering."

The day the Israeli pilots stopped the Egyptian ground forces from overrunning Tel Aviv has been immortalized in Israeli history as "to here and no further."[8]

Decades later, I introduced Lou Lenart to Johnny Eder in a New York restaurant. They understood their lives had intersected thousands of miles apart at a special, unforgettable moment. So much had depended on it.

I was fascinated by their low-key demeanors, despite one of them having spent a lifetime peddling high-quality stolen jewelry, and the other a war hero and often-called-upon operative for the Mossad (the Israeli intelligence and special operations).

These two soldiers of fortune now together in a Manhattan restaurant putting on their eyeglasses to choose their Early Bird Specials.

I shared with them how it was such an emotional moment for me. It didn't, however, seem unusual or in any way remarkable to either of them.

Lou Lenart is one of my heroes.

He was also my late father-in-law.

[1] Ben-Gurion wanted two million Jews to migrate from Palestine to Europe. He had no idea at the time of this meeting in July 1945 that over six million Jews had been killed in the Holocaust.

[2] One of the most impressive movie tracking shots of the 1990s is in the 1990 Martin Scorsese film *Goodfellas*. The shot, which lasts over three minutes, starts with gangster Henry Hill (Ray Liotta) and Karen (Lorraine Bracco), his wife-to-be, on their first date exiting his car across the street from the Copacabana. Instead of going through the front entrance, he guides her down a metal staircase into a series of narrow hallways, wise guys greeting him along the way. They turn into a huge hyperactive kitchen, winding past steam tables, stoves, dishwashers. Chefs, waiters, and bus boys frantically pass in front of the camera. The same shot takes them into the nightclub. The maître d' sets up a table for them in front of the stage. Two men send over a bottle of champagne from a nearby table. Curious as to how Henry knows these men, Karen asks, "What do you do?" He says, "I'm in construction." She feels his hands, "They don't feel like you're in construction." He shrugs. "I'm a union delegate."

[3] Johnny Eder also told of being awoken on a Sunday morning in the 1950s at his hotel room in New York City by two Irish police inspectors. Johnny thought he was being arrested. Instead, they told him to dress quickly. They took him to another hotel. Men were seated around a dining table ordering breakfast. David Ben-Gurion had called the meeting. He was then Prime Minister of Israel. He wanted to thank the people who supported the Haganah in New York City. One of the Irish police inspectors ordered ham and eggs for breakfast. The other said, "You stupid bastard, these Jews don't eat ham." Ben-Gurion said, "He saved the State of Israel, he can eat ham."

4 According to Lawrence J. Epstein, in his fine work *Americans and the Birth of Israel*, William Levitt, the builder of Levittown, was asked for the $1 million for the Czech planes. He couldn't be told what it was to be used for or even if the loan would ever be repaid. Nonetheless, Levitt understood the gravity of the moment and wrote the check. He was repaid one year later.

5 In February 1946 Lucky Luciano was deported back to Italy as part of the commutation of his New York prison sentence. He arrived in Naples on February 28, 1946. Coincidentally, Lou Lenart and many other American volunteers arrived in Italy at the same time.

It was the beginning of the Haganah forces and the by then disbanded Jewish Brigade intensifying their activities on the Eastern coast of Italy.

6 Ezer Weizman was the nephew of Israel's first president, Chaim Weizmann. Their last names have often been spelled differently.

7 Decades after these events, and still long before smart phones, I was on my home landline arranging to buy marijuana from a friend. The operator interrupted with an emergency call (as people did regularly in those days). It was Ezer Weizman, the president of Israel. He was calling my late wife, Nina, looking for her father, Lou Lenart, who was in Los Angeles. I told him I would have Lou call him. The President of Israel had interrupted my drug purchase! Nina and I laughed about it for a long time after. So did Lou.

8 Although the events in Czechoslovakia and the attack on the Egyptian column have been widely recounted, I relied mostly on Lou Lenart's many conversations with me, as well as his autobiography, *Destiny*, which he wrote for his family, friends and lifelong admirers.

In the documentary *Above and Beyond* (2014), directed by Roberta Grossman and produced by Nancy Spielberg, Lou Lenart is one of the many heroes of these events interviewed.

NAME : Joseph LANZA

ALIASES : Socks Lanza, Joe Zotz.

DESCRIPTION : Born 8-18-1900 NYC, 5'8½", 200 lbs, brown eyes, black-grey hair, heavy build.

LOCALITIES FREQUENTED : Resides 300 W. 23rd St., Apt. 14 H, NYC. Frequented Angelo's Neapolitan Restaurant, 146 Mulberry St, & lower East side dock area of Manhattan.

FAMILY BACKGROUND : Married to Ellen Connor; brothers: Harry, Anthony & Salvatore (dead); sisters: Mrs. Sara Guma, Mrs. Rose Christopher, Mrs. Ann Demeo, Mrs. Frances Viggiano, Mrs. Eleanor Jannizzi.

CRIMINAL ASSOCIATES : Frank Costello, Joe Profaci, Mike Clemente, Frank Mancino, Vincent Rao, Vito Genovese, [redacted], all of NYC, Lucky Luciano & Sebastiano Nani of Italy.

CRIMINAL HISTORY : FBI #785896. NYCPD B#65346. Arrests since 1917 include burglary, extortion, homicide, conspiracy & extortion.

BUSINESS : Has been affiliated with several Teamster Locals in NYC.

MODUS OPERANDI : A powerful & feared member of the Mafia in NYC. Has been one of the most accomplished terrorists in connection with labor racketeering in the lower east side Fulton Fish Market area. Received his weekly "shakedown" from a teamsters local even during his incarceration for extortion.

Property of U. S. Govt – For Official Use Only
May not be disseminated or contents disclosed
Without permission of Commissioner of Narcotics

Note: redactions by the government, not the author

Author's family album

Lou Lenart flew this barely airworthy ME-109 at the beginning of Israel's War of Independence. It had been a Nazi Air Force Messerschmitt fighter during World War II. The irony was not lost on Lenart or the other Jewish pilots that they were flying Nazi planes in defense of Israel.

The dockworkers on the East Coast of America and the sympathetic underworld in America made certain that secret arms shipments destined for Israel got to their destination. Arms en route to Egypt and other Arab countries were often rerouted to Uruguay or South Africa.

Author's family album

Lou Lenart with David Ben-Gurion, the founder of the State of Israel and its first prime minister. Lou was thrilled to have played such a heroic role in the battles for Israel's independence. He had never heard of Lucky Luciano before he arrived at the secret Haganah bases in Italy. He quickly learned that Luciano, on behalf of his American based Jewish underworld associates, was supporting the fight for the Jewish state in Palestine.

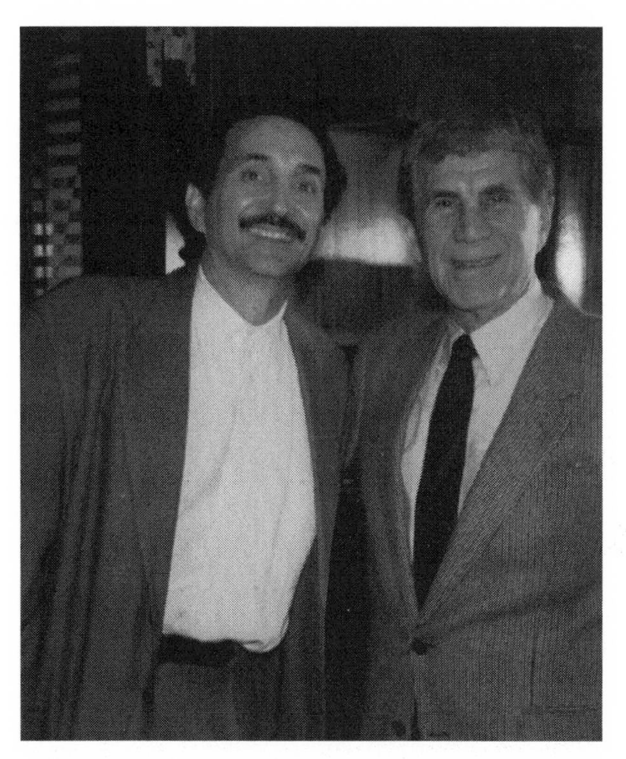

Author's family album

Lou Lenart and Me. My brother Bernard, a former NYPD detective, loved hearing Lou's exploits as a fighter pilot and working with the Mossad (the Israeli intelligence agency).

Lou enjoyed meeting some of the surviving NYC crime figures who helped supply the Israeli military during its War of Independence.

24

LAS VEGAS AND CUBA —IT'S LEGAL

The Mounds Club heist in September 1947 and the newspapers' investigations of the Cleveland Syndicate's decades-long control of Ohio motivated them to find friendlier surroundings for their casino gold mines. They already had other locations in sight.

In the early 1930s Meyer Lansky, along with Moe Dalitz, had already paid off Fulgencio Batista, the political power in Cuba, and established organized crime's control of gambling on that island. Batista served as president of Cuba from 1940 to 1944, then he was out—the Cuban constitution barred him from succeeding himself as president. Batista moved to a comfortable retirement in Florida, but with the backing of organized crime, he was still a power broker in the Cuban government.

Developments in a dusty desert town in Nevada in 1946 would present another opportunity for the Cleveland Syndicate. Benjamin "Bugsy" Siegel, a charter member of the National Commission, and a leader of the Meyer Lansky and Lucky Luciano gang since the early 1920s, had come across Las Vegas—a town that had seen action during the building of the nearby Hoover Dam in the 1930s. The brothels and sawdust joints abounding there attracted soldiers from bases in Southern California during the war years.

In 1946 Siegel started construction of his obsession; The Flamingo, a hotel and casino to be built with East Coast mob money. He soon ran into cost overruns. He underestimated the cleverness of the local contractors, who fleeced him at every turn. They just saw him as a "city slicker" without experience in construction—especially something as grand as this hotel/casino. His mob backers were getting nervous.

Siegel's girlfriend, Virginia Hill, attracted mob suspicion—perhaps, they thought, she encouraged Bugsy to swindle his lifelong partners back East? She had a history of involvements with mobsters, and who else but "a dame," they concluded, could entice Siegel, a respected member of the inner sanctum of organized crime, to possibly cross the deadly line of cheating his partners?

The New York outfit dispatched Moe Dalitz to scout the Flamingo operation. He was a logical choice—for the past two decades he had been the leader of the most successful illegal gambling syndicate in America. To complicate the drama, Dalitz had been Virginia Hill's lover before she met Siegel—so had other mob figures.

Dalitz reported that Siegel and Hill might be pocketing money from the mob investment in the Flamingo and depositing the proceeds in Swiss bank accounts.[1] Dalitz had a reason to dramatize this claim; he saw the future of Las Vegas, which was only a few hours' car ride from the post-war boom of Los Angeles and Southern California. Even better, Nevada had legalized gambling in 1931.

In 1946 Meyer Lansky and Lucky Luciano presided over several days of meetings at the Hotel Nacional in Havana. Siegel's possible embezzlement of mob funds was a sensitive matter, given his lofty stature in mob circles, but it couldn't be ignored. Moe Dalitz was also present at these Havana meetings. He indicated that Siegel might try to flee the country given he had Swiss bank accounts.

The Flamingo reopened after an earlier faulty start on March 27, 1947 but it was of no help to Bugsy Siegel. He was assassinated while he sat reading a newspaper in the living room of Virginia Hill's Beverly Hills, California, home on June 20, 1947. The New York mob immediately took over the Flamingo operation.

Virginia Hill was in Paris at the time of the murder.

The murder was never solved.

* * *

At the same time that Siegel's face had holes blown into it in a Beverly Hills living room, legal gambling in Cuba once again became the new shiny object for the East Coast mob. It was Meyer Lansky's personal realm; he had nurtured the vision for the previous fifteen years. After the war, Lansky built the Riviera in Havana and gave the Hotel Nacional, the crown jewel of Havana casinos, to the Cleveland Syndicate to operate.

The mob financed Batista's successful run for the Cuban Senate in 1948. He never even had to leave the comfort of his Florida home. They would continue to fund Batista's political trajectory for the next four years when he, in 1952, finally seized control of the government and assumed dictatorial powers.

In 1948 Moe Dalitz met a promoter, Wilbur Clark, who had started construction of the Desert Inn, a hotel and casino in Las Vegas. Clark ran out of money, and the Cleveland Syndicate stepped in with $3.6 million they raised from sources back East. In May 1949 the Syndicate took controlling interest in the Desert Inn. The Desert Inn opened in April 1950, and as the Syndicate had done so many times, they stayed in the background.[2] They promoted Wilbur Clark as the front man; from then on, the hotel was known as Wilbur Clark's Desert Inn.

Uncle George later recounted disagreements within the Cleveland Syndicate. They were enthused about the future of Las Vegas as a legal gambling destination. In Ohio they had local officials paid off and neutralized. In Nevada they had even greater allies. Pat McCarran, a Nevada senator and a champion of gambling, would be their lobbyist in Washington. It was a slam-dunk—they would be legitimate for the first time ever.

Cuba, however, was never as certain an investment for the Cleveland Syndicate. They had the same concerns as expressed in any corporate boardroom when financing a subsidiary in another country—especially one with as unstable a government as they had observed in Cuba. They would be investing in one man: Batista. What happens if he loses control? Didn't that happen all the time in these "banana republics?" Why invest there when they have a sweetheart deal in Nevada?

The discussions continued, but according to Uncle George there was ultimately just one overriding consideration: "How do you say 'no' to Meyer Lansky, who was counting on us to invest money and to bring our casino knowledge to a foreign country?"

Saying 'no' to Cuba and just concentrating on Las Vegas was not an option. They would lose their place at the table, and that was something they could not allow to happen. They would move forward with their Cuban interests, hoping for the best outcome. It reassured them that Meyer Lansky controlled the operation.

* * *

In June 1950 liquor tax agents raided the Pettibone Club, a popular casino near Cleveland. The manager refused entrance to the agents, who then promptly broke down the door. They arrested the club's manager and several employees. At the court hearing, the manager identified himself as Joe Green. He paid the $50 bail and immediately disappeared.

A few days later, the *Cleveland Plain Dealer* identified Joe Green as George Gordon—Uncle George. The newspaper also reported that the one person who had known of "Joe Green's" real identity was Sheriff Steward M. Harland, whose longtime patron was Uncle George.

Uncle George, while a fugitive, went to Los Angeles carrying a message to the Southern California gangsters angling for a piece of the Las Vegas action—it was in their backyard, after all. The message was simple and direct: The same people who controlled illegal gambling all over the country—the Cleveland, New York and Chicago mobs—would control Las Vegas.

The public outrage over George skipping bail created too much attention back home. Eight months after he disappeared, he just as easily reappeared in Geuga County, Ohio. In March 1951, he was indicted on twenty-four counts of illegal gambling and resisting the agents during the Pettibone Club raid. He was sentenced to two months in the county jail and a fine. This should have ended the local newspapers' fixation on the raid, but a scandal soon followed.

Newspaper investigations revealed Uncle George's two-month sentence to be more like a stay in a full-service hotel than in a county jail. The jail's phone bill doubled in the two months of his detention—he had called the Desert Inn numerous times to check in with Moe Dalitz. A local tavern, a favorite of George's, made regular food deliveries to his cell through the jail's back door. Flashy cars were parked in a nearby alleyway well into the early morning hours. Aunt Mildred (George's second wife) parked her Cadillac there many times.

My father remembered his visits to his older brother's jail cell. Uncle George ordered steak dinners for them from the tavern. At least this one time, Sheriff Harland picked them up and brought them to the dining table in George's cell. A nearby empty cell served as a closet for Uncle

George's expensive suits, silk shirts, diamond studded cuff links and two-tone shoes.

* * *

These revelations led to Sheriff Harland's indictment for "pampering a prisoner who had been sentenced to imprisonment in the county jail."[3] He went to trial and was found guilty.[4] In 1952 an Ohio appellate court reversed the lower court decision, ruling that the code under which the sheriff was charged did not extend to criminal liability. The sheriff was fined.

Nonetheless, for years after, the mob guys laughed remembering Uncle George as the one who "got the sheriff arrested and convicted."[5]

---

1 Michael Newton, *Mr. Mob: The Life and Crimes of Moe Dalitz* (Jefferson, NC: McFarland & Company, 2009), 123. *Mr. Mob* is a fascinating biography of Moe Dalitz, who, as I mentioned, Meyer Lansky considered a trusted equal.

2 Ibid. 146. Moe Dalitz signed on as a vice president at the Desert Inn, and Ruby Kolod, Uncle George's partner in crime since their teenage years on the Lower East Side, became manager of the casino.

3 *State v. Harland, 94 Ohio App. 293 (1952)*.

4 One of Sheriff Harland's many amusing claims was that, during his several previous inspections of the Pettibone Club, he had "never found anything more significant than a fast game of ping pong." Cleveland Plain Dealer May 7, 1951 *Gordon Adept At Geuga Contempt*

5 The regal treatment Uncle George received in the county jail lent credibility to his role in the manhunt for the Mounds Club armed robbers just a few years before—described earlier in this account. So much Syndicate money had been given to law enforcement they couldn't possibly treat one of their generous patrons any less preferentially than they did.

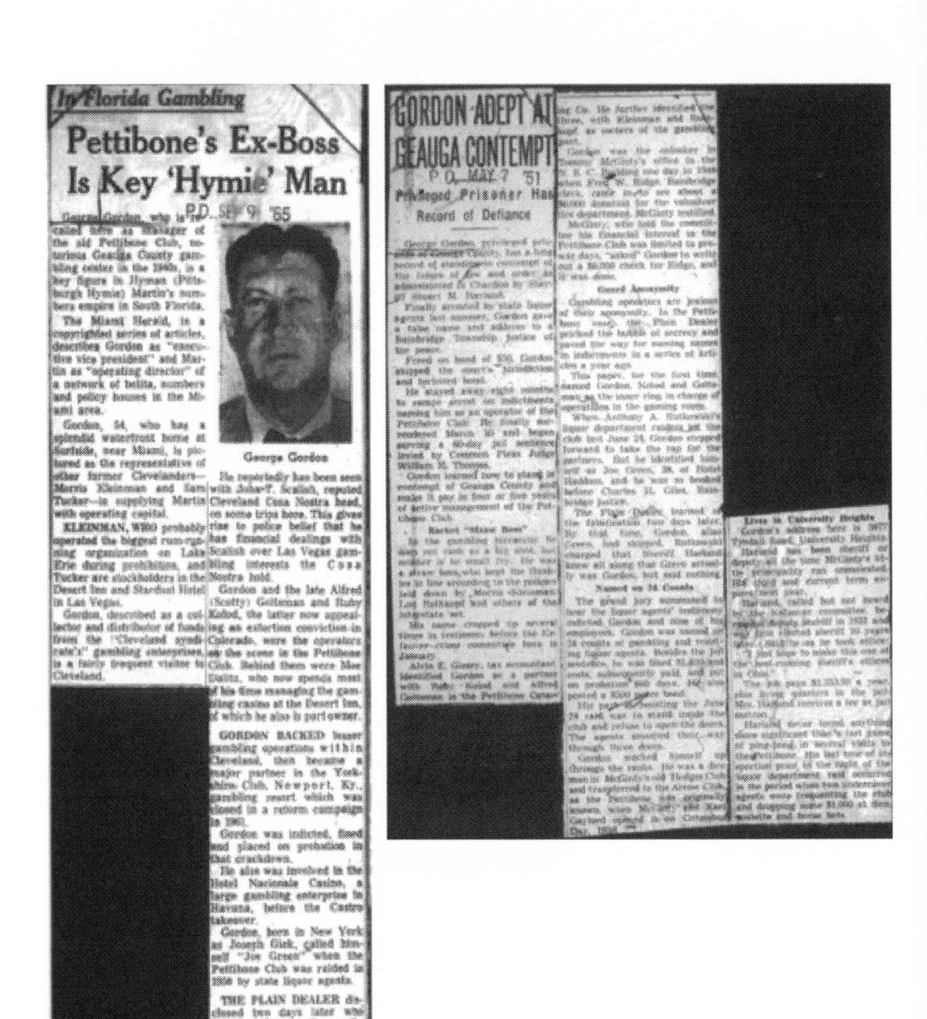

In Florida Gambling

Pettibone's Ex-Boss Is Key 'Hymie' Man

P.D. SEP 9 '65

George Gordon

GORDON ADEPT AT GEAUGA CONTEMPT

P.D. MAY 7 '51

Privileged Prisoner Has Record of Defiance

Special Collections Michael Schwartz Library, Cleveland State University

May 7, 1951 newspaper coverage of Uncle George's Pettibone Club bust that led to later complications with the Nevada Gaming Commission

Author's family album

Uncle George and Aunt Mildred at my brother's bar mitzvah in 1951. Uncle George had just been in jail in Ohio for two months for illegal gambling operations at the Pettibone Club. George also evaded the Senator Kefauver hearings for most of that year, but still had time to come to a family event, put on a yarmulke and light a candle. Nice!

"GIVE 'IM A BUCK"

– Lou Geik, my dad, at Yankee Stadium circa 1952

At ten or eleven years old I absorbed two profound life lessons. They occurred on the same day—and in Yankee Stadium.

I've been a baseball fan ever since I could remember. Neither Lou, my father, nor my older brother, Bernard, cared about baseball, or any sport, for that matter. I had watched baseball games on the little black-and-white televisions in bars throughout Manhattan while my father drank and reminisced with old friends. Lou was, I might add, like Uncle George, a functioning alcoholic. As an adult I always thought of both of them as gentle, shy men despite Uncle George's reputation as an organized crime figure.

I was a die-hard New York Yankees fan. I took my enthusiasm a step further. Often when the Yankees were playing day games at home, I would race back to our apartment after school and ride my bicycle down the Grand Concourse eight blocks to Yankee Stadium. I would arrive at about the seventh inning. I chained my bike to a rail, and with no ticket takers at the gates I could sit anywhere I wanted. I knew every section in the stadium.

I collected autographs from the Yankees and the visiting team after the games. I even learned the ingenious tactic of handing self-addressed postcards to players who didn't want to stop to sign an autograph.

Instead, they stuffed the cards in their jacket pockets. I looked in our mailbox every day for cards postmarked from far away cities—Boston, Chicago, Washington. And there would be an autograph on a postcard. Sometimes two or three signatures. Years later I imagined a player in a bar pulling the postcard out of his pocket and having a few drunken teammates sign it.

My father's friend, Willie Danker, had a box of eight seats right off the field between home plate and first base, near the Yankee dugout.[1] Every Yankee emerging from the dugout seemed nine feet tall. So did every other player in the major leagues.

One special player on a visiting team was a super star to me and to a generation of Jewish kids in the Bronx, Al Rosen, the Cleveland Indians' All-Star third baseman. We idolized him—not just because he was one of the few Jews playing in the major leagues, but also because he had been an amateur boxer, a street fighter. He would challenge opposing players who said anything about his religion. He got in their faces.

* * *

Which brings me to that memorable day in Yankee Stadium when I learned two of life's great lessons. My father would sometimes come home with tickets for Willie Danker's box seats. They were the best in the house. I often asked a friend to go with me. This time my father said he would be going. I loved being with him—it was always an adventure going around Manhattan with him.

But going with him to Yankee Stadium was a different story. He had no interest in the game or the players, but what the hell, I thought, it's time I can spend with Dad. Then he told me Uncle George was in town and he would meet us there. Uncle George was a living legend in the family—someone who had made it out of the Lower East Side and was a well-known gambler and crime figure in New York and Cleveland.

Uncle George slid into the seat next to my father soon after the game started. I greeted him. He was wearing leisure clothes that I could tell were expensive. He and my father talked. The Yankees were playing the Cleveland Indians, and that was exciting.

George, living in Cleveland, might have been a fan of the Indians, I thought. I leaned over my father and asked him if he liked the Indians. He nodded. "I get to a few of the games. I know some of the players," he said casually. He knows them!!

My father, Uncle George and another man spent much of the game in animated conversation. In the sixth inning they said they were going to the clubhouse, a bar restaurant on the mezzanine level, open to season ticket holders. I could have stayed in my seat and watched the game, but I went along with them. I noticed that men in the clubhouse turned to look at Uncle George and then turned away, nodding in his direction. They knew him in a way they didn't know my father.

The bartender put a bowl of pretzels and an icy glass of ginger ale in front of me. That was always the payoff for hanging in a bar all day.

It was the first great contradiction of my life—there I was with a box seat ticket to a baseball game in Yankee Stadium, and I was watching it on television in still one more bar. I told my father I was going to watch the game from the mezzanine seats outside the clubhouse.

I left. I walked down the steps of maybe fifteen rows to the first row. A number of seats were empty. I was looking down at home plate. Perfect.

An usher leaned over me. He asked for my ticket. I showed it to him.

"You can't sit here," he said, "your seat is down there." He pointed over the railing to the box seats I had just left. I went back to the clubhouse. My father nodded sympathetically as I told him what happened. He put his hand in his pocket. He pulled out a few bills and gave me a dollar.

"Give 'im a buck. They'll let you sit where you want."

"Just like that?" I asked myself. I took it and turned to leave, not sure how it would work out.

Uncle George stopped me. "Make sure you find the same guy who told you couldn't sit there. Give it to him." My father nodded his approval. I became nervous. The guy was big, surly. Would he be angry? What would he say? He had just told me to leave.

I went out to the mezzanine. The same usher stood at the top of the steps. I took a deep breath. I handed him the buck. He looked at it. "Where do you want to sit?" I pointed down to the first row of the mezzanine overlooking the field. He walked down ahead of me. The ushers carried phony fur mitts so they could wipe off a seat with a flourish and be rewarded with a tip for their efforts. He did it for me. I thanked him. I was amazed. That's how it's done. It came to me in a flash—"give 'im a buck."

I looked up the row of stairs. To my surprise, my father and Uncle George were standing at the top. They seemed to be nodding. They turned and went back into the clubhouse.

* * *

When the game ended, there was another revelation awaiting me in the clubhouse. A crowd had gathered around the bar. The room was filled with cigar smoke. My father and Uncle George sat at a table with two other men. I think they were also from Cleveland. Uncle George asked me if I liked the game. "Yes, we won," I answered. He nodded.

After a while more men came into the room—I recognized them. Cleveland Indians—the players right next to me. I couldn't believe it. They all greeted Uncle George. Mel Allen, the Yankee announcer, came over to say hello. Mel Allen, another hero. His real name was Melvin Israel, a Jew born in Alabama. Uncle George knew him.[2] Amazing!

Uncle George waved Al Rosen over to our table. Rosen responded immediately. I was in shock. He called my Uncle, "Mr. Gordon." George introduced me to him, saying I was a fan of his. He laughed.

"Not a Yankee fan?" he asked.

I said, "Yes, but I'm a fan of yours also."

Uncle George leaned in. "He's a fan of yours because you don't take shit from the goyim (Christians)."

I nodded. They all laughed.

The men in the Yankee clubhouse did not look at Uncle George as they did the ballplayers. Uncle George was a very big shot. It came to me in a flash.

---

1 Willie Danker, the owner of the box seats in Yankee Stadium, had a steel shelving company in Midtown Manhattan. I went there with my father many times. The back office was always crowded with gamblers and police captains and commanders with bottles of booze on the tables. It was a hangout. It was called the A&D Steel Company. The name is as branded in my brain as it was on the nameplate on the rail of his box seats at Yankee Stadium.

2 Decades later, it occurred to me that of course the gamblers, the Cleveland players and even Mel Allen would know Uncle George. He was part of the Cleveland Syndicate. In every city, sports figures and entertainers always gravitated to gamblers and crime figures. Uncle George also had notoriety from the much-publicized Pettibone Club bust only two years earlier. You can bet (as these guys would say) that most of the players had been in the club during their years playing for the Indians.

Cleveland State University

Al Rosen—Cleveland Indians All Star third baseman.

He was one of the few Jews in the major leagues—also an amateur boxer, a street fighter who didn't take crap from the anti-Semites on the other teams. Our hero.

THE SKIM

"Their casinos in Las Vegas were legal, but they had
to steal something."
–Johnny Eder, 1989

Legal gambling in Las Vegas became the Golden Goose for the Cleveland Syndicate in 1950. They were the most experienced casino operators in America and had the backing of Meyer Lansky and the New York mob. Everyone wanted a piece of Las Vegas, and it would all flow through the Cleveland Four (the Cleveland Syndicate), led as always by Moe Dalitz. Meyer Lansky, back in New York City, would do what he had done best all his life; keep order among the greedy, suspicious, already wealthy crime families around the country.

The Cleveland Four used OPM (Other People's Money), and it was readily available to them. They invested in shopping malls, and funded synagogues and non-profit organizations. They built the Sunrise Hospital in Las Vegas with Teamsters Union Pension Fund financing. They pieced together dozens of financing deals just as they had done for the preceding twenty-five years. It's a safe bet that they laughed amongst themselves about their evolution to civic leaders.

But with legality came government oversight. Nevada tax agents and the IRS would now be counting the take from the casinos. As they had done so many other times, the Syndicate improvised new scams for these new circumstances. Criminality was, after all, in their DNA, and they just couldn't give a government agency an honest accounting of anything. So they "skimmed" money before the tax agents ever touched it, thus insuring that there would be far less to count.

There were no credit cards or computers monitoring slot machines in the 1950s, so no paper trail—it was all cash. Nickels, dimes, quarters, half dollars, and silver dollars from thousands of slot machines weighed on tampered scales in the off-limits counting rooms insured a lighter count for the taxman. The skimmed coins were changed into big bills in minutes and never became part of the official take.

Casino bosses signed IOUs ("markers") at the gaming tables for tens of thousands of dollars in chips. They changed the chips for bills at the cashier cages. The cash would disappear into suitcases destined for out-of-state crime families. The floor men would tear up the markers before the bosses' signatures dried.

The skim was enormous. One newspaper investigation revealed that Las Vegas casinos skimmed $500,000 per month.[1] An FBI estimate was $1,000,000 a day by the late 1960s. There would never be an exact accounting of how much money was sent out of Las Vegas in those suitcases. And it went on for years.

It would last for more than two decades—until the mob guys got sloppy and wire-tapping techniques improved. When the Racketeer Influenced and Corrupt Organizations (RICO) Act became law in 1970, skimming had already evolved into an intricate tax evasion conspiracy—an ideal target for that federal statute, which also mandated long prison sentences.[2]

* * *

In 1951, because of his recent Pettibone Club arrest, and the "coddling" scandal that kept the story alive in the newspapers for another year, Uncle George wasn't likely to get a gaming license in Las Vegas. He stayed behind in Cleveland and managed the Syndicate's still lucrative illegal casino operations in Ohio and Florida with Lou Rothkopf, one of the Cleveland Four.

Senator Estes Kefauver began an investigation into organized crime at the end of 1950. He held hearings in cities across America. As the hearings moved from city to city, some criminals evaded the subpoenas, others didn't. Uncle George was in Miami when the hearings were conducted in Cleveland, and then in Cleveland when the Kefauver Committee came to Miami. He never appeared before the committee.

As expected, the committee findings were of no consequence to organized crime. One determination was that "organized crime does exist" and another "the connivance of local authorities is necessary" for rackets to thrive. Not exactly stunning revelations.

Moe Dalitz had one of the US senators from Nevada, Pat McCarran, working hard to defund the Kefauver Committee investigations and to subvert the hearings at every turn. When McCarran later died of a sudden heart attack in September 1954, the Nevada casino owners lost their fully purchased Washington lobbyist in the Senate. But there were, as always, others to take his place.

On March 10, 1952, Cuba again moved back into the spotlight for the New York underworld. Fulgencio Batista, a player in Cuban politics since he'd left the presidency in 1944, and always on the mob payroll, led a military coup against the government. He quickly took dictatorial control. Mob investments flowed back into Cuba.

The Cleveland Syndicate continued managing the Hotel Nacional casino until the end of the decade. FBI informants throughout the 1950s reported Uncle George was one of the casino bosses of the Nacional.[3] He moved to Surfside, Florida, in 1958 so he could manage the Syndicate's growing operations wherever he was needed—Miami, Havana, Cleveland, or Kentucky.

* * *

In June 1955 tragedy struck Lou Rothkopf, one of the Cleveland Four. It would change Uncle George's fortunes overnight. Rothkopf's wife, Blanche, shot herself on their thirty-seven-acre estate in Bainbridge, Ohio, just thirty miles from Cleveland. It was a stunning act—nobody expected that the wife of a semi-retired mob boss would take her own life. She had been with Lou since his 1920s ascent to the top of the Cleveland business-crime syndicate.

Johnny Eder, the longtime fence and confidant of Uncle George and my father, recalled:

> *"Blanche had been depressed. She was ill—a few people in her family thought it might have been cancer, and she didn't tell her husband. Her death devastated Lou. I saw a lot of him and George back then. They owned a store, more like a warehouse, in Cleveland. It was called something like A&E Merchandising. It was a front for stolen merchandise. I picked up a lot of jewelry from them and brought it back to New York. Even though they were already rich, they still couldn't keep their hands off of stolen jewels, stolen anything, really.*

"I could see Lou becoming more depressed. Everybody saw it. Still, it was a shock when he committed suicide in his garage. It was a year after Blanche died. He died of carbon monoxide poisoning. The death certificate said it was accidental, but we knew Lou took his own life."

Uncle George took over Rothkopf's interests. He had come a long way from the Lower East Side tenements. His new status in organized crime arrived at the perfect time. There was still another venture the Cleveland mob couldn't pass up. It was in Las Vegas, and Uncle George would be called upon to play a crucial role—one that fit his street tough reputation and his decades long relationships of trust with the Italian crime families.

* * *

Tony Cornero, a West Coast gambler with the usual resume of bootlegging, illegal gambling casinos, unsolved murders around him, and an assassination attempt on his life that left him with bullets in his stomach, had been hustling financing for the construction of a 1,000-room hotel in Las Vegas.

It would be called the Stardust Resort & Casino.

Cornero had the same problem the other bootleggers and criminals encountered in Las Vegas—he needed approval for a Nevada gaming license. The rumor on the Strip was that Moe Dalitz was plotting against Cornero; if the gaming commission shut out Cornero, the Cleveland group could take over the Stardust—sure to be a prime property.

Always in need of additional financing for his huge Stardust project, Cornero came to Dalitz for cash. Dalitz would much rather Cornero go bankrupt than have him as a partner. He turned Cornero down. On July 31, 1955, Cornero, just another incurable gambler at heart, threw the dice at a Desert Inn crap table on still another losing night. Moe Dalitz was somewhere on the casino floor. A waitress brought Cornero a drink. He knocked it back and fell to the floor dead.

The whiskey glass disappeared in seconds. A physician signed the death certificate immediately. Cornero's body was taken to a mortician. His body was in the ground in a Los Angeles cemetery eight hours later—without an autopsy.[4]

The ownership of the Stardust quickly passed into the hands of the Cleveland Syndicate. The powerful Chicago mob took a piece of the action, with the usual trading of hidden interests. The casino was an immediate success. The combined skim of the Desert Inn and the Stardust was enormous. More suitcases stuffed with cash were destined for crime families all across the country.

Johnny Eder remembered:

> *"The skim was unbelievable. Georgie knew everybody, so he became even more important. Everybody trusted him. He had been traveling the country since 1930. Sometimes he would even take a small footlocker filled with cash on a train. Nobody ever looked in passengers' luggage. I went to Vegas a lot back then. It was a high-class market for stolen jewelry. We met in hotel suites. Ruby [Kolod] was the manager of the Desert Inn casino. He still liked those deals. He was excited—just like back on the Lower East Side when he and Georgie stole that crappy stuff when we were kids."*

In July 1966 the *Chicago Sun-Times* investigated the hidden ownership and skimming in Las Vegas casinos. They named Sam Giancana as the boss of the Stardust Hotel, and another gangster partner of Uncle George and the Cleveland Syndicate, John Scalish, as the boss of the Desert Inn.[5]

The Cleveland Syndicate would never object to Italians named as sole owners of the casinos. The Jewish gangsters were in the counting rooms and executive suites of the hotels where the skim would be put into numbered envelopes for the couriers. That was important to them—not publicity.

The *Chicago Sun-Times* estimated that Giancana received $65,000 a month from the skim of the Desert Inn and Stardust hotels by the early 1960s. John Scalish received $52,000 per month. If the proceeds from each share held by hidden interests were accurate, Uncle George would have received $44,000 per month.[6]

The couriers carried cash-filled suitcases around the country. No excuses were accepted if they didn't arrive or if the count wasn't right. It was serious business—and because of that the casinos often arranged protection when the couriers arrived in other cities. It was from an unexpected source—the police.

Neither the *Chicago Sun-Times'* July 1966 skimming exposé nor FBI reports took note of the police protection of the Las Vegas couriers.

Rather than leave the courier alone in a strange town where independent stickup men might be aware of their mission, local detectives often met the couriers at the train stations or airports. It made sense—a cop unaware of the operation might stop a local gangster driving a courier around town. How do you explain a passenger holding $50,000 in cash in a suitcase on his lap? With a local detective behind the wheel, that possibility was eliminated.

My father once recalled:

> *"Right after the war, Frank Sinatra was the biggest star in America. He loved being around Italian wise guys. He would go out of his way to act like them. Sometimes he carried money for them on his tours. They always came to his shows, so did the police commanders who were on the mob payroll. It was through Sinatra the police started guarding the couriers. Nobody thought cheating the taxman was a big crime, anyway. They paid off the police. It worked out for everyone."*

When Uncle George came to New York in the late 1950s, he stayed at the Essex House or the Hampshire House on Central Park South. I was impressed—this was power and wealth to a teenager from the Bronx. Lieutenant Arthur E. Schultheiss, the commanding officer of the 14th Detective Squad of the NYPD, was a regular visitor in Uncle George's suite. I learned later on from my brother that Lt. Schultheiss often assigned detectives as Uncle George's driver when he came to town with mob money. Local law enforcement would be unlikely to detain a car with a Lt. Schultheiss detective behind the wheel.

Arthur Schultheiss looked the part—a red-faced German Irish man with white hair. He was the stereotype of New York City high-level police commanders often portrayed in cop movies of the 1980s–1990s.

Ten years later Arthur Schultheiss would be my detective brother Bernard's "rabbi."[7]

[1] Controlling Crime Through More Effective Law Enforcement, Hearings Before the United States Committee on the Judiciary, Ninetieth Congress, First Session, on Mar. 7–9, Apr. 18–20, May 9, July 10–12, 1967, p. 1058.

Professor Blakely testified for the need to increase electronic surveillance of criminal activities, including the skimming of money in Las Vegas casinos. A series of articles in the *Chicago Sun-Times* in July 1966 were entered into the hearings record. The amount of skim was estimated at $500,000 per month.

[2] The RICO Act became law in 1970. It changed the rules of engagement in the federal fight against organized crime. It specified that racketeering activity could be prosecuted as part of an ongoing criminal conspiracy. Now, crime bosses could be charged along with their underlings who actually committed the crimes. The sentencing was more drastic than it had been previously, insuring that co-conspirators would more likely flip on their associates.

[3] Special Agent Robert A. Schwartz 6/30/59, File number (92-399) Title: George Gordon, aka, Danny Levine, George Geik, Anti-racketeering

[4] Michael Newton, *Mr. Mob: The Life and Crimes of Moe Dalitz* (Jefferson, NC: McFarland & Company, 2009), 165.

[5] Controlling Crime Through More Effective Law Enforcement, Hearings Before the United States Committee on the Judiciary, Ninetieth Congress, First Session, on Mar. 7–9, Apr. 18–20, May 9, July 10–12, 1967, p. 1058.

Sam Giancana ("Little Momo") had worked his way through the labyrinth of intrigue and street warfare to become the head of the Chicago organized crime family. John Scalish did the same in Cleveland. Scalish became the face of the Cleveland Mafia—which was, as noted many times, fully integrated with the Cleveland Four and the Jewish mobsters, who always received less media and government scrutiny.

[6] Controlling Crime Through More Effective Law Enforcement, Hearings Before the United States Committee on the Judiciary, Ninetieth Congress, First Session, on Mar. 7–9, Apr. 18–20, May 9, July 10–12, 1967, pp. 1061, 1062.

[7] In the police or fire department, a "rabbi" is someone who could move a friend or family member up the through the bureaucracy. Every entrant, regardless of ethnicity, wanted a "rabbi."

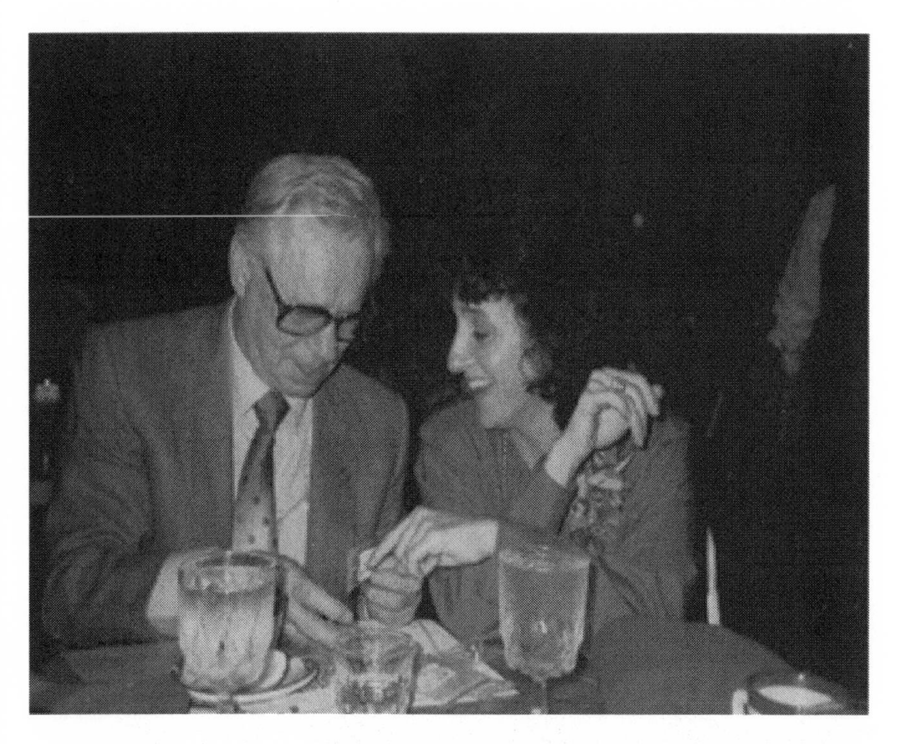

Author's family album

My sister, Iris, looking over one of Johnny Eder's many rings, earrings and necklaces that were always close at hand. At one time he was a major fence. Johnny was a great source for much of this history, as he was the most reflective on what career criminality was all about. He also lived the longest. He told the stories with great humor—we always laughed, no matter how grim the details.

144

NAME : Sam GIANCANA

ALIASES : Sam Mooney, Sam Malone

DESCRIPTION : Born 7-16-08, Chicago, Ill.; 5'9", 175 lbs., hazel eyes, dark chestnut hair, fair complexion and medium build.

LOCALITIES FREQUENTED : Resides at 1147 Wenonah Ave. Oak Park, Ill. Frequents the Army Lounge, Norwood House, Villa Venice, all of Chicago, Illinois.

FAMILY BACKGROUND : Wife, Angeline DeTolve, died in 1954. Has three daughters, Annette, Bonita Lou and Francine. Mother deceased, father is Tony Giancana, and sisters are Mary, Josephine and Victoria. Sam's consort is Ladana Collins, 20 E. Delaware, Chicago, Illinois.

CRIMINAL ASSOCIATES : Tony Accardo, [redacted], [redacted], [redacted] [redacted], Sam Battaglia and Leonard Gianola, all of Chicago, Illinois.

CRIMINAL HISTORY : FBI #58437, Chicago PD #E-27465. Subject has record of 13 arrests dating from Sept. 1925, on such charges as murder, grand larceny, auto theft, burglary and liquor law violations with two felony convictions.

BUSINESS : Owns the Forest Lounge, the R & S Liquor Co., the Lohmar Dist. Co., Chicago, Ill., and has gambling interests and an interest in the shrimp business in Cuba.

MODUS OPERANDI : A top ranking member of the Mafia in the State of Ill. and a director of the organization's activities in Chicago and vicinity.

Property of U. S. Govt — For Official Use Only
May not be disseminated or contents disclosed
Without permission of Commissioner of Narcotics

Note: redactions by the government, not by the author

A PASTRAMI SANDWICH WITH MEYER LANSKY

It had to have been 1958—probably in the spring or summer— when I met Meyer Lansky. I was fifteen or sixteen years old.

My father asked me to come to Uncle George's suite at the Essex House on the Southern edge of Central Park. It was a late spring afternoon. I think we were going to the hospital to visit a relative.

When I entered, my father, Uncle George and another man sat on two couches around a coffee table. I noticed someone else in a comfortable armchair reading a newspaper by a window overlooking the park. I knew who he was.

My father said, "Meyer, this is my younger son Alan." I shook his hand and perhaps shuffled awkwardly. He smiled kindly.

Meyer looked like every other old Jewish man in my neighborhood; white shirt opened at the collar under a nondescript sport jacket, alert to everything around him but tired. There was nothing about him that attracted attention. The description was, and would remain over the years whenever I thought about him, unassuming.[1]

He asked, unexpectedly for sure, "Do you want a pastrami sandwich?" I didn't know what to say. I shook my head.

He said, "Alright, you can have half of mine?" Again, I didn't know what to say. I nodded.

He shrugged and said quietly, more to himself, "Yes, half is enough. Pastrami killed more Jews than Hitler."

I laughed out loud. I couldn't help it. He smiled, appreciating my response. I repeated that joke many times throughout my life without giving him credit for it. (After all, what would I say, "Meyer Lansky once told me...?")[2]

Meyer turned to the unidentified man with my father and Uncle George. "Henry, call the Stage [deli]. Order four pastrami sandwiches. Don't use my name."

Meyer asked me. "Do you know where the Stage Deli is?" I nodded. "Pick up the sandwiches. The order is for 'Henry.'"

I completed the assignment and for three decades I joked with my father and his friends that I shared a pastrami sandwich with Meyer Lansky.

---

1 One reason Uncle George often stayed at the Essex House (sometimes it was the Hampshire House next door) was because Meyer Lansky had a hideaway apartment there. That would account for his leisurely clothing the day I met him. He may have just crossed the hall, as someone would have done visiting a neighbor in a Bronx apartment building.

2 A few years later our father had a serious operation. Meyer Lansky called him. He told Dad not to believe the doctors, that "they were all full of shit." Reba, always one to normalize these men, smiled pleasantly hearing of Lansky's call and his concern for Dad. She forever after referred to him as "that nice Mr. Lansky."

3 I should note here that, of course unknown to me at the time of my encounter, there was considerable F.B.I. activity regarding Uncle George's role in disposing of the Cleveland Syndicate's interests in the Hotel Nacional in Havana. He was negotiating with both Meyer Lansky and also with Meyer's brother Jack in Havana. A later chapter details the politics and outcome of the negotiations. I also include the relevant F.B.I. memos.

Library of Congress, Prints and Photographs Division, NYWT&S Collection

Meyer Lansky booked in Manhattan in 1958 for vagrancy. It was amusing in the underworld that the man at the center of organized crime—a multi-millionaire running casinos in Cuba, was "a vagrant." It was pointless harassment by law enforcement. Charges were soon dismissed.

This is perhaps the most often published photo of Meyer Lansky. For me it has a special relevance—shortly before or after it was taken, I met him in Uncle George's Essex House suite. We shared a pastrami sandwich. I remember thinking he was an old man at the time. He was fifty-six.

FD-204 (Rev. 9-23-58)

UNITED STATES DEPARTMENT OF JUSTICE
FEDERAL BUREAU OF INVESTIGATION

Copy to:

Report of: SA PAUL A. CAJIGAS Office: MIAMI
6-26-59

MIAMI (92-458)

GEORGE GORDON

Character: ANTI-RACKETEERING

Synopsis:

Subject is known as a gambler who came from Cleveland, Ohio. He now has a residence at Surfside, Florida. He formerly had financial interest in the Hotel Nacional gambling casino. Most recent information indicates he has financial interest in Desert Inn, Las Vegas. No known criminal activities available for GORDON. He is known to associate with notorius gamblers such as MEYER LANSKY and SAM TUCKER, and was allegedly a member of the Mayfield Road Gang of Cleveland.

- P -

DETAILS:

This document contains neither recommendations nor conclusions of any kind. It is the property of the FBI, and is a loan to your agency; it and/or its contents are not to be distributed outside your agency. 16—74025-1 GPO

This June 1959 F.B.I. memo notes the association between Uncle George, Meyer Lansky and Sam Tucker, one of the Cleveland Four. The association between the three of them began almost thirty years earlier.

28

A CIA SCIENTIST FALLS 170 FEET

"Everything the CIA does is illegal, which is why the government provides it with an impenetrable cloak of secrecy... . Everything the CIA does is deniable. It's part of the Congressional mandate. Congress doesn't want to be held accountable for the criminal things the CIA does."

– Douglas Valentine, author of The Phoenix Program, an exposé of the CIA torture/counterintelligence program in Vietnam[1]

After World War II the CIA evolved from the Office of Strategic Services (OSS), the wartime intelligence agency. Given the real or imagined threats presented by the Cold War, the lack of congressional oversight, and its secret unaudited budget, the Agency quickly infiltrated every corner of American society.

In addition to infiltrating the media and academia, the CIA targeted local police departments during the Korean War. The Agency supplied specialized training at their facilities, and donated equipment the local police departments couldn't afford—all with the intent to create the same personal relationships they had so successfully nurtured with foreign police and military personnel.

The police departments returned the courtesy by conducting surveillance and break-ins, providing local police credentials and other support to the agency that was prohibited from operating within the US.

The CIA, so quickly engulfing every post World War II American institution, intersects with some of the organized crime characters inhabiting these pages—and also with my brother's role in the NYPD.

This penetration was enabled by a wartime good-old-boy network of intelligence agents and military officers who later were dispersed throughout the business, science, law enforcement and intelligence worlds.

After World War II, Fort Detrick, an Army base fifty miles outside of Washington, DC, became the CIA's center for biochemical warfare and mind-control experimentation. Their work was top secret and had little oversight even within the agency. The prevailing "need to know" allowed widespread experimentation on unwitting military personnel and locals in small town America, and one experiment that went terribly wrong in a small village in France in 1951.[2]

On November 28, 1953, Frank Olson, a bacteriologist at Fort Detrick, "fell or jumped" to his death from a thirteenth floor window at the Statler Hotel, across the street from Pennsylvania Station in Manhattan. The bare details released by the military noted that Dr. Olson had been "despondent over ill health" and was in New York, sharing a room with a colleague and receiving psychiatric help.

It wasn't until Congressional investigations in 1975 that the truth surrounding Dr. Olson's death became public knowledge—and the full story would still not be known for another twenty-five years. In 1975 the CIA admitted that Dr. Olson had been given a dose of LSD from the laboratory of Dr. Sidney Gottlieb, the chief CIA scientist, a week before his death. The agency claimed the intent was to evaluate the effects of the drug and acknowledged that the experiment was a contributing factor to his death. Frank Olson's family was awarded a $750,000 settlement.

That was the beginning of the unraveling of the cover-up. Decades later, Dr. James Starrs, a forensic scientist, conducted an independent investigation. The body was exhumed. One of the many determinations was that a hole in Dr. Olson's skull came from the butt of a gun, not from a fall from the thirteenth story window.[3]

The most unsettling revelation from interviews decades later with the by-then elderly former CIA employees was that Dr. Olson had made comments about his discomfort with experiments he had been overseeing. The Agency was concerned that he could become a whistleblower—all of their secret operations and experiments could become public knowledge.

They administered the LSD a week before Dr. Olson's death, not to evaluate its effects as they claimed during the 1975 Congressional hearing, but rather for "enhanced interrogation" to determine whether he intended to publicize the secret experimentation. He spent the next week in an agitated and unpredictable state. He was to be taken the night of his death to a military facility, but something went terribly wrong and he was thrown out the window.

In 1953 the CIA started damage control immediately after Dr. Olson's "suicide."

Only five hours after Frank Olson's death, a young CIA investigator, James McCord, interviewed the scientist who had shared a room with him. McCord established that the scientist was asleep and was awakened by a crash through the window. He looked out and saw Olson's body on the sidewalk, thirteen floors below.

On December 2, 1953, McCord interviewed the two NYPD detectives assigned to the case, James Ward and Dave Mulle. He read their written reports. McCord was interested in the account of the first policeman on the scene, who had recommended the "case remain active." The detectives informed McCord they had closed the case as a "suicide" even though there had been no autopsy. They assured McCord of their continued cooperation.

Part of this recounting of McCord's visit to the 14th Precinct is from the well-researched *A Terrible Mistake* by H. P. Albarelli (2009). The author at this point raises the question (on page123): How did McCord introduce himself—as a CIA investigator? Questions might also occur to the reader—who gave the detectives authority to speak about the case? Would that have been common practice?[4]

My brother Bernard had the definitive answer. Fourteen years later he may have been in one of the chairs that Detective Mulle or Ward sat in across from James McCord. If he wasn't in the same seat, at least he was working with their commanding officer, Lt. Arthur Schultheiss.[5] That was the same Arthur Schultheiss who at the time of the Olson "suicide" was Uncle George's guardian on his trips to New York with the Las Vegas skim.

"There is no way a detective under Schultheiss would give information to someone just walking into the precinct—especially in a case where a government scientist was dead on a New York City sidewalk," said Bernard. "No way they would show him the written reports unless Schultheiss ok'd it."

Bernard added, "That may have been the first time McCord worked with the NYPD, but it wasn't the last. McCord was around throughout my time in the SIU (Special Investigative Unit) and after. He probably worked with other commanders around the city besides Schultheiss. The CIA used the department a lot."

James McCord may sound familiar. Twenty years after his work burying the Olson investigation, he was one of the Watergate burglars caught in the act at the Democratic National Committee offices. His acknowledgment at the arraignment that he once "worked for the CIA" led to the unraveling of the Watergate conspiracy.

Another New York based government operative at the time of Dr. Olson's death was Robert Maheu, an FBI agent. He worked with James McCord throughout the 1950s and into the '60s. He would be closely involved with the Agency's attempt to assassinate Fidel Castro using organized crime's contacts in Cuba in the early 1960s.

Later the same Robert Maheu negotiated Howard Hughes' purchase of the Desert Inn from the Cleveland Syndicate as well as several other Las Vegas casinos. He had long been involved in the intricate post WWII web of CIA/FBI, organized crime and media intrigue. Small world!

---

[1] Lars Schall, "The CIA: 70 Years of Organized Crime," *Counterpunch*, September 22, 2017.

[2] On August 16,1951, a postman making his rounds in a small French village, Pont-San-Esprit, fell ill with nausea and hallucinations. He was put in a straightjacket in a village hospital. Within days, dozens of other villagers experienced the same hallucinations. Five deaths were attributed to the mysterious outbreak. It was first suspected that a fungus in bread might have been the culprit. Decades later, it was revealed that a CIA LSD experiment was probably the cause. Dr. Frank Olson, the CIA science officer who led LSD research in the CIA at the time, had expressed profound regrets for the deaths of innocents that had occurred in the village.

[3] Jeremy Kuzmarov, "There's Something Rotten in Denmark": Frank Olson and the Macabre Fate of a CIA Whistleblower in the Early Cold War," *Class, Race, and Power*, Volume 8, Issue 1, Article 3, 2020, p. 3.

Also, *A Terrible Mistake* by H. P. Albarelli Jr, (Walterville, OR: TrineDay, 2009) details the Olson death and secret programs the unbridled CIA engaged in since its inception.

The 2017 Netflix seven-part series *Wormwood* is an excellent reenactment of the events surrounding Dr. Olson's death in 1953.

[4] Albarelli notes, in his fine work *A Terrible Mistake,* that the two New York detectives discussed with McCord other mysterious "suicides" from upper floors of buildings in the years preceding Olson's death. Many of these deaths were suspicious and involved men in the intelligence world.

The best known was the "suicide" of James Forrestal, who had been the Secretary of Defense before his admittance to Bethesda Naval Hospital. He allegedly jumped from a sixteenth-story window. While at the Department of Defense, he was an advocate of biochemical warfare and instrumental in the establishment of Fort Detrick's Special Operations Division, the unit that employed Frank Olson.

[5] *A Terrible Mistake* by H. P. Albarelli Jr, (Walterville, OR: TrineDay, 2009) p.661

AN EXIT FROM HAVANA— NONE TOO SOON

The Cleveland Syndicate partnered in Meyer Lansky's first payoffs to Batista in the early 1930s, but later they were not all-in with organized crime's love affair with Cuba. They had their illegal casinos in Ohio and Kentucky—every one a cash machine. Once they opened shop at the Desert Inn in Las Vegas in 1950, their interest in Cuba waned even further.

Las Vegas was their future.

Their outward enthusiasm for Havana was driven by an overriding factor: They never wanted to show a lack of support for Lansky's Havana dream. They were seeing huge cash flow from Cuba, so it wasn't too painful to be involved.

One event moved the Syndicate closer to the exit from Cuba; it played out on the streets of Havana. In November 1956, a force of eighty-two revolutionaries waded ashore in Niquero, a municipality jutting out into the Caribbean on the distant southeast coast of the island. The initial report indicated that the rebel leader Fidel Castro was killed, along with most of the other men. It wasn't true, nor would be most of the government reports on rebel activity over the next few years.

Uncle George, one of the Cleveland Syndicate men in Havana, perhaps had a better view of the reality of Cuban street life than did Meyer Lansky. Lansky's exposure to Cubans was limited to those in

Cuban generals' uniforms. Until the very end, he believed Batista's dismissals of the rebel threat.[1]

Uncle George's fondness for Cuban nightlife led him into bars and clubs. He saw the strength of revolutionary fervor in that demi world. He didn't share the East Coast gangsters' belief that Batista could maintain control of the streets.

George witnessed celebrations on the streets around the Hotel Nacional after every rebel victory in the distant provinces. He had the ear of the growing Miami Beach colony of semi-retired criminals. Soon their growing discomfort with Batista made its way back to Moe Dalitz, who had emerged as the upstanding "Godfather of Las Vegas."

The Cleveland Syndicate devised still one more scam—laundering Cuban casino proceeds through Miami and New Jersey banks. Cash and personal checks deposited in these banks were transferred to shell companies and other banks in Europe. Money just vanished.[2]

This money-laundering operation ran effortlessly throughout their stay on the island. There is no realistic estimation of the amount sent through these banks throughout the 1950s. Despite this tax-free cash cow, the Cleveland Syndicate still looked for a graceful exit from Cuba. It wouldn't be easy for them to walk away from their cut of the untaxed proceeds the mob was taking out of Cuba from their casinos and whorehouses.

The opening of the Stardust Hotel in Las Vegas in July 1958 under the control of the Dalitz crew made a departure from Cuba an even easier decision. Also, revolutionary activity had reached the big cities of Cuba, right up to the doors of the casinos. How to depart without appearing disloyal to Meyer Lansky was still the problem.

Coincidentally, just as the Stardust was being readied for its grand opening, the Nevada Tax Commission made a ruling that gifted cover to the Cleveland Syndicate's exit from the island.

The tax commission in April 1958 "discovered" that some holders of gaming licenses in Nevada had also invested in Cuban casinos. The commission ruled that, because of the growing international disapproval of gaming in Cuba and the tense political situation on that island, the holders of Nevada licenses would have to choose between Cuba and Las Vegas. They were given an ultimatum; divest their interest in the Nacional if they wanted to keep their licenses in Las Vegas. No doubt Moe Dalitz did all he could to have the tax commission render this blessing-in-disguise "ultimatum."

The Cleveland Syndicate looked for buyers for their Nacional interests—they wanted out as soon as possible. It is noted in the F.B.I. memos at the end of the chapter that Uncle George was negotiating the Syndicate's exit with Meyer Lansky's brother Jack in Havana.

The Syndicate once again had a streak of good fortune. A manager at the Bank of Miami Beach who had worked for years with the Nacional casino operators clearing cash and checks and transferring the proceeds out of sight managed to interest Mike McLaney, another of his clients, in the Nacional casino purchase.

McLaney, a promoter, pulled together a group of investors. He was a golf hustler and onetime policeman who claimed to have then Senator John Kennedy as a friend. The deal was probably completed by October 1958.

Unrelated to the rapidly changing Cuban casino outlook, on November 24, 1958, J. Edgar Hoover under the Top Hoodlum Program, ordered each FBI field office to prepare a list of ten local gangsters—no more, no less—for intensive surveillance. So many gangsters had migrated to the sunny beaches of Southern Florida that the Miami field office had difficulty limiting the list to just ten gangsters. Uncle George was put under "intensive surveillance."[3]

As a result, there were extensive FBI reports on Uncle George's interest in the Nacional and on his move to the town of Surfside, a haven for semi-retired gangsters, just one block north of Miami Beach. The reports and confidential informants verified the cover story of pressure from the Nevada Tax Commission as the reason for the sale.[4]

Less than two months later, Batista fled Cuba on New Year's Eve. The next day, January 1, 1959, Castro took power. The Cleveland Syndicate got out without losing their investment. The same wasn't true for the other mobsters, including Meyer Lansky. They held out hope that they could, as they had always done before, make a deal with the new political powers—this time, Fidel Castro.

Months later, it became apparent gambling was done and they would be shut out of Cuba. They looked for other locations in the Caribbean, but no place looked safe, especially after the surprise upheaval of their business in Cuba.

McLaney, one of the Havana casino bag holders, stayed in Cuba looking for an inside track to continue gambling at the Nacional. A representative of the Castro government become his contact, advising him on the gaming possibilities. He drove McLaney around Havana and took him for a large amount of Yanqui dollars for payoffs to other "insiders" in the new government. Only after Castro shut down the casinos did McLaney learn that he had been taken—the "insider" was just a Havana street hustler who had no influence within the Castro government and was last seen a few years later working in a Miami restaurant.

[1] Meyer Lansky's life experience would have validated the belief that every politician had a price. He might not have seen any difference between Batista and Castro, and so he never viewed the revolution as a long-term problem.

[2] The Cleveland Syndicate money laundering was revealed in a newspaper investigation. A cashier's check was purchased on August 5, 1960, by Morris Kleinman, one of the Cleveland Four, for $299,000 from the Bank of Las Vegas, made payable to himself. In November 1960, Uncle George cashed the check after Kleinman endorsed it. The money vanished—there was no trail to follow.

[3] 6/12/1959
Federal Bureau of Investigation Memo
To: SAC
From: Special Agent Elmer. F. Emrich

Subject: George Gordon, Surfside, Florida

"This office is in receipt of a communication from the Bureau dated June 10, 1959. It is pointed out that in connection with the Bureau's drive against organized crime and racketeering the Attorney General's Special Group has advised the Bureau of 386 individuals in whom they are interested. Very limited identifying information was made available to the Bureau with respect to these individuals.

"In the list of names previously referred to appears the above captioned individual."

I visited with Uncle George and Aunt Mildred several times throughout the 1960s. There were often two men in suits seated in the front seat of an unmarked car parked outside their home.

[4] 6/26/59 Department of Justice
Federal Bureau of Investigation
Special Agent Paul Cajigas
Miami (92-458)

On December 16, 1958 Chief of Police of Miami Beach Andy Murcia advised the FBI that his department "maintains an index file on the hoodlums in the Town of Surfside...a recent addition was George Gordon and his wife who purchased a home in Surfside in October 1958." It was "heard that Gordon had a piece of a gambling casino located in the Hotel Nacional in Havana Cuba but that he reportedly sold his interest...before coming to Miami in November, 1958."

The chief of police added, "It was rumored that Gordon sold his interest in the Havana hotel because of a recent law passed in Las Vegas that anyone who has an interest in a gambling casino is not permitted to operate a gambling casino in any other city."

MM 92-458

During May of 1958, T-5 stated GEORGE GORDON, who is reported to represent certain Cleveland interests, and who is presently working at the Desert Inn, Las Vegas, had come to Havana to discuss with JACK LANSKY the possible sale of the concession at the Hotel Nacional. T-5 said it appeared efforts were being made to have GORDON "front" for a new group of buyers of the casino.

On June 4, 1958, this source advised GEORGE GORDON had turned down the offer made to him by the Desert Inn group to be the front man for the Nacional Gambling Casino.

On July 14, 1958, T-5 said GEORGE GORDON had recently been at the casino in the Hotel Nacional because SAM TUCKER, FBI #377258, had been absent due to the death of TUCKER's brother-in-law in Cleveland. T-5 said an individual named BOBBY KAY represented the Cleveland group at the Hotel Nacional casino a year ago during SAM TUCKER's absence in Europe. T-5 noted he believed GEORGE GORDON maintained a residence in West Palm Beach, Florida, since GORDON had placed a telephone call to his wife there. T-5 advised further, GORDON recently made a telephone call to JOE ROGERS (an alias of JOE STASSI, FBI #559327, a business associate of SANTO TRAFFICANTE, FBI #[illegible]5318) and influenced ROGERS to place an individual by the name of LOU ROSS in the Hotel Havana Hilton as a dealer.

F.B.I. FOIA document MM-92-4458

For those readers inconvenienced by this hard-to-read F.B.I. memo I transcribed the first two paragraphs verbatim.

During May of 1958, T-5 [an informant] stated GEORGE GORDON, who is reported to represent certain Cleveland interests, and who is presently working at the Desert Inn, Las Vegas, had come to Havana to discuss with JACK LANSKY the possible sale of the concession at the Hotel Nacional. T-5 said it appeared efforts were being made to have GORDON "front" for a new group of buyers for the casino.

On June 4, 1958 this source advised that GORDON had turned down the offer made to him by the Desert Inn group to be the front man for the Nacional gambling casino.

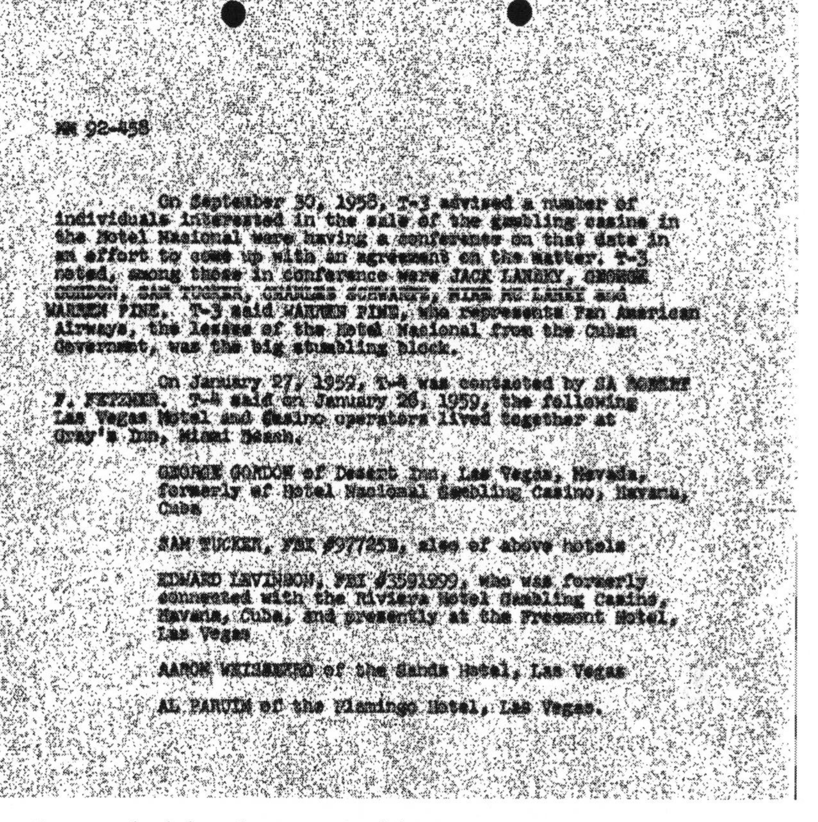

MM 92-458

On September 30, 1958, T-3 advised a number of individuals interested in the sale of the gambling casino in the Hotel Nacional were having a conference on that date in an effort to come up with an agreement on the matter. T-3 noted, among those in conference were JACK LANSKY, GEORGE GORDON, SAM TUCKER, CHARLES SCHWARTZ, MIKE MC LANEY and WARREN FINE. T-3 said WARREN FINE, who represents Pan American Airways, the lessee of the Hotel Nacional from the Cuban Government, was the big stumbling block.

On January 27, 1959, T-4 was contacted by SA [illegible] F. [illegible]. T-4 said on January 26, 1959, the following Las Vegas Hotel and Casino operators lived together at Gray's Inn, Miami Beach.

GEORGE GORDON of Desert Inn, Las Vegas, Nevada, formerly of Hotel Nacional Gambling Casino, Havana, Cuba

SAM TUCKER, FBI #97725B, also of above hotels

EDWARD LEVINSON, FBI #3591999, who was formerly connected with the Riviera Hotel Gambling Casino, Havana, Cuba, and presently at the Freemont Hotel, Las Vegas

AARON WEISBERG of the Sands Hotel, Las Vegas

AL PARVIN of the Flamingo Hotel, Las Vegas.

I transcribed the relevant part of this F.B.I. Memo MM 92-458.

On September 30, 1958, T-3 [an informant] advised that a number of individuals interested in the sale of the gambling casino in the Hotel Nacional were having a conference on that date in an effort to come up with an agreement on the matter. T-3 noted that among those in conference were JACK LANSKY, GEORGE GORDON, SAM TUCKER, CHARLES SCHWARTZ, MIKE McLANEY, and WARREN FINE. T-3 said that WARREN FINE, who represents Pan American Airways, the lessee of the hotel Nacional from the Cuban Government, was the big stumbling block.

MM 92-515

Investigation at Las Vegas indicates MORRIS LANSBURG, a big hotel operator at Miami and Las Vegas, paid $11,250.00 cash for the machines.

MICHAEL MC LANEY, Miami Beach, Fla., a former operator of the casino at Hotel Nacional, Havana, is interested in taking over the operation of the Wappen Von Hamburg, if it can be done in a strictly legal manner and divorced completely from any known hoodlums.

MM 509-C on 12/4/62, advised that on 12/3/62, MICHAEL COPPOLA (Miami File 92-101) who has been out of prison since 11/27/62, spent some time in the office of JOE MASSEI (Miami File 92-122) at 23rd and Collins, Miami Beach, Fla., and individuals observed to be conversing with COPPOLA there were, JIMMY COPPOLA, MASSEI, JOE BOMMARITO (Miami File 92-144), ABE KAUFMAN, a bookmaker and friend of GEORGE GORDON (Miami File 92-458) who was also there. He also advised COPPOLA does not desire to hang out at any of the present clubs or hangouts on Miami Beach and is seeking a place where he can meet with his "Corp" and acquaintances. MM 509-C pointed out that ALLIE HARRIS, one of the COPPOLA group, remained in New York City, where he reportedly is running some floating dice games, but that HARRIS' son, MEL HARRIS and his wife came to Miami and are staying at the Fontainebleau Hotel.

F.B.I. memo MM 92-515

Of interest here is that McLaney despite losing everything he invested in the Nacional and being scammed by a "Castro insider" was still hunting around the world for a friendly gambling environment.

Also of note is Trigger Mike Coppola was released from prison on 11/27/62 and a few days later (12/3/62) quickly reassembled his closest associates, including Uncle George of course.

KILL EL COMANDANTE

"No matter how much money these guys had, they still could not resist another scam."
– *My father, Lou Geik*

By the end of the 1950s the cash flow from Nevada casinos vastly surpassed any amount imagined at the beginning of the decade. Despite US Senate hearings and investigations into mob control of the casinos by federal agencies and newspapers, the biggest fear of the casino operators was that new federal laws would allow the government a long look into their web of hidden ownership. One tactic in American industry is to keep government regulators at arm's distance by enacting easy-to-ignore pretenses of self-regulation. Nevada casinos and their elected allies were no different.

In 1959 the Nevada legislature established the Nevada Gaming Commission. The Commission would act upon the recommendations of the Gaming Control Board and would make all decisions in gaming licensing matters.

Unexpectedly, this legislation would enhance Uncle George's stature in Las Vegas and his standing in the Italian world of organized crime.

In 1960 the Gaming Control Board produced an Excluded Person List—"the Black Book." It was their public show of exercising oversight by banning arbitrarily chosen characters for life from every casino in the state. Of course, no state legislation would ever address the hidden mob interests or the massive skim of casino profits that had evolved into an art form.

Most of the blackballed characters stayed away from the casinos, but it didn't always work out well. Owners of the El Rancho casino ejected Chicago mob enforcer Marshall Caifano based on his Black Book entry. Later the same night, arsonists burned the building to the ground.

Sam Giancana and "Trigger" Mike Coppola —two of the original Black Book entries—were close associates of Uncle George. They both chose Uncle George to be their on-the-ground representative in Las Vegas.

A *Chicago Sun-Times* July 1963 investigative series on Las Vegas mob control identified Giancana as the Chicago mob boss with controlling interest in the Stardust Hotel. The series claimed that Giancana never trusted Moe Dalitz, who operated the casino. Now with his inability to enter any Nevada casino, Giancana relied on Uncle George to represent his interests in the counting room.[1] The close, personal relationship put Giancana at ease, and Dalitz didn't have to deal with disputes with the powerful Chicago mob.

Johnny Eder recalled, *"George was valuable to everybody. He was close to Sam Giancana. They knew of each other for a long time and finally met. Sinatra introduced them in the early '50s. Giancana respected George. They stayed close friends for years."*

International intrigue soon linked Uncle George and Sam Giancana in another scam. For months after Castro's takeover of Cuba, the mob calculated Fidel's durability, waiting for a chance to return. The CIA had different intentions—they set about to kill Castro. However, operatives of colonial powers often underestimate the strength of an insurgency.

The CIA was no different. They were destined to misjudge Cuban politics for the coming decades. In August 1959 the CIA failed to kill Castro with a poisoned cigar.

After that failure, the CIA turned to organized crime. They reasoned that the Havana casino operators, having lost their investment, had motivation to want Fidel dead. This opened the door to still another organized crime improvised scam. The only constant over the next three years was the gangsters' amusement with the gullible government operatives.

Johnny Eder said,

> *"The guys in Miami joked about those government spooks. They smoked pipes and were educated in Ivy League schools. Not one looked like he had ever been on a street corner. They must have had desk jobs together during the war or something. They were fraternity guys talking to criminals who had spent their lives in gang wars and prisons. It didn't take much to get them to part with a few bucks."*

The first week in October 1959, CIA officials met with underworld leaders, including Sam Giancana, at the Fontainebleau Hotel in Miami Beach. Giancana's groupie, Frank Sinatra, was close to Senator John Kennedy, the likely Democratic candidate in the following year's presidential election. Kennedy's father no doubt was already plotting with Giancana and Richard Daley, the Mayor of Chicago, to steal the votes in that city in what they knew would be a close election against Richard Nixon.

The Fontainebleau was only four miles from Uncle George's house in Surfside. George met Giancana right after the meeting. Giancana turned to Uncle George who a year earlier had, along with the rest of the Cleveland Syndicate, sold out their interests in Havana. Giancana wanted George's Havana contacts. George, according to my father, had no current contacts in Havana and was clear about that.

My father recalled:

> *"The CIA was desperate. The wise guys sensed it and took them for as much as they could. Right from the beginning they were content with just seeing what they could get out of the government. For the first time, instead of being arrested by government agents, they were partners with them; and to make it an even bigger joke, the next president of the United States was supposedly in on the plan."*

Later the same month, October 1959, J. Edgar Hoover stated in a memo to CIA officials: *"During a recent conversation with several friends, [Sam] Giancana stated that Fidel Castro was to be done away with very shortly...that he had already met with the assassin-to-be three times. When doubt was expressed regarding this statement, Giancana reportedly assured those present that Castro's assassination would occur in November."*

According to many in the growing Miami Beach semi-retired wise guy community Giancana just wanted to see what angle could be worked to cut a deal to ease up on federal prosecution of organized crime.

The CIA called the Castro assassination project "Operation Mongoose." The mobsters understood that nothing would ensure a faster CIA career advancement more than being the agent who orchestrated the assassination of Castro. The mobsters tried to work that goal to their advantage for the next three years—until Kennedy's assassination.

Two tales from the mob/CIA "partnership" always amused me. The first is documented: The mob guys claimed someone—a probably fictional character "close to Fidel"—would slip poison into El Comandante's food. A CIA chemist prepared a slow-acting poison to be smuggled into Cuba.[2] The poison didn't get that far—the mobster running that scam flushed it down a toilet in Florida.

Hardly a dime of CIA funding for organized crime's efforts to kill Castro over three years made it to a single Cuba-based "operative"—most of it stayed in mob hands in Miami.

The second scam was more improvisational. A Miami based boat captain had the lead role. Two Italian hoodlum friends of Uncle George's involved the captain in an improbable scheme to "kill Fidel"—the captain would be contracted to smuggle assassins onto the island. It was part of another scam to shake a few bucks out of the CIA. The captain was never made aware that his co-conspirators had no intention to follow through on the plan once funded by the CIA.

Uncle George met the two scammers and the boat captain at a Miami marina restaurant. They discussed the "operation." Then the captain surprised them—he wanted to be in "the Mafia." He asked if they could sponsor him. They were stunned by the request. They later joked that the captain thought that "joining the Mafia" might be the same as joining a neighborhood bowling team. However, they were not so stunned that they couldn't find a way to make a few bucks from the captain.

After a few meetings they forgot the "kill Fidel" scam and told the captain they had set up a Mafia initiation. Their crime family boss, Don Rico Rigatoni (great name!), was coming down from New York City to initiate him.[3] The captain could barely restrain himself—he was going to meet a crime boss.

Vincent, a local limo service owner, was elevated to mob boss. Now as Don Rico, Vincent sat in the back of one of his limos for a change. The limo swooped under the carport of the restaurant, and two bodyguards jumped out. Don Rico made a grand entrance through the restaurant. He kissed the two hoodlums on their cheeks. He spoke Italian to one of them.

Don Rico had the captain cut his thumb and put his blood on an ace of spades playing card (they omitted messing up their own fingers as reenacted in TV portrayals of this supposed induction ceremony). They guided the captain through whatever other crazy shit came to mind. Don Rico solemnly told the captain to go back to his daily life and to never reveal any details of the induction.

The captain also was to await further instructions from the Godfather in New York. He was not to contact anyone again. He agreed. They all hugged. He never heard from them again.

Uncle George learned that the captain had paid $275,000 in cash for the honor of being "a Mafia guy."

---

[1] Controlling Crime Through More Effective Law Enforcement, p. 1062

[2] Dr. Sidney Gottlieb, who prepared the poison pills for Castro, was the same CIA doctor who gave Frank Olson his fatal LSD dosage in 1953.

An excellent account of the CIA attempts to assassinate Castro between his taking power on January 1, 1959, and Kennedy's assassination on November 22, 1963, can be found in *Mafia Spies*, by Thomas Maier (New York: Skyhorse Publishing, 2019).

[3] In the mid-1970s I read that the FBI conducted a yearlong sting operation in Washington, DC. Dozens of DC-area thieves sold stolen items to a warehouse fencing operation—run by undercover FBI agents posing as "Mafia" guys. Finally, word went out that "the Don" was coming down from New York to thank each criminal personally at a banquet hall with food and drinks. The "Don" was an FBI official. He arrived in a limousine and was introduced as "Don Rico Rigatoni." I laughed and wondered if the FBI had heard the Miami boat captain scam and stole the "Don's" name. The thieves were taken into a smaller room one at a time to meet "the Don" and arrested.

31

UNCLE CHARLIE LEAVES PRISON

Our father was laid off from his office job at the Midtown Manhattan music publisher. It was traumatic for the family. I was working and taking classes at City College of New York at night; a few years later, my sister would be doing the same at Hunter College. Our brother, Bernard, would soon be taking a test for the New York Police Department. It was the beginning of 1961.

Lou was a forty-five-year-old unskilled worker, but with great street smarts—he only had this one job since he was sixteen. Job opportunities were limited, but he did have a lifetime of contacts around the city, in the business world and in the underworld.

My sister and I went to the practically tuition-free City College of New York (CCNY). I was grateful, as it allowed me to roam the city at night, seeking out after-hours clubs in the South Bronx and Manhattan. The clubs were mob owned. The front men came to know me, and it was soon known in my father's world that that was my beat. I think they lived vicariously through me, as I seemed more unencumbered than they were with families and the never-ending politics of fronting nightclubs for organized crime.

An exciting family event occurred on March 10, 1964. Charles Workman, Uncle Charlie, was released from the New Jersey prison system. He had been there since I was born. It was hard for me to imagine that someone had been in prison throughout my whole life.

I had read that he killed more than fifty people—even though these guys always laughed at newspaper estimations of kill rates, or the amount of money they had stashed away.[1] We were aware Uncle Charlie would be released from prison a short time before it happened.

What do I say to someone who had been in prison for twenty-three years? He had never been in a home with a television set in the living room. What did he think about Kennedy's assassination only four months earlier? Was that a big deal in prison? I joked with my brother, "Does Uncle Charlie have a professional opinion of the Kennedy hit?" Did he ever hear of Bob Dylan or the Beatles? Was he a baseball fan? Would he be easy to talk to?

Iris's birthday is March 10. We waited to celebrate until Uncle Charlie could join us. It was postponed a few times, as he had other family and old friends to meet. Consorting with known criminals was a parole violation, so he had to be careful to avoid the usual suspects.

* * *

At the end of the month, we finally met in a restaurant on Mott Street in the heart of Chinatown. It had changed ownership and names many times, but Uncle Charlie remembered the address—it had been his favorite. When we arrived, he was already seated at a large table in the back. He stood up as we approached. He was well dressed—his silver hair combed straight back.

He hugged my mother affectionately. "You're as beautiful as ever, Reba."

He turned to Iris, "And you're Iris, the youngest and as lovely as your mother." Iris smiled, appreciating the comment. Charlie's charm hadn't dulled in prison.

He hugged Dad.

"Thanks so much, Lou."

It was all he needed to say. I could see he wanted to say it in person in front of the family. It was thanks for my father—someone without a criminal record—a bearer of funds and checking in on his family those years he was away. My father smiled, nodded, and pointed for us to sit.

Charlie looked toward the entrance. "Here they are," he said. I turned. It was Sam Red Levine, who I knew as the owner of The Spot, a bar on Grand Street. He was also still feared even though he had long since semi-retired into a world of part-time labor union racketeering—the underworld survivors always had a soft landing in New York City.

Sylvia Lorber had her arm looped around Red's. She had been my mother's friend since their teenage years on the lower East Side. Sylvia had become Red's constant companion since her previous man, Ben Kass, had gone to Sing Sing along with his brother Sammy, an often called-upon narrator in this account. They had been busted in a federal undercover operation aimed at the one-time New York crime boss, Waxey Gordon.

I always thought of Sylvia as a glamorous single woman in the mob world who lived so differently than our mother. She was uninhibited and laughed easily. They sat down—my sister and mother next to Sylvia. Red, Charlie, my father and brother sat on the other side. I felt like the outsider, but it was an exciting encounter for me. I would listen to every word—of the men, that is. The women's stories didn't interest me as much back then. I resisted their efforts to bring me into the conversation—it was just that I wanted to hear everything these men would say. I learned later that the women's life stories put this crime culture into a different context.[2]

I didn't expect the conversation that unfolded.

Charlie laughed. "Red, I know you don't eat this stuff. I can't go anyplace that wise guys congregate. They're sure to know me in a Jew joint. They'd all come over to say hello. Then they'd get me on a parole violation—consorting with known criminals. I'm glad you're sort of retired now. Nobody's following you around anymore. This place is better anyway—there ain't a Chinaman in New York who knows me." They laughed. We all did.

* * *

I spent the next two hours listening to Uncle Charlie and Red Levine remind each other of the shopkeepers on the Lower East Side and the neighbors they both knew. I watched two of the best known, now retired, Murder Inc. assassins laugh about the "old days" in New York City, not unlike any two old men sitting on the steps in front of any building in the Bronx. (I laugh now, as Uncle Charlie was only about fifty-five and Red sixty years old.)

The questions I wondered about before now seemed unnecessary to ask. Charlie acted like any uncle I might have never met before—one who might have been living in Buenos Aires or Israel for much of my life. I was sure there would be time for a relationship—and luckily, there was.

My brother Bernard had joined the New York Police Department the year before, and that attracted both Charlie and Red's interest. Charlie said, "Bernard, I hear Schultheiss has his eye on you. It's great having someone with his juice."

It never occurred to me that Arthur Schultheiss even knew my brother.

"Yeah," Bernard said, "I went to see him last week. He told me how close he is to Uncle George. I didn't know you knew him."

Both Charlie and Red laughed. Schultheiss had been on the force in the 1930s and made his way up the chain to a Manhattan commander of detectives. He knew every criminal as well as they knew him.

Bernard's move up the ranks in the police department was to be guided by Lt. Schultheiss—an unseen power broker. His journey started off as a patrolman in the NYPD and later would be central to the greatest New York City Police department scandal. Oddly, Bernard would not only survive it—roughed up by the publicity and arrest—but he ended up in even better standing in the criminal underworld of the Garment Center.

---

[1] I learned early on that most of the lower-level organized crime figures died broke. Their families struggled while their wise guy fathers and husbands were in jail, or spending their bounty on women, gambling, and always, defense attorneys. One mobster was indicted, went to trial, acquitted, and then arrested again on the courthouse steps as he was leaving a free man—rinse, repeat for years. The government objective was often to impoverish the soldiers in crime families.

[2] Later, my sister, Iris, told me that while the men were engaged on one side of the table, Sylvia was telling her and my mother about the frustrations of being with criminals like Red Levine and Benny Kass—Sammy's brother—before he went to Sing Sing. Sylvia never knew when the FBI would knock on her door and she would be alone and never sure what to say—or knowing that because they had wives somewhere she could never go to their funeral—and the family, especially the women, would hate her. I was to hear these sad life stories from these women many times—second-hand, mostly through my mother and sister.

Warren M. Winterbottom/AP/Shutterstock

Charlie Workman leaving New Jersey State Penitentiary March 10, 1964, after serving twenty-three years for Dutch Schultz's murder. For the next decade Uncle Charlie always dressed dapper, even if it was to meet my NYPD detective brother Bernard and me at a restaurant in the basement of a tenement building in Chinatown. He never lost that stone cold stare—I'm sure it was the last thing more than one person ever saw.

Author's Family Album

(mid 1950s) Sylvia Lorber, posing front and center, with a flower in her hair—Sam "Red" Levine's girlfriend for several years and would remain so until he passed away in the 1970s. She came alone to this family event, as Red Levine would have had to be there with his wife—of course.

Sylvia, my sister Iris, our mother and I went on a great adventure shortly before this photo was taken. We went to Cape Cod and then drove to Montreal. Our driver and my roommate for those several weeks was a family friend who was also a great New York Yankee fan.

Years later Iris told me the unspoken drama; we went on this trip because Sylvia wanted to leave Red Levine—she didn't. Our mother wanted to leave our father—she didn't. I, nonetheless, had a great time. I was twelve years old.

32

LONDON—THE COLONY SPORTS CLUB

The mid-sixties action unfolded in Las Vegas, Miami, and New York. I didn't learn the stateside drama because I was living in London from 1966–1968, a great era to be there—sex, drugs, rock and roll, the Beatles, The Rolling Stones. I was an anti-Vietnam War agitator.

I arrived in London to attend the London School of Economics & Political Science in September 1966. I saved $1,200, had a student loan for $1,200, and my mother gave me her last $600 of savings that she still had after my father's several years of unemployment. Remarkably, that total of $3,000 lasted me over one year in London. The year's master's degree program was just $79.00—tuition for a prestigious British university.

I don't know why I was attending graduate school—I wasn't very interested in it at the time. This degree would, however, allow me to roam the world attending tiresome conferences for senseless international agencies. That seemed to be the goal of most of the graduate students, many from Britain's former colonies.

Robbie Margolies called a few months after I arrived. He invited me to dinner. Robbie had been a longtime friend of my family. He and his brother Abe owned jewelry stores in Manhattan, and both were known in New York's sporting world. Both had the same affliction: gambling on any sport at any time, never a pursuit that offered long-term profitability. To support his gambling losses, Robbie also fenced jewelry and had done many deals with Johnny Eder. The Margolies brothers gambled on everything. They were especially fond of the regularly fixed fights in Madison Square Garden in the 1950s and '60s where Frankie Carbo, still another Murder, Inc. alumni, was the overseer of the sport.[1]

After Castro closed the Cuban casinos, the East Coast underworld looked for locations to open new operations. Recently enacted British gambling laws legalized casinos and also the same games that organized crime had refined since the 1920s. Meyer Lansky opened the opulent Colony Sports Club in London in the mid-1960s.

Robbie Margolies was one of the managers of the Colony Sports Club, representing Lansky. Robbie invited me to stop by the casino. I did. George Raft, a Hollywood movie gangster, was the front man. He carried off the role of debonair gangster effortlessly.

Raft told me about his longtime friendship with Uncle George. He claimed to have modeled himself after two gangsters: Uncle George and Owney Madden, a legendary bootlegger in the 1920s and once owner of Harlem's famous Cotton Club. I had the feeling that Raft told many gangsters that he modeled his onscreen persona after them—knowing how narcissistic they could be.

* * *

A few weeks after our first dinner, Robbie called again with a one-evening job offer. A "whale" (a high roller always catered to by casinos everywhere) had arrived in town unexpectedly. He was a German auto manufacturer and an organized crime groupie. The club managers treated him as European royalty. He was certain to lose a huge amount of money at the tables.

There was a small inconvenience that needed tending. The whale's daughter, Mila, was with him. She was a graduate student in Germany.

The casino operators wanted her occupied while they kept the whale at the tables. They didn't want Daddy to wonder if Mila was bored.

"Why don't you be a tour guide for her while Daddy is getting cleaned out at the tables?" Robbie asked me, perhaps not that cynically. I can't remember, maybe it was that cynically. "Take her around—a show, nightclub, dinner whatever? Size her up; see what she wants to do. $200 should be enough. Right? Come by the club. " Two hundred dollars! That was huge money for me at the time.

So I meet Mila. She was a delightful, attractive, bright lady, and a frigging graduate student in some kind of physics—but still a daddy's girl. We went for dinner at a restaurant I could never afford if I didn't have that casino stash.

We walked through the theater district. She asks, "Are you free till Sunday night?" It was Thursday night. I was surprised. I didn't know what to say. "Uhhh, yes."

"Let's go to Paris. Dad will pay for it." She goes to a pay phone and calls the Colony Sports Club. "No, I don't need to talk to him. Just tell him I met a girlfriend from school and we're going to Paris." She hangs up.

Pot, booze, sex, jazz clubs, even a museum (I think) and we are back in London Sunday night. Robbie hears about the adventure. He tells George Raft, whose eyes narrow theatrically as he looks at me. "I'll tell your Uncle George you're a fucking gigolo. Forget that college crap."

The next year the British government deports George Raft.

The British government also deports Robbie Margolies.

Scotland Yard investigated the Colony Sports Club and concluded that it was owned by American organized crime figures. It took Scotland Yard a few years to find out that American gangsters owned the club! Scotland Yard also determined that, unlike the games in America, the

Colony Sports Club games were rigged. They shut down the London casinos.

In 1972 Meyer Lansky and a few other club operators were indicted in the US for income tax fraud relating to their Colony Sports Club operations. Lansky was acquitted.

In the 1990s Robbie Margolies jumped from his upper story balcony to his death. He had huge gambling losses by that time. I asked my former detective brother if it had been suicide or someone guiding Robbie over the balcony railing. He shrugged his shoulders, "We called them all suicides—less paperwork."[2]

---

1 I trained for two years in Stillman's Gym, on 54th Street four blocks up 8th Avenue from the old Madison Square Garden. Stillman's was the iconic gym in the boxing world in that era. I was lucky enough to train and get hit hard by several world champions-to-be. Years later someone asked me what my best memory was of Stillman's. My answer "taking a punch and pretending it didn't hurt." I broke my nose, ribs and a knuckle, which were all proudly displayed over the years.

The positive fallout from this experience was that gamblers who hung out in Stillman's knew I was George's nephew. It made me more than just "a college guy." Because of that connection, old-time fighters, trainers and managers sometimes recounted the many fixed fights.

I realized that the Friday Night Fights, a regular TV presentation from Madison Square Garden that aired on the screen above the bar in every tavern in New York City, were a nice earner for the mobsters who had cut themselves into the purses of the exploited fighters. They decided who would be in the main event. Wins and losses were casually orchestrated. The mob had become behind-the-scenes producers of a popular TV program. What should anyone expect—that the mob would produce a musical comedy?

2 In 2000 Randy Gordon, a boxing blogger, paid tribute to the passing of Teddy Brennan, the well-known boxing matchmaker. "A few years ago, Brenner slipped into deep depression after one of his closest friends, Robbie Margolies, died after plunging several stories from his balcony. It is still unsure whether Margolies was murdered. Regardless, he was gone, and so was Brenner's longtime pal." ("Randy's World of Boxing by Randy Gordon" *The Cyber Boxing Zone Journal*, January 2000.

Author's family album

A family gathering: Most of the men were NYC construction union officials who would be indicted within the next few years. The man in the foreground on the left is Robbie Margolies: a jeweler, a gambler, and a fence. He was not indicted. He was to play a part in an exciting adventure of mine in London in 1967. Deeply in debt in the 1990s he either jumped from, or was thrown from, his Queens, N.Y. apartment balcony.

In the foreground center is Sol "Blubber" Bloom of naked-Nazi-in-the-trunk-of-a-car fame.

NAME : Solomon BLOOM

ALIASES : Sol Bloom, Saul Berman, Solly, Mutton Head, Sol Rosen, Blubber, Blubberhead.

DESCRIPTION : Born 9-7-09 NYC, Jewish, 5'8", 183 lbs, black greying hair, grey eyes, heavy build, ruddy complexion.

LOCALITIES FREQUENTED : Legal Address is 1120 Brighton Beach Ave, Brooklyn, NY, c/o Mrs. Sarah Berman, sister. Frequents Hotel Olcott, Hotel Bancroft, Westover Hotel, Sidney Garage, Tomaldo Rest., Tony's Bar, all of NYC. Town Pump & Colony Club of Detroit, Mich., also Miami, Fla.

FAMILY BACKGROUND : Father: Julius Bloom (deceased); mother: Fannie Weinstein; sisters: Sarah Berman & Anna Taub of Brooklyn, NY; brother: Sam Bloom of Brooklyn, NY.

CRIMINAL ASSOCIATES : Anthony Teramine, Joe (scarface) Bommarito, Peter Licavoli, Anthony Giacolone, of Detroit. Florio Isabella, Nathan Behrman, Anthony Vellucci, Harry Stromberg, of NYC.

CRIMINAL HISTORY : FBI #198796. Detroit PD #97106. NYCPD #B84213. Record dates back to 1928 for burglary, grand larceny, assault and robbery, narcotics, violation state gambling laws, stench bombing.

BUSINESS : No legitimate occupation.

MODUS OPERANDI : Close associate of important Mafia and other narcotic smugglers and traffickers. Engaged in the interstate distribution of narcotics.

Property of U. S. Govt – For Official Use Only
May not be disseminated or contents disclosed
without permission of Commissioner of Narcotics

33

THE MOB SCAMS HOWARD HUGHES

The Cleveland Four—men who had together assembled a gambling empire (legal and illegal) in Ohio, Kentucky, Havana, Florida, Las Vegas and wherever else they could buy into or extort a piece of the action—were now in their early sixties. The gambling life, regardless of how successful it had been, had taken its toll.

Lou Rothkopf was the first of the Cleveland Four to die, in 1956, and that it was a suicide affected the remaining partners. Sam Tucker and Morris Kleinman found semi-retirement in Southern Florida with the ever-growing class of gentlemen fishermen, formerly gangsters.

Moe Dalitz, tiring from organized crime politics, and the exhaustion of being the main man in Las Vegas—now an international destination—along with the constant pressure of more intense federal investigations and congressional hearings, decided to step back from the daily operations as head of the still thriving Cleveland Syndicate.

In April 1963 the FBI reported Uncle George would assume Moe's place in the Syndicate. The report indicated however that Dalitz's partners, Tucker and Kleinman, could never accept Uncle George as an executive, certainly not to replace Moe Dalitz.[1]

Although they admired Uncle George's street toughness and his lifelong willingness to get messy when the need arose, the job description called for an ability to look a few moves ahead on the intricate chessboard of organized crime.

They never questioned Uncle George's loyalty, but they also knew him to have a recurring addiction, one deadly to casino operators—he was as much of a loser at the craps tables as any of the hopeless gamblers the Syndicate had impoverished over the decades.

In 1959 months after the Syndicate had sold their Cuban casino interests, George had returned to Las Vegas and quickly amassed heavy gambling losses.[2] Dalitz sent him to Florida to manage the Syndicate's growing interests there. He still returned to disburse the skim from the Stardust to the organized crime families, but his high-level executive possibilities were severely tarnished. He would remain a presence in both Las Vegas and Miami until his death in the early 1970s.

Moe Dalitz reconsidered his retirement and remained chairman of the board of the dwindling Cleveland Syndicate until the 1980s.

In May 1966 an unrelated event changed Las Vegas history. A federal court ruled Howard Hughes' ownership of TWA and Hughes Aircraft to be a conflict of interest. He had to divest his interest in one of these entities. He sold his TWA stock and became a billionaire with cash that needed to be invested to avoid a huge tax bill.

In 1966 he hired Robert Maheu as his CEO—Maheu, the same FBI agent in New York at the time of the Frank Olson "suicide," and the same CIA operative running the organized crime/CIA collaboration to kill Castro earlier in the decade.

In November 1966 the sizable Hughes entourage moved into the top two floors of the Desert Inn. They were the most unlikely residents in Sin City—many were Mormons with no interest in gambling or the other attractions of the city. They were secretive and cast a glum aura over a property whose owners had worked hard to project a carefree setting for their guests.

A month later Ruby Kolod, Uncle George's lifelong partner in crime from the Lower East side, confronted Maheu. Kolod, now president of the Desert Inn, wanted the Hughes people out of the hotel.[3] Other customers had reserved those top floors for the Christmas week—whales, guaranteed to lose big at the gaming tables over the holiday season. Hughes refused to move and instead negotiated to buy the property, which he did in March 1967.

It was a dumb deal; the agreement only gave him control of the casino and hotel for fifty-five years. It was more of a lease than Hughes appreciated at the time. The Cleveland Syndicate retained ownership of the land and buildings.

Hughes displayed his naiveté by turning over the operations of the casino to the Dalitz group—the same scammers who had pocketed millions in skimmed cash over the previous two decades. Robert Maheu negotiated the purchase for Hughes. He was never one to measure up to the mob's street smarts in any deal he made with them.

Hughes and Maheu magnified the dumb Desert Inn deal—they made the same deals with the Frontier, Sands, Castaways and Landmark hotels and casinos and the Silver Slipper. Hughes tried to purchase the Stardust, but after many legal battles he left that casino to other investors who would ultimately get busted by the FBI for their part in the skimming operation.

Hughes left all of the casinos in the hands of the same pit bosses, managers—every co-conspirator in the long-running skimming operation. Of course, they continued skimming under Hughes' management.

The Las Vegas casinos remained cash cows, but for the same hidden interests around the country. For Hughes, with the mob doing the counting, the expected cash flow of course could never possibly materialize. It surprised many that someone with Hughes' experience—a daredevil aviator, a Hollywood film producer and studio owner, perhaps the most important innovator of his generation in the aircraft industry—never understood the simple principle of watching the cash registers, which in this case were the casino counting rooms.

In 1976 Nicholas "Peanuts" Donalfo described the very brief "Las Vegas Hughes Era." Peanuts, a long-time casino manager, came from Cleveland after the Syndicate bought the Desert Inn. I was in Las Vegas in 1976 for the first time and met Peanuts. He laughed, recollecting the years of Hughes "control, "As soon as Hughes bought the place, we pocketed as much as we could. Your Uncle George even had a crew— a few guys in security. They burglarized hotel rooms a couple of times. They would take a couple of pieces of jewelry, cash, whatever. It didn't matter—it wasn't their hotel anymore. We were all thieves at heart." He shook his head in admiration.

Peanuts continued, "It was the best time for all of us. Maheu put all these retired FBI agents in charge of the casinos. Not one of them ever gambled anywhere. They never drank. They were Mormons. So we stole them blind. Who cared? What were these retired FBI guys going to do to us? It wasn't like when the mob ran the town. If we did the shit to them we did to Hughes we would have disappeared in the desert."

One study concluded that by 1970 just three years after his first Las Vegas casino purchase, Hughes had lost $50 million.[4] In the same year he left his Las Vegas properties and, in poor mental and physical health, moved to the Bahamas to again avoid US taxes.

[1] Michael Newton, *Mr. Mob: The Life and Crimes of Moe Dalitz* (Jefferson, NC: McFarland & Company, 2009), p. 199.

[2] FBI Special Agent Joseph G. Fregs
7/9/1959 Subject: George Gordon

[3] Kolod's confrontation with Maheu was his last known act for his long-time co-conspirators. In August 1967 he died of a heart attack. Ruby was only fifty-seven years old. Despite his lifetime of criminality, he died of a broken heart—his son had drowned in a boating accident in Lake Mead two years earlier. His body was never recovered.

[4] Michael Newton, *Mr. Mob: The Life and Crimes of Moe Dalitz* (Jefferson, NC: McFarland & Company, 2009), p. 231

DETECTIVE BERNIE GEIK

"To be trusted by other detectives you had to be alright with four things: cheating on your wife, drinking, taking bribes, and shaking down drug dealers."

– My brother, Bernard Geik, long after he left the NYPD

Bernard joined the police department in 1962 and was immediately known as Lt. Schultheiss' guy. He was assigned to the TPF—the Tactical Patrol Force—a highly visible police unit that flooded areas of high crime. TPF cops would be noticed and marked for speedy career advancement.

Arthur Schultheiss had my brother promoted to detective a few years later. He became one of the youngest detectives on the police force at the time. Arthur Schultheiss assigned Bernard special functions, including sometimes meeting organized crime characters at the airport and staying with them for their time in New York. Schultheiss automatically trusted Bernard with these assignments because he was Uncle George's nephew.[1]

The CIA had already dug deep into many police departments in Big City America, even before their ill-fated collaboration with organized crime to kill Castro. The CIA identified commanders like Schultheiss, who then had their favorite detectives carry out the covert operations. Bernard was one of them.

Bernard recalled:

> *"We knew we were involved with the CIA but it wasn't as dramatic as movie stuff. Some of it was ordinary. The guys I teamed with were not the only detectives doing this. But we would never know because the CIA probably had other commanders like Arthur [Schultheiss] assigning guys to these jobs.*
>
> *"The CIA might want us to trail a small-time drug dealer or criminal. We would take him to the station or someplace out of the way. A CIA agent using phony NYPD credentials would interrogate him about a relative, maybe a high-level official in a foreign country. If they threatened to charge the Sad Sack Dealer with whatever they could, they might be able to work a deal with the relative in freakin' Ghana or wherever to spy for the Agency."*

New York City was of special interest to the CIA—it was the site of the United Nations.

This was New York, the prized assignment for every foreign diplomat. The United Nations is on the East River, in Midtown Manhattan, as are the residences of the foreign delegations—Bernard's beat, Arthur Schultheiss' domain. Bernard's team put in illegal wiretaps using the Agency's more modern equipment so they could listen in on diplomats' calls.

Part of the lure of New York for foreign delegations is its nightlife, at nightclubs operated and protected by organized crime—many of them by Uncle George's close friend and one of the several guardians of my father's Garment Center trucking business, Matty "The Horse" Ianniello.

The detectives might follow foreign delegates targeted by the CIA. Sometimes the trail led into nightclubs. That information came in handy if the CIA wanted to get that delegate or employee out of the country. Bernard, with a lifetime of knowing the underworld characters, was of special usefulness on these operations.

Bernard: "Just like in the movies, undercover cops might start a fight with a diplomat or his bodyguards. Make a lot of noise. The club bouncers—we knew them all—would always want to accommodate us, especially if it was at the expense of a foreigner who'd be too scared to say anything. The delegates would tell the CIA guys anything they wanted to hear."

Sometimes the target might be the wife of a diplomat visiting her lover in another part of town. Police would shake her down for information or induce her to spy in whatever way the Agency could negotiate.

And then there were the gay bars of Manhattan. It was a different era; a police car parked in front of a gay bar was enough to keep it empty for the night. With the patrons always under threat of arrest, the operators, fearing closure, had found it worthwhile to cut in the better-connected organized crime bosses as partners. The police disappeared.

Why the CIA targeted someone didn't matter—the detectives just did their job. Bernard remembered:

"Trailing a closet gay delegate to a bar where he's sure nobody knows him; the next thing he's standing on a Manhattan street in handcuffs. He has to be thinking how this is going to play back in Egypt or the Congo. Not too well. He'll likely cooperate.

"The CIA had a guy in the United Nations Headquarters security services working with them. Frank Acinapura—you

met him once when we went to dinner with Dad in that place on 72nd Street. He was close to Schultheiss also. Frank had personal information on the foreign delegates and their staff—phone numbers, addresses, contacts. He had dozens of sources inside the UN."

When the Watergate burglars were arrested in May 1972, Bernard recognized Jim McCord's photo in the newspapers. McCord, one of the burglars, was the same CIA investigator who began the Agency whitewashing of the Frank Olson "suicide" hours after it happened in 1953.

As soon as the Olson "investigation" began, Schultheiss' detectives had quickly closed the Olson case. McCord ran other operations through the NYPD in the 1950s and '60s. Bernard worked on at least one of them.[2]

* * *

By 1968 something far deadlier and more destructive than the police/CIA/organized crime collaboration saturated the streets of Big City America.

Heroin.

Were CIA freelancers, under cover of their Vietnam War operations, responsible for bringing heroin into the cities of America? Congressional hearings and investigative reporters have laid out that case. Regardless, the painful reality is that the tsunami of heroin coming to America beginning in the 1960s required a huge distribution network that included organized crime, law enforcement and probably lone operators within the federal government.

In that era, too few public servants in the NYPD or criminal justice system could keep themselves from getting dirty. It was an unsettling story—even to me, a New Yorker who knew about police corruption as a child and had taken it for granted as an adult.

Narcotics had changed everything. There was just too much money to be made.

In 1962 two detectives, Eddie Egan and Sonny Grosso, tracked 50 kilograms of heroin to the trunk of a Buick owned by a popular French television host. The host was revealed to be a runner for a notorious Corsican drug cartel. The ensuing drug bust was popularized in the movie *The French Connection*.

The two detectives became rock stars in the NYPD. Department officials formed the Special Investigative Unit (SIU), intending that selected detectives would concentrate on major busts, leaving other detectives to deal with the more mundane street drug arrests.

Bernard's next stop on his fast track was to be promoted to the SIU. He remained part of the SIU for a few years of its approximately ten-year existence. The Special Investigative Unit, instead of performing as a group of dedicated crime fighters, soon devolved into extorting the high-value targets they were charged with building solid criminal cases against.

The extent of the unit's corruption was astonishing by any standards. A Hollywood script detailing it would have been rejected as unrealistic, even if it had been set in a Middle Eastern, African or Latin American country, the usual stereotypes of corrupt governments.

During his time as an NYPD detective, Bernard was an alcoholic, as were many of the other detectives. To his credit, he never blamed his actions on alcohol. He later took full responsibility for them. Throughout the 1970s and '80s I often met with him and one or two other former detectives who also were never able to recover from their decades of largely self-inflicted physical abuse.

Shit food diets, nights prowling the city, and fallen down drunkenness all took their toll. They also honorably protected the public. Fights with junkies and street criminals left them with unhealed broken bones and other injuries that plagued them the rest of their lives. Bernard had been stabbed with dirty needles—it was an occupational hazard at the time.

My brother fought cancer, heart problems, Hepatitis C, and high blood pressure for the rest of his life. He was sober for the last twenty years of his life. Bernard died when he was sixty-eight years old.

* * *

Often at the core of drug investigations are the informants law enforcement enlists to ensnare the higher levels in a criminal organization. The methods used for these cases are the same as those used for investigating white-collar or any other crime: wiretaps, surveillance, using informants, reviewing bank records, and working with prosecutors to build a solid case for conviction.

The SIU detectives had another use for informants, illegal wiretaps, surveillance, and subpoenaed records—and it was not always to partner with prosecutors. When the evidence was convincing, they sometimes instead "arrested" a high-level target, handcuffed him, and then drove to a desolate location—that was enough to get the attention of even the most hardened criminal.

They'd let him know how strong their case would be if they went to trial. He'd offer to make a deal to let him walk—the payoff would be huge. That was the point of the "investigation." If the vibes were right, or a future with the drug boss looked promising, the detectives would give up the informant, who would never be seen again. It didn't matter.

Often the detectives supplied defense attorneys with confidential information, or even the prosecution strategy and secret grand jury transcripts. That, too, didn't matter to them.

"We were the reason some of the defense attorneys had great reputations. Drug bosses paid them big retainers and they'd cut us in for the information we gave them," one of my brother's reformed partners recalled.

> "The SIU was the most corrupt law enforcement unit in American history."
>
> *- Assistant US Attorney Gregory Wallance*[3]

> *Bernard: "Prosecutors, judges, bail bondsmen—they saw we had money, cars, expensive clothing. Not like the other detectives. Everyone wanted in on the action. Sometimes we made deals between prosecutors and defense attorneys of the drug bosses. Even judges. We could do whatever we wanted."*

The result was almost a decade of an elite unit turning in an arrest record of small-time dealers. Rarely were the major dealers convicted, or even arrested.

* * *

Robert Daley, author of *Prince of the City,* a narrative of the SIU's demise, wrote: "Someone once called them the Princes of the city, for they operated with the impunity, and sometimes with the arrogance, of Renaissance princes...they could enforce any law or not enforce it, arrest anyone or accord freedom. They were immune to arrest themselves."[4]

My brother was arrested on January 31, 1974, and charged with bribe receiving and bribery. He had resigned from the department three years earlier. He was in a different unit for several years before he resigned, but his arrest was related to the SIU scandal.[5]

Of the seventy detectives assigned to the SIU, fifty-two would be indicted. There would also be two known suicides.

The scandal has often been referred to by the romantic name *Prince of the City*. It was the title of Robert Daley's book, and then a movie by the same name released in 1981, directed by Sidney Lumet. Both purport to tell the story of Robert Leuci, an SIU detective, a team leader. He is supposedly pained by the corruption in the New York City criminal justice system. He is convinced to work undercover with prosecutors who are attached to the Knapp Commission, established in 1970 to investigate criminal justice corruption.

Leuci insists the prosecutors not focus on the police but instead on judges, bail bondsmen, prosecutors, defense attorneys—all the guilty components that had always evaded punishment, leaving the police to take the brunt of the public's scorn for the system's corruption. He also stresses his resolve to never testify against his fellow detectives—his "brothers." He wants to bring down the "big shots" in the system.

That is the premise of the book and movie. The SIU detectives are cast in the then-prevailing *Dirty Harry* mode—frustrated with a system that favors the rich and well connected, police work hampered by politicians, and with easy convictions overturned by liberal judges.

"Almost everything about the book and the movie is bullshit," Bernard said. He and I had already had many conversations about the underlying premise of the story. We saw the movie as soon as it opened, along with another former SIU detective. They both laughed afterwards.

"We weren't frustrated by anybody. We were criminals looking to pocket everything we could: cash, jewelry, drugs," the other former detective said.

Leuci, portrayed as troubled by the extent of the criminal justice system's corruption, admitted to a few illegal acts before he went undercover. "Leuci was as bad as any of us—otherwise he would have never been trusted by anyone," Bernard said. "He was probably busted for something big and just went undercover to save his ass. He had no sudden guilt crisis. None of us did."

My brother found the first undercover action described in the opening pages of *Prince of The City* as proof of Leuci's own corruption. Once he decides to go undercover, Leuci tells the prosecutors that with one phone call he could buy the location of every wiretap in the city. The prosecutors don't believe him.

> *Leuci made the call—to Detective Bernie Geik in the Criminal Investigation Bureau—and later Leuci met with Geik on a midtown sidewalk wearing a recording device.*[6]

Bernard asked, "How could he be so sure he could get that information from me? Only because I knew him for years. I gave him information like that before. He gave me whatever I wanted. Yet they made him out to be cleaner than the rest of us."

Bernard's former partner said, "The real big lie was that Leuci insisted he would never testify against another cop. The first thing we tell an informer is, "You'll tell us everything. If you lie, we will fuck you up even worse than you are now.'"

Oh, yes—that 50 kilos (approximately 110 pounds) of *French Connection* heroin the NYC detectives Egan and Grosso had turned in as evidence to the property clerk's office at police headquarters in 1962—it disappeared.

By the time an audit of the facility was done in 1972, over 400 pounds of heroin and cocaine had been removed—replaced with flour that over the years had become infested with red beetles. All of the drugs stolen from the property clerk's office went back on the street.

The drug evidence, although held in an impregnable installation with bombproof walls and bank vault steel doors, was easily accessible with a detective's badge. An SIU detective, Joseph Nunziata, had signed out much of the heroin. He was thirty-nine years old when he put a bullet through his heart in February 1973, at the height of the investigation.

By 1973 New York City was in the midst of a deadly heroin epidemic far surpassing its extent a decade earlier when the SIU had been formed to combat drugs on the city streets.

The criminal justice system had failed its citizens miserably.

---

[1] In 1968, Frank Sinatra's company produced *The Detective* on location in New York City. He starred in the movie. Sinatra hired his old friend Lt. Arthur Schultheiss as the technical advisor. Schultheiss had a few of his detectives work on the film as tech support—Bernard was occasionally one of them. Schultheiss introduced him to Sinatra, who was amused that George Gordon's nephew was an NYPD detective.

[2] Robert Maheu was also known to the NYPD as a government intelligence agent. Bernard never knew him, but once Maheu became Howard Hughes' dealmaker in 1966, other NYPD detectives remembered him working the same operations that McCord had worked.

[3] Nicholas Pileggi, "The Not Quite Prince of the City" *New York Magazine*, August 31, 1981, p. 29.

[4] Robert Daley, *Prince of the City* (Boston: Houghton Mifflin Company, 1978).

[5] Bernard's charges were reduced and he never served time—a combination of good lawyering and probably connections in the prosecutor's office. He had been pressured to inform on other detectives but never did. Neither did many of his former detective colleagues. This served him well when he took over my father's Garment Center business—he was considered a "stand up guy."

[6] Robert Daley, *Prince of the City* (Boston: Houghton Mifflin Company, 1978). P.26

Author's family album

My brother Bernard, our father Lou and me on the right—at Matty "the Horse" Ianniello's Little Italy restaurant, SPQR. It was our father's retirement party from his Garment Center trucking company.

Author's family album

My father Lou (front right). Tommy Dioguardi (front left) and (second from the left) Johnny Dioguardi, Lucchese family member and Teamsters Union official. I believe the other men are Uncle George's Cleveland associates. Photo taken at Manhattan's Copacabana probably in the mid 1950s.

DAD BECOMES A GARMENT CENTER TRUCKER

Robbie Margolies, the jewelry fence and casino manager, mentioned to me when I visited him at the Colony Sports Club in London that he had introduced my father to his cousin, a small New Jersey garment trucker. His cousin wanted to expand into the Garment Center, which was controlled by organized crime and their close associates, the Teamsters Union. Robbie thought my father might be able to help him make the right connections.

I listened politely, but New York was so far away. Perhaps I was also caught up in my own exciting life in London—it never occurred to me that the introduction Robbie made would so quickly change my family's fortune.

A few months later, the company couldn't get a teamster truck driver to deliver to Macy's main store, a few blocks away—organized crime had to sign off. It was a carefully orchestrated dance. No trucks moved without their approval. There were no exceptions.

Uncle George, watching from a distance, came to New York. He and my father met with the Teamsters Union officials at JFK. The Gambino and Lucchese crime families had the airport tightly locked down. The airport was a goldmine—extortion of shipping companies, cargo thefts, stolen airline tickets; anything was possible.

Johnny "Dio" Dioguardi, a childhood friend and longtime associate of my father and Uncle George since their days on the Lower East Side, by then controlled the Teamsters local at the airport. Even though it was family, details still had to be resolved, and everyone still needed to be paid off. It was just business, but to get a seat at the table to make a deal, you needed to be connected.

It took months to make a deal, but it was done. I don't know the details and never asked. Whatever it was, it was more than a great deal for Dad and his trucking company partners. They could operate all over the Eastern Coast. They had contracts with major department stores and clothing manufacturers. Business boomed.

* * *

Matty "The Horse" Ianniello and "Fat Tony" Salerno protected the company for the next few decades—they did it out of respect for Uncle George and my father. Matty Ianniello was a huge earner for organized crime. He controlled dozens of bars and nightclubs in Manhattan, including the Stonewall, where the modern Gay Rights movement began in a riot in 1969, as well as the Metropole in Times Square and Umberto's Clam House in Little Italy. Matty also controlled Manhattan's private garbage haulage. Madison Square Garden was one of his clients.[1]

Matty's business operations were one of the many extremely profitable Italian and Jewish mob partnerships that flourished for decades. Benny Cohen, another long time family friend, became partners with Matty probably in the late 1950s.

Their company, the M&M Trading Company, operated from an unremarkable office in Midtown Manhattan. Benny remained in the background while Matty attracted the notoriety. Their tight control of the nightclubs and bars lasted until the mid 1980s when Benny Cohen, Matty and several others were indicted for a number of federal charges, including the usual tax evasion, money laundering, loan sharking etc. I include a 1977 New York Times article that elaborates on the charges and attempts to trace the maze of corporations they established over the years.[2]

In the early 1960s Trigger Mike Coppola retired from his lucrative numbers rackets in the Bronx and Manhattan. He handed his numbers action off to Fat Tony Salerno and moved to Miami Beach. Salerno respected Uncle George's lifelong relationship with Mike, so he let it be known on the street that my father's company would always be protected.

My brother, an SIU detective, in turn could be of use to them. I don't know how much he was, but he and Matty the Horse became good friends. My brother became a partner in the family trucking company. His publicized corruption bust, conviction, and not informing granted him respect in that world. Their relationship was perhaps a case study of organized crime's allowing franchises within its hard-won turf to well connected "civilians"—a business plan refined over forty years.[3]

---

[1] Matty Ianniello invited me to call whenever I wanted tickets to Madison Square Garden. "I'll get you better seats than the players' wives have." I took him up on it for a few Rangers hockey games and a boxing match when I was in town. The only day his office was closed for visitors was on Monday. Bernard told me that mob guys or off-duty detectives kept everyone out—it was the day the nightclub and bar managers came with the weekend cash receipts.

[2] New York Times August 1, 1977 *Crime Group Leader Said to Rule Many Bar Businesses in Midtown*

[3] A joke circulated in some circles in the Garment Center for a while; one afternoon my father noticed a young woman with a news film crew outside his shipping storefront on busy, narrow West 37th Street. One of the workers pointed toward my father. The woman entered the store and asked if she could interview him standing next to one of their trucks.

"Interview me about what?" he asked—charmingly, I'm sure.

"The US attorney is investigating organized crime in the Garment Center. One of your partners, John Roncoroni, has been subpoenaed to testify at the Grand Jury."

"And...?" My father asked.

"We know that the trucking company next door to you is owned by the sons of reputed mob boss Carlo Gambino. Have they ever threatened or harassed you?" She asked brightly.

"I've known those boys for years," Lou said. "Where are you from?" he asked, certain that she couldn't be from New York.

"Minneapolis. I was hired by ABC New York five weeks ago."

"So you've been in New York for five weeks. Do you really think someone in the Garment Center is going to go on television and say he was threatened by whatever mob you are referring to?"

The story always got a laugh, as did the understanding that whenever a law enforcement agency wanted to investigate mob influence in the Garment Center they sometimes subpoenaed my father's partner, John Roncoroni. John lived in New Jersey, hated Manhattan, was never in a Garment Center bar—even for a minute—knew everything about trucks and trucking, and nothing about organized crime.

But he did have an Italian last name.

NAME : John Ignazio DIOGUARDI

ALIASES : Johnny Dio, Diao, Dioguardio, Die, Dioguardia

DESCRIPTION : Born 4-29-1914, NYC, 5'8", 165 lbs, brown eyes, black hair, dark complexion.

LOCALITIES FREQUENTED : Resides 109 Freeport Ave., Pt. Lookout, L.I. Frequents 250 W 57 St, Lower East Side of NYC & NYC night clubs.

FAMILY BACKGROUND : Wife: Ann Chrostek; daughter: Rose; son: Dominick; father Dominick; mother: Rose Plumeri; brothers: Thomas & Frank; uncles: William, Joseph & James Plumeri.

CRIMINAL ASSOCIATES : James Plumeri, [redacted], Frank Caruso, Lucien Ignaro, Anthony Corallo, [redacted].

CRIMINAL HISTORY : FBI #665273 NYCPD #B-114267 Record dating from 1932 includes arrests for coercion, extortion, felonious assault, bootlegging, state tax violation, bribery & conspiracy. Indicted in acid blinding of labor columnist Victor Riesel. 1958 sentenced to 15 to 30 years for labor racketeering, conviction reversed on appeal, matter still pending (1960).

BUSINESS : Equitable Research Ass'n, 250 W 57 St, NYC (firm through which he instrumented his labor racketeering).

MODUS OPERANDI : A ranking member of the Mafia. At one time engaged primarily in illicit alcohol operations on a grand scale. Graduated to labor racketeering when, after the death of Louis "Lepke" Buchalter, he, his brothers and James Plumeri gained control of labor racketeering in New York City's garment center.

Property of U. S. Govt – For Official Use Only
May not be disseminated or contents disclosed
Without permission of Commissioner of Narcotics

Note: redactions by the government, not by the author

Author's family album

My father, Lou, with Johnny Dioguardi (on the left) at a family gathering. By the time I was a teenager, Johnny was one of the main labor racketeers in New York. Johnny came up as a young thug for Lepke. He gave my father the blessing of the Teamsters Union and organized crime to operate a trucking company in the Garment Center.

Author's family album

The man sitting behind the woman turned toward the camera was one- half of the most understated, most profitable Jewish/Italian mob operations in New York City throughout the 1960s -1980s. Benny Cohen, then beginning his decades long partnership with Matty "the Horse" Ianniello. They soon owned, operated and financed many dozens of bars, strip clubs and nightclubs. Our father Lou is standing on the right.

Author's family album

Matty "the Horse" Ianniello urged my father to retire so my brother could run the business.(It was more of a joke than a mob boss "urging.") Matty offered my father a retirement party in the private upstairs banquet room of his Little Italy restaurant S.P.Q.R. My father agreed. Dad and me at the bar—that's my John Travolta suit I guess. Note: Benny Cohen couldn't attend this family event as he had just been indicted for a number of federal charges—loansharking, tax evasion, racketeering—the usual stuff.

Author's family album

My father (right) with Sammy Kass, who was, in his later years, one of "Fat Tony" Salerno's close associates. Tony ran the New York numbers rackets, had a hand in Garment Center trucking, and he and Sammy always watched after my father.

NAME : Samuel KASSOP

ALIASES : Sammy the Jew, Sam Cass, Samuel Kass.

DESCRIPTION : Born 10-26-11 NYC, Jewish, 5'9", 185 lbs, stocky, black hair, brown eyes.

LOCALITIES FREQUENTED : Resides 96-09 66th Ave, Queens, NY. Frequents Lower East Side and Upper East Harlem areas of NYC. Currently incarcerated.

FAMILY BACKGROUND : Married Evelyn Reiss; daughter: Adrianne Sacks; father: Isadore Kassop (deceased); mother: Rose Meshlam; brothers: Dr. Harry Kassop, Benjamin Kassop.

CRIMINAL ASSOCIATES : John Ormento, Carmine Locascio, Joseph Vento, Frank Borelli, Rocco Mazzie, Arthur Repola, Anthony Ciccone, Saro Mogavero, Anthony Castaldi.

CRIMINAL HISTORY : FBI #425901A. NYCPD B#304312. Has been arrested twice for narcotic violation. Currently serving 7½ - 15 yrs on State narcotic conviction.

BUSINESS : No legitimate employment.

MODUS OPERANDI : Though Jewish he has always associated almost exclusively with East Harlem (NYC) Mafia racketeers. Distributed wholesale quantities of heroin in NYC and interstate with assistance of his Mafia associates.

NAME : Anthony Michael SALERNO

ALIASES : Fat Tony, Punchy, Tony

DESCRIPTION : Born 8-5-13 NYC, 5'8", 180 lbs, black hair, brown eyes, part of left ring finger missing.

LOCALITIES FREQUENTED : Resides 344 E 116th NYC, frequents Lizzi's Bar, 116th & 2nd Ave, parking lot 111th & 1st Ave., NYC.

FAMILY BACKGROUND : Father: Alfio; mother: Mary Corroccio; brothers: Alfred & Angelo.

CRIMINAL ASSOCIATES : Michael Coppola, Joseph Stracci, Joseph Rao, Charles Albero

CRIMINAL HISTORY : FBI #574465, NYCPD B#101580, record dates from 1932 and includes arrests for robbery, policy, assault & coercion & conviction for Federal Narcotic Law violation.

BUSINESS : Parking lot, 111th & 1st Ave., NYC.

MODUS OPERANDI : With other East Harlem Mafiosi engages in policy, bookmaking and narcotic trafficking.

36

A GOOD DAY TO END THE STORY

Sometime in 1971, I went to my father's Garment Center storefront on West 37th Street. I often stopped by. If he wasn't there, someone knew which bar he was in—that was where he conducted his real business. Dad functioned in the classiest mob-owned bars as well as the most run-down, busted-out gambler bars. He always ordered the same drink—VO (Seagram's VO Canadian whiskey) straight. The bartenders had it on the bar when they saw him walk through the door.

My brother had asked me to meet him.

"Let's stop by to see Fat Tony for a minute. He's at that factoring place," Bernard said.

In addition to the numerous construction extortion rackets, numbers banks and trade unions Fat Tony Salerno controlled, he even had one legitimate company on Broadway—well, sort of legitimate. It was a factoring company. He was rarely in the Garment Center or anywhere else other than in East Harlem, so it was a good time for Bernard to see him.

Factoring is particular to the garment industry. Garment manufacturers experiencing short-term cash crunches—unexpected expenses or customers delaying payment—sell their account receivables, the invoices, to a factoring company at a discount and receive cash up front.

Of course, when criminals are involved, sooner or later even a seemingly solid, boring business will be a front for a scam. Over those next ten years commercial banks seeking new sources of income bought many of the factoring companies. They soon discovered that the factoring companies had vastly inflated the value of their one main asset—the invoices—many of which were fictitious. There was at least one murder associated with the factoring fraud uncovered in 1983.[1]

Tony was cheerier than I would have expected, judging from his reputation. He had a stub of a cigar in his mouth. He alternated taking it out of his mouth when he spoke and leaving it in his mouth when he spoke. His voice was softer than I imagined it would be.

Bernard introduced me.

"So you're the college guy," Tony said.

"That's me," I said.

He nodded. "You can make more money in the Garment Center than in college."

We later turned to leave. He said, "Your Uncle George will be at your father's place in a while. Ask him to come see me. The walk will do him good."

* * *

Thirteen years later, in 1984, I saw Fat Tony for the next and last time. It was at the Copacabana, the famous nightclub and the scene of the secret meetings in the kitchen between the mob and the Haganah, the Israeli paramilitary organization, during the Israeli War of Independence.

Tony co-hosted my parents' fiftieth anniversary party. He was there for awhile. He saw Bernard and me talking. He said, "Bernie (I'm sure he didn't remember my name), I was just telling someone about the Sammy Kass thing on Ninth Avenue awhile ago. Did ya hear the story?"

Sammy Kass had become Tony's close advisor and friend, as well as a fixture in East Harlem, Tony's turf.

My brother said, "I know something about it."

Fat Tony was only too happy to tell the story once again: "So, Sammy still gets up early every morning. His friend from the old neighborhood has a bagel store over on Ninth Avenue. Sammy stops there every morning to pick up bagels for the people in the belt shop we gave him. He parks his Cadillac in front of the store.

"A hooker on the sidewalk says something to him. He doesn't like it, so he slaps her or something. You know Sammy. He goes inside. A few minutes later a big colored guy comes in. He's wearing a fur coat, big hat and those high heel shoes they wear.

"He says to Sammy, 'You fucking with my woman. I'll fuck you up.'

"Sammy says, 'Don't hurt me. I'm an old man. I have money in my car. I'll give it to you.'

"So the guy follows him to the car. Sammy goes around and opens the driver's door."

Tony laughs and puts his cigar back in his mouth, or takes it out. I can't remember—he talked the same either way.

"Sammy says, 'As soon as I opened the car door the guy was as good as dead.'

"He pulls out a shotgun. The guy sees it and starts running down Ninth Avenue. That's not good enough for Sammy. He gets up on the sidewalk and lets go with both barrels. At seven in the morning. The guy grabs his ass like he got hit and keeps running."

Bernard and I laughed.

Tony stopped us. "But that's not the end of it. So Sammy comes uptown and tells me the story. I say, 'Ok, you don't go back to that bagel shop. That colored guy will want revenge. Don't go back. That's an order.'

"I know Sammy won't listen—he'll go back— so I have two cars go down and park outside the bagel shop the next morning. If the muliyam (Italian derogatory slang for Black people—from melanzane—eggplant) shows up, it'll be the worst day of his life—that's a guarantee.

"So Sammy drives up to the bagel store the next morning. He sees my guys in the cars. He knows them and gets pissed off. 'Who the hell needs you here?' he asks them. So he comes uptown to see me in the restaurant, all pissed off and everything.

"'What's the matter Tony, didn't you trust me?'

"I laugh my ass off. 'No, I didn't trust you. I knew you'd go back and you did, didn't you? So I was right?' Sammy goes into the kitchen and orders something from the cook and never says another word."

After Bernard and I left Tony's factoring company office we returned to the trucking company shipping floor.

Uncles George and Charlie, Red Levine and two other men stood in a far corner of the floor near a pay phone and a worn desk with a phone connected to the wall. Uncle George waved us over to them.

"I'll call from the pay phone," I heard Uncle George say as we were closer to them.

"You know my nephew Alan," he said to the two men I didn't know. "He went to graduate school in London."

Wow, I thought, that impressed him. How cool.

He digs a twenty-dollar bill from his pants pocket and gives it to me.

"Here, professor, go find me some quarters."

So much for graduate school.

I picked up a roll of quarters at the corner cigar store. When I returned, Sol Bloom "Blubber" came in. He was nervous.

"Two colored guys are following me," he said. It was a cause for concern—Joey Gallo, a low-level mobster, was using black ex cons he had met in prison to kidnap organized crime guys. He held them for ransom. It wasn't an activity that promised a long career. Gallo was killed the next year in Matty "the Horse" Ianniello's Umberto's Clam Bar.

My brother said, "I'll go check them out."

He came back fifteen minutes later. "They're detectives. I know them both. I talked to them. They left."

Blubber laughed. "The cops are following me. That's great—I have police protection from the gangsters."

Uncle Charlie had made an effort to help me get into the cameraman's union—it was a tough union to get into at the time. He said he had talked to a union representative a month earlier.

He apologized, "You know Alan, in the old days, before I went away, if I wanted anything from a union guy all I had to do was open his window and say, 'It's a long way down.'"

I laughed, but felt bad that he was embarrassed because he couldn't come through.

When we left, my brother shook his head. "I can't believe these guys. I told Dad a few times that the payphone on the wall was tapped just like the office phones are."

The comments were funny, but I mention this day because it was the last time I would see many of these characters.

Sam Red Levine died soon after.

So did Uncle George.

Uncle Charlie died in 1979. I had moved to California a few years before that, and we just spoke on the phone a few times.

It was the end of that era.

* * *

My Father, Lou, died on April Fool's Day, 1988. He was seventy-three.

On November 19, 1986, Fat Tony Salerno and the heads of the other New York City crime families were convicted on RICO charges.

On January 13, 1987, they were each sentenced to 100 years in prison without parole. Fat Tony was seventy-seven years old.

While that trial was underway, he was indicted in a separate federal racketeering case involving hidden interests in a concrete company. He was also charged with Teamster Union labor racketeering. He was convicted on all charges.

He received another seventy years without parole.

Tony supposedly asked, "Is there time off for good behavior?"

THE END

---

[1] "Turbulant Times in Factoring," August 30, 1983, *New York Times* (yes, it is spelled "turbulant" in the headline.) The *New York Times*!!!

Made in the USA
Las Vegas, NV
07 January 2023